Manager's

HANDBOOK

Manager's
HANDBOOK

*Everything you need to know about how
business and management work*

Editor-in-chief
ROBERT HELLER

London, New York, Munich,
Melbourne, and Delhi

Editor **Christine King**
Design **Cooling Brown**

DORLING KINDERSLEY
Senior Editor **Jacky Jackson**
Senior Art Editor **Sarah Cowley**
Assistant Editor **Richard Gilbert**
US Editors **Gary Werner
and Margaret Parrish**
DTP Designer **Rajen Shah**
Production Controller **Elizabeth Cherry**

Managing Editor **Adèle Hayward**
Managing Art Editor **Karen Self**
Category Publisher **Stephanie Jackson**

First American Edition, 2002

02 03 04 05 10 9 8 7 6 5 4 3 2 1

Published in the United States by
DK Publishing, Inc.
95 Madison Avenue
New York, NY 10016

A CIP catalog record for this book is available
from the Library of Congress

ISBN 0-7894-8422-6

Reproduced by Colourscan, Singapore
Printed and bound at TBB, Slovakia

See our complete product line at
www.dk.com

CONTENTS

Managing Your Career

Understanding Organizations

International Management

The Role of the Manager

CONTRIBUTORS

PAUL DONKERSLEY

DEVELOPING YOURSELF

A successful freelance writer on many management and employment topics, Paul Donkersley's books include the best-selling guide *Britain's Top Employers*. He has extensive commercial experience, and in 1999 he set up Terrier, his own "virtual" international agency, specializing in web content strategy.

BOB GARRATT

THE LEARNING ORGANIZATION
(Pages 35–51)

Professor Garratt is the chairman of several companies, including Media Projects International in London (UK), and a consultant on board development and organizational learning and change. His academic posts include visiting professor in corporate governance at The Management School, Imperial College, London University. He wrote the original book on *The Learning Organization* in 1986, revised in 2000. His other books include *The Fish Rots from the Head: The Crisis in Our Boardrooms* (1996).

TERRY GASKING
(FCCA, MIMIS, MIMgt, FRSA)

FINANCIAL MANAGEMENT

A very experienced management consultant, since 1989 Terry Gasking has specialized in helping many companies release money from idle assets, resulting in an increase in profitability and a focused, well-motivated workforce. He has written *How to Master Finance* (1999) for the nonfinancial manager, and *Perfect Financial Ratios* (1993).

COLIN BARROW

MANAGING RESOURCES
(Pages 90–9)

Colin Barrow is head of the Enterprise Group at Cranfield School of Management (UK), and director of a UK program for entrepreneurs, the Business Growth and Development Programme. He has taught extensively, and was a visiting professor at Suffolk University, Boston, Mass. He has held senior appointments in industry, and is now also a strategic consultant and a non-executive director in a number of companies.

PAUL SPENLEY
(CEng, MIEE)

OPERATIONS MANAGEMENT

Paul Spenley is a founder and managing director of The Leading Change Partnership. A chartered engineer with a degree in electronics and a master's in the leadership role of managers in the development of information systems, he has had an accomplished career in line management, most notably as system and quality manager for an award-winning operation for ICL. Author of two books in his own right, he is also coauthor with Robert Heller of *Riding the Revolution* (2000).

MALCOLM MCDONALD
(MA (Oxon), MSc, PhD, DLitt, FCIM, FRSA)

MARKETING AND SALES

Malcolm McDonald is a professor of marketing and deputy director at Cranfield School of Management (UK). He has extensive industrial experience, and is chairman of several companies, working with multinationals. His best-selling books include *Marketing Plans: How to Prepare Them, How to Use Them* (1999) and *Key Customers: How to Manage Them Profitably* (2000).

SUE CLEMENSON

MANAGING PEOPLE

Sue Clemenson is a leading consultant on change communication and joint founder of Archangel Associates. With much experience across a range of different industries, she is a specialist in the areas of organizational effectiveness and employee commitment, and the architect of award-winning change programs.

ANGELA M. PINNINGTON

PROBLEM-SOLVING AND DECISION-MAKING

After a successful career in the pharmaceutical industry, Angela Pinnington joined international consulting and training organization Kepner-Tregoe as a partner. She manages their UK and Ireland offices and their training programs throughout Europe. She has helped managers worldwide to improve their thinking skills.

CHRIS DOWNING

THE IMPACT OF THE INTERNET

An e-strategist, Chris Downing specializes in business internet consulting. After 20 years in the computer and technology industries, he created leadership positioning for British Telecom's corporate clients in the internet marketplace by helping industry leaders become aware of the need for a business internet strategy.

GEORGE BOULDEN

(DMS, FIMC, MIM)

CHANGE AND INNOVATION

George Boulden is the chairman and managing director of ALA International Ltd., which promotes the use of action learning in solving business problems. He has written many papers, and a recent book, *Organizational Restructuring*, for the International Labour Organization.

TERENCE BRAKE

(MA)

OPERATING A GLOBAL BUSINESS

Terence Brake is the president of TMA-Americas in Transnational Management Associates. He is the author of *The Global Leader: Critical Factors for Creating the World-Class Organization* (1996), and coauthor of *Doing Business Internationally: The Guide to Cross-Cultural Success* (1994). He has written many papers and is a keynote speaker at international conferences. He has designed, developed, and delivered programs for many clients worldwide.

FONS TROMPENAARS

MANAGING ACROSS CULTURES
(Coauthor)

Professor Dr. Fons Trompenaars was the original founder of THT Consulting (Amsterdam). He began to research the influence of cultural differences on cross-cultural business while working on his PhD at the Wharton School in Pennsylvania, using Royal Dutch/Shell as his "laboratory." He is now the author of best-selling books, a keynote speaker, and a worldwide authority on cross-cultural values. He is also a visiting professor at the University of Nijmegen, the Netherlands.

PETER WOOLLIAMS

MANAGING ACROSS CULTURES
(Coauthor)

Professor Dr. Peter Woolliams is a professor of international business at the Anglia Business School, UK, and a visiting professor to THT (Amsterdam), the Netherlands. He has worked closely with Fons Trompenaars since 1989, and has been concerned with the development and analysis of their cross-cultural database. He is a frequent speaker at international conferences, and publishes extensively with Dr. Trompenaars.

INTRODUCTION

Managers have never before needed to know so much, and across so broad a front. There was a time, not that long ago, when managers needed solely to concern themselves with their own specialization: finance, or marketing, or information technology, or human resources, and so on. The need to know about subjects outside their field belonged to somebody else. Management was divided into separate compartments – despite the self-evident fact that none of the elements could function adequately, let alone well, without the others.

Today, this separatism is recognized as artificial and self-defeating. If every process must begin with the customers' needs, and end with their full satisfaction, every manager must understand the principles and practice of marketing. If "adding value" is another imperative, every manager must understand the fundamentals of the financial mechanisms – the machinery of profit and loss – that determine value. If the superior mobilization of superior people is the key to achieving superior results, every manager must learn to be expert in handling and helping "human resources."

If, moreover, all these areas of management each depend for full effectiveness on the deployment of the latest technology of information and communication, then managers cannot leave IT to the specialist. The "age of the internet" is inclusive. Managers who learn how to communicate, analyze, and serve the customer by tapping the infinite resources of cyberspace must have the advantage over those who understand none of these necessities. In an all-around world, the edge belongs to the all-around executive.

To know, however, is not enough. Management is about action. Acting more effectively on more effective knowledge is the objective of the modern manager, and the end to which *Manager's Handbook* is dedicated. The chapters of this book cover many more subjects than those mentioned above, each of them just as vital to the success of the enterprise and the individual. Paradoxically, the latter – the lone man or woman – cannot fulfill his or her ambitions except through the activities of the collective. Learning to work with and through others therefore becomes a prime asset of the individual manager.

Manager's Handbook is a complete introduction to the wide field of modern management. For all managers, it opens the door to the other interrelated disciplines that have an effect on their own, and whose mastery will make their own activities more successful. For example, planning – which used to be the reserve of staff specialists – is now quite plainly a requirement for all line managers. Not only that: "staff managers," too, need to be able to plan, to organize present activities to achieve future outcomes. In fact, the whole division between line and staff, inherited from management's military beginnings, is obsolete. Finance is very much a case in point. There should be no such thing as a "nonfinancial manager." Every manager should have the costs and revenues of his or her unit under full control without calling on financial specialists. These specialists are still urgently required for vital tasks such as checking, consolidation, and analysis; but their most important work lies in devising and managing the business and financial models that drive the business forward.

The term "business models" is a relatively new entrant into the stockpile of jargon with which managers are asked to be familiar. *Manager's Handbook* explains jargon, but, more importantly, substitutes true understanding of what lies behind the fashionable (and even the unfashionable) words such as Total Quality Management (TQM) or Business Process Re-engineering (BPR). The management world is given to the odd practice of seizing on new "cures," elevating them to the status of panaceas, reacting to the results with extreme disillusion – and then throwing out the baby with the bathwater.

Such ideas may look like fads or fashions, but the presentation should not be allowed to obscure their lasting value. Total Quality Management, for example, enshrines basic truths: that each and every practice or process can be significantly improved forever; that this improvement can be achieved only if before-and-after results are meticulously measured; that planning and implementation should be entrusted to those directly involved; and, finally, that the involvement and the improvement have an energizing effect on the whole enterprise – and a wonderful impact on both the bottom line and the top.

The all-too-familiar drive to downsize, rightsize, and rationalize is not concerned with the top line, which is where the revenues are recorded. This is a serious mistake, and one that *Manager's Handbook* explicitly avoids. The customers are the masters of the top line. They are deeply concerned with the quality of the product and the processes they encounter firsthand. Improvements in that quality have a direct impact on what products or services they buy and what prices they are prepared to pay. Whether or not a company practices TQM, this driving force cannot be denied and must not be ignored.

The moral of BPR is much the same. You break down, analyze, and reconstruct processes, starting at the very beginning with the customer need, and driving toward customer satisfaction, not to cut costs in absolute terms, but to reduce them relative to the realized price – and to the competition. *Manager's Handbook* aims to equip its readers with the knowledge they require to outmanage and outwit competitors who, in this new millennium, are more numerous and determined than ever before, in all businesses. Their competition will not lessen in the years to come: only intensify.

The most important instruction in these pages is therefore action. The contributors have all sought not only to show managers what must be done, but also how to do it – and to do it now. In the past, many managers believed that there was no need to read or learn: their job was simply to act, usually within a narrow field. *Manager's Handbook* is an action manual, but one that recognizes fully that, while action speaks louder than words, ideas and understanding are the indispensable weapons of the active and effective manager.

The hope of the editor and contributors is that readers will use this handbook as a practical guide to their daily actions, but equally as a longer-term aid to the constructive thought and planning on which all successful enterprise must rest.

Robert Heller

ROBERT HELLER

Robert Heller was the founding editor of *Management Today* magazine, and supervised the launch of such highly successful magazines as *Campaign* and *Accountancy Age*. Since the best-selling *The Great Executive's Dream* (1973), he has confirmed his position as a leading business author with many other books, including Dorling Kindersley's *Essential Managers* and *Business Masterminds* series. He is coauthor, with Edward de Bono, of *Letter to Thinking Managers*, and is in demand all over the world as a speaker and consultant.

For *Manager's Handbook*, Robert Heller has contributed the topics Stating the Vision and Mission, and Maintaining Image and Reputation in the chapter "The Learning Organization"; the topics The Essentials of Planning, Planning for Action, Pursuing Total Quality, and Implementing Feedback in "Managing Resources", and the complete chapter "Communication."

Managing
Your Career

developing
YOURSELF

A SUCCESSFUL CAREER IS COMPATIBLE WITH
YOUR UNIQUE PERSONALITY, INTERESTS, SKILLS,
AND AMBITIONS. TO ACHIEVE SUCCESS, YOU NEED
TO MANAGE YOUR WORKING LIFE ACTIVELY AND
EFFECTIVELY. THIS IS A LIFELONG PROCESS, AND
GOES HAND-IN-HAND WITH YOUR PERSONAL AND
PROFESSIONAL DEVELOPMENT.

Traditional career ladders have been relegated to the past:
you can no longer expect an organization to take full
responsibility for your development. In what is now a
complex career maze, it is up to you to define your goals
and find ways of reaching them.

A fundamental need is planning: you must identify
what you want, and how this may be achieved. It is essential
to develop the right skills, both technical and interpersonal.
You can increase your chances by building a truthful
personal profile, which in turn helps to identify the right
organizational fit. Once in a new job, there are specific
routes to success, while a personal development plan will
identify how to make further progress. Finally, when a job
no longer satisfies, you need to know the best time to change.

PLANNING YOUR CAREER

PLANNING YOUR CAREER IS MORE THAN JUST MAPPING OUT STAGES IN YOUR WORKING LIFE: IT IS ABOUT TAKING CONTROL OF YOUR OWN DESTINY. FOR THIS, YOU NEED A GOOD UNDERSTANDING OF THE WORLD OF WORK, AND WHAT YOU REALLY WANT FOR YOURSELF.

WORK AND PERSONAL DEVELOPMENT

Your jobs, and the order in which you take them on, structure your career. Within this structure, you will develop certain learning skills and values, both formally and informally.

The two aspects interact. What you learn determines which future jobs and roles are available to you. In turn, your jobs and roles affect what you learn. Some people find themselves in career and development cul-de-sacs, developing highly specialized skills in work that offers little or no growth. Others develop skills and accumulate experiences that are increasingly in demand; their career options broaden accordingly. Either path can develop through luck or chance, but being aware of the processes means that you can manage them.

CAREER SECURITY

Few people talk about "jobs for life" any more. For "job security" now read "career security." Both employers and employees have recognized that each benefits from increased job mobility.

It is in the company's interests to sustain your career. By providing career development services, the company can derive bottom-line benefits across a wide range of activities. In return, you are expected to be fully productive while in their employ.

If you are willing to learn, and the company provides the necessary resources, you can manage your own career in a healthy two-way contract.

KNOW YOURSELF

Before you plan anything that will affect your life, you need to know yourself. Self-knowledge gives you control. There are various ways in which you can help yourself. Psychometric tests are useful; you can take them yourself at any time, including on-line, as they are not just a tool for employers in the recruiting process. Encourage feedback from those

The benefits of career management
Managing your own career gives significant benefits to both your work and your personal life, allowing greater control over each, and encouraging a healthy balance. You develop an in-depth awareness of what you really want from work, and are able to create positive means of achieving it.

Clearer view of longer-term goals

Greater self-awareness

Alleviation of work-related stress

Enhanced job satisfaction

Regular career "health checks"

around you and talk openly with other people to find out how you are perceived in the workplace. You need a thorough understanding of yourself and a realistic awareness of your own strengths and weaknesses – and your potential.

Recent years have seen an increasing level of awareness of the importance of "emotional intelligence," as opposed to the traditional intellectual yardsticks. Good personal relationships are the key to happiness and success in both work and life. Emotionally literate people know themselves very well, appreciate others, and empathize with them.

DARE TO DREAM

You need to have career goals. They should be realistic and achievable, but also highly ambitious. Follow the "dare to dream" philosophy, and aim high. Do not be satisfied just by short-term targets that can be achieved now. Think ahead in terms of bigger, longer-term goals: becoming a senior manager or director by a certain date, for example.

And apply your mind. Your mindset, focused on your objective, will actually increase your chances of reaching it. The early days of many successful managers and entrepreneurs are distinguished by

ANTICIPATING THE IMPACT OF CHANGE

In a well-managed career, you will change jobs when the time – and the opportunity – is right. Or, of course, change may be forced on you, by a pink slip for example. Unwelcome change can be very distressing and you may experience negative reactions. It is important to recognize such feelings and cope with them.

Whatever the impetus to change, it is common to be seized by doubt and panic. You need to keep a sense of perspective. Many people experience the same kind of emotional turmoil – the "change curve" illustrated below. Early phases of reaction are often marked by

feelings of shock and denial, a loss of self-confidence and a fear of the consequences. At your worst, you may feel low, even depressed.

A key phase is the gradual acceptance that nothing will change what has happened. You let go of the past and start looking ahead. This can be an important time to explore your needs, goals, and options.

As time passes, you will assess what the change has meant for you and, in the final phase, take on board what you have learned and transfer it to other situations in your personal and working life.

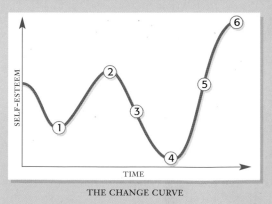

THE CHANGE CURVE

The change curve
An important life change, such as leaving a job, is bound to have an emotional effect on you. Typically, the early negative feelings gradually give way to acceptance, adaptation, and a growing awareness of new possibilities. You will have gone through a true learning experience.

KEY

1 Shock	5 Acceptance
2 Denial	and reflection
3 Self-doubt	6 Learning
4 Rock bottom	and growth

their strong self-image of future success. While such confidence may not come easily to all, it is a worthwhile tactic. Compelling and positive thought can lead to compelling and positive action.

BREAK THE BOUNDARIES

In the course of a varied career, you will probably have to reinvent yourself to fit different professional contexts. You could, of course, retrain in some way, or acquire new qualifications. But do not confine yourself to thinking just in terms of job titles and specific functions. Go beyond this and assess the skills you have that could be applied anywhere: for example, leadership, problem-solving, and project management. You may well find that career paths that looked beyond your reach will suddenly open up.

DEVELOPING THE RIGHT SKILLS

MANY ORGANIZATIONS HAVE CHANGED THE WAY THEY APPROACH AND ORGANIZE WORK IN RESPONSE TO FUNDAMENTAL CHANGES IN THE GLOBAL ECONOMY. YOU NEED TO DEVELOP THE RIGHT SKILLS TO MATCH THESE DEVELOPMENTS, SO MAKING – AND KEEPING – YOURSELF MARKETABLE.

GLOBAL TRENDS AND USEFUL SKILLS

The changing nature of the worldwide marketplace is reshaping the career landscape. While some companies are expanding by acquisition and growth, other big companies are shrinking by demerging, downsizing, delayering, and outsourcing. Organizations in both the private and public sectors are outsourcing functions to suppliers or joint ventures, thus opening up a range of opportunities for entrepreneurial people.

The global workplace has also been revolutionized by new technology. Now, small businesses can often compete with multinational corporations. The Internet, with its dot-com and e-commerce businesses, has fundamentally redefined the concepts of location, distribution, remote working, and supply chains.

As the work landscape shifts, and organizations become flatter in structure, there may be fewer career paths than in the past. Also, expanding organizations will demand job applicants with specific, sometimes different, skill-sets and work experience. For the individual, "jobs for life" has been replaced by "skills for life."

Key developments in the market include the following:
● the Total Quality Movement, as a result of which organizations work much more closely with customers and seek to get things right the first time
● a streamlined management of the supply chain, thus reducing stocks and inventories.

These approaches have led to a change in traditional emphases. They demand a greater degree of organizational learning, teamwork, problem-solving, and staff involvement. People are now expected to hold a broader portfolio of skills than was

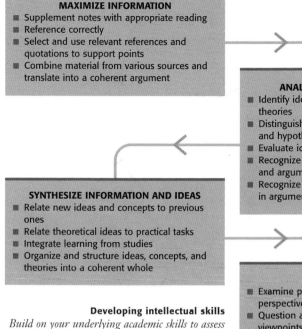

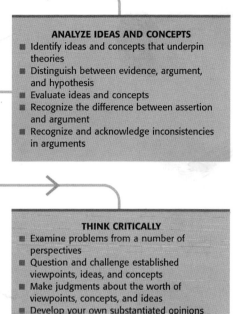

MAXIMIZE INFORMATION
- Supplement notes with appropriate reading
- Reference correctly
- Select and use relevant references and quotations to support points
- Combine material from various sources and translate into a coherent argument

ANALYZE IDEAS AND CONCEPTS
- Identify ideas and concepts that underpin theories
- Distinguish between evidence, argument, and hypothesis
- Evaluate ideas and concepts
- Recognize the difference between assertion and argument
- Recognize and acknowledge inconsistencies in arguments

SYNTHESIZE INFORMATION AND IDEAS
- Relate new ideas and concepts to previous ones
- Relate theoretical ideas to practical tasks
- Integrate learning from studies
- Organize and structure ideas, concepts, and theories into a coherent whole

THINK CRITICALLY
- Examine problems from a number of perspectives
- Question and challenge established viewpoints, ideas, and concepts
- Make judgments about the worth of viewpoints, concepts, and ideas
- Develop your own substantiated opinions

Developing intellectual skills
Build on your underlying academic skills to assess and assimilate the mass of information available. Work on your powers of analysis and synthesis, and learn to marshal arguments effectively, while always remaining receptive to new ideas.

required in the past. Today, single-issue specialists are disappearing and being replaced by multiskilled generalists who can identify solutions to a broad range of problems, and implement them.

In particular, people with high-level technical knowledge and professional specializations find that they also need an active understanding of the principles of modern management.

These developments have given careers important new patterns. Most people can now expect a number of career moves in their working life (not all of them voluntary) and an accompanying need for significant periods of training.

THE RIGHT SKILLS

When they start work, people adapt their generic academic skills to the job. You need to develop these to keep pace with the wide range of intellectual, technical, and personal skills required in the modern marketplace.

KEY PERSONAL TRANSFERABLE SKILLS

Many skills will remain specialized and vocational, but there are some transferable skills that all managers should possess. These will help you immeasurably if you choose to change career, allowing you to adapt your experience to new jobs.

KEY PERSONAL TRANSFERABLE SKILLS

KEY SKILL	APPLICATION
Communication	■ Adapting reports, documents, memos and other written material to target audience. ■ Speaking effectively in different formal and informal contexts.
Organization	■ Identifying available resources and using them effectively. ■ Developing a flexible approach to time management and work-in-progress. ■ Recognizing the demands of multiple and related tasks.
Information Management	■ Gathering information (e.g. source data, statistics, market research) and developing effective storage/retrieval systems. ■ Interpreting, analyzing, and synthesizing information into valuable knowledge.
Technology	■ Creating, storing, sending, and retrieving data (e.g. word processing, email, websites, databases, spreadsheets, graphics). ■ Making effective use of information from various sources.
Self-management	■ Showing initiative, self-motivation, and resourcefulness. ■ Decision-making and problem-solving autonomously. ■ Assessing progress, and monitoring, reviewing, and learning from your own performance and achievements.
Teamworking	■ Working cooperatively in teams, sharing decision-making and negotiating with others. ■ Listening to relevant opinions before reaching decisions and relating the ideas of others to the task at hand. ■ Adopting various roles in changing circumstances. ■ Evaluating the strengths and weaknesses of group effectiveness and of your own performance within the group.

SELF-RESPONSIBILITY

"Self-responsibility" is an enduring buzzword in business circles. It identifies a certain kind of personality and a certain way of working: enterprising and self-reliant people, who constantly monitor what is happening in business globally, nationally, and locally.

Such individuals actively search for opportunities and are able to withstand setbacks. Whether self-employed or locked into an organization's payroll, they invariably enjoy what they do. They are ready to work both independently and in a team, and excel during times of rapid change. You will find that employers place a very high premium on these qualities – they are in great demand.

You do not need to run your own business to be enterprising. Working within an organization, these so-called "intrapreneurs" can show the same entrepreneurial characteristics. You might recognize some of them: enthusiasm, decisiveness, confidence, resourcefulness, resilience, open-mindedness, flexibility, and the ability to handle risks and stress. Underlying all these are excellent time-management and organizational skills, and a highly developed sense of humor.

SKILLS FOR THE NEW ECONOMY

In a time of unprecedented technological change, the Internet and the associated new economy have transformed many aspects of business and life. Throughout the work landscape, the Internet touches people and organizations in different ways, and different specific skills are required in the web world.

Few managers will have to double as fully fledged computer programmers or IT systems analysts. However, it is generally a safe bet that the more knowledgeable you are in information technology, computing, and the Internet and the huge impact they have on business, the better manager you will become.

A good manager will at least be aware of the power of the Internet, of the new skills that it demands, and of its potential to transform commerce. Even if you lack the core technical skills, you may well need to know enough to manage others who do possess them.

CREATING YOUR PERSONAL PROFILE

BEFORE YOU BECOME INVOLVED IN PURSUING CAREER AND DEVELOPMENT OPTIONS, BUILD UP YOUR PERSONAL PROFILE. IDENTIFY YOUR SKILLS AND EXPERIENCE AND YOUR STRENGTHS AND WEAKNESSES. MATCH THEM TO THE MARKETPLACE AND THEN PURSUE THOSE OPTIONS THAT WILL BRING YOU THE GREATEST PROGRESS AND FULFILLMENT.

SELF-ASSESSMENT

Making a rigorous self-assessment is an essential stage in planning for your future. Prepared honestly and clearly, it can open the way to more choices and broader options. Whatever format you choose to record your details, on disk or on paper, it helps if it can be updated.

It is relatively easy to identify your priorities and to record past experiences, but it is harder to analyse your own personality and attitudes. You need to ask yourself some searching questions to evaluate who you really are now, not the person you would like to be.

Priorities

Try to decide what really matters to you, and how these priorities could be integrated into your working life. Start by answering these questions:

- Is working a means to an end or an end in itself?
- Is it important to you to have a job that involves your personal interests?
- How ambitious are you? Do you want to get to the top at any cost?
- Do you see home life as more important than work?
- Is money your top priority?
- Is it important to you to have time to pursue leisure interests outside work?
- Do you think it is worth giving up free time for work-related training?

Work experience

List all your jobs so far, starting with the most recent. Include your position and your main responsibilities, and whether you worked in teams or independently, as an employee, contractor, or freelancer.

Skills and abilities

List any skills gained in leisure activities as well as at work. In previous jobs you may have utilized underlying functional skills, such as working with information or people. You may also have exercised other transferable areas of expertise such as leadership and problem-solving.

Achievements

Itemize all your best, most positive achievements. Typical examples are:

- negotiating a difficult contract
- raising money
- resolving a strategic issue
- doing something earlier/faster/better/more often than others
- being commended for consistently high quality of work
- winning awards
- exceeding targets
- leading a successful team.

Preparing your personal profile
To present yourself effectively in the marketplace, start by creating a personal profile. Be as honest and objective as you can, in both the professional and personal areas of your life.

Personal attitudes

How you interact with the world, your relationships with other people, gives a strong indication of the kind of work with which you will be most comfortable. Try to assess what your attitudes and reactions would be in different situations. The following questions may help you to clarify the way you feel:

- Do you become energized by being around people?
- Do you prefer to spend time alone?
- Do you think out loud or need time to think before speaking?
- Do you pursue a few interests deeply, or many interests superficially?
- Do you share personal information freely?
- Do you tend to live in an orderly way, where life is structured?
- Do you tend to live spontaneously, remaining open to possibilities?
- Do you feel happier after decisions are made?
- Do you try to understand life rather than control it?

Work satisfaction
Register aspects of work that are most satisfying

Priorities
Identify what is really important in your life

Work experience
Create a comprehensive portfolio of your work so far

Decision-making style
Distinguish your approach to decision-making

Skills and abilities
Include those gained in both work and leisure

Information processing
Analyse the way in which you absorb information

Personal attitudes
Clarify how you interact with the world

Achievements
Itemize your most impressive achievements

Information processing
We are bombarded with data of all kinds. Try to identify your way of taking in information. For example:
- Do you concentrate on what you take in through the five senses, i.e. the real and concrete?
- Do you value imagination?
- Do you look at a situation and think about its meaning and the possible consequences?
- Are you able to sift through a mass of information to find what is important?

Decision-making style
It is a significant part of a manager's working life to make decisions, whether major or minor, routine or unexpected. People have their own style of making decisions: rational or intuitive and all points in between. Try to identify yours. For example:
- Do you always rely upon logic and objective analysis?
- Are you heavily influenced by personal values?
- Do you trust your instincts?
- Do you rely on one set standard?
- Can you cope with ambivalence and shifting priorities?

Work satisfaction
Can you analyse your current job and identify any aspects that you positively enjoy? If you can register any "quality moments" when your work is especially rewarding, you will have useful clues to sources of satisfaction.

CHOOSING THE RIGHT ORGANIZATION

ORGANIZATIONS COME IN EVERY TYPE, SIZE, AND ETHOS, AND YOU NEED TO FIND ONE THAT IS RIGHT FOR YOU. WHICHEVER YOU CHOOSE WILL HAVE A SIGNIFICANT EFFECT ON YOUR CAREER AND PERSONAL DEVELOPMENT, SO MAKE SURE THAT YOU ARE AWARE OF THE OPTIONS.

WHAT IS A "RIGHT" COMPANY?
There is no one "right" company, but there are right companies for each individual. Such a company will offer what you need in order to feel that you are making a contribution. The right company will also want what you value most in yourself.

Do not put too much faith in companies' own literature; this can often describe a world that is unrecognizable to employees, who know better from their work and the realities of the workplace. It is far more important to know how it feels to be part of that company. What are its core values? How are you expected to perform if you are to be valued? What challenges will you face if you join?

Beware, too, of independent research and reports into which are the best organizations to work for. The best source of genuinely independent opinion must be people who currently work, or have recently worked, for a company you are considering joining. Find these people and talk to them if you can. Career consultants and search agencies can also provide impartial advice.

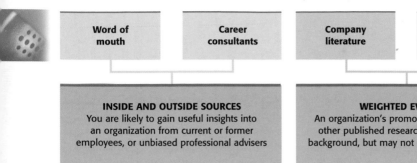

Word of mouth	Career consultants	Company literature	"Independent" research

INSIDE AND OUTSIDE SOURCES You are likely to gain useful insights into an organization from current or former employees, or unbiased professional advisers	**WEIGHTED EVIDENCE** An organization's promotional material (like other published research) may give useful background, but may not otherwise be reliable

Finding out about an organization
You have a much better chance of choosing a compatible organization if you carry out some background research. Try to look behind the public face to find the living, working reality.

MATCHING THE ORGANIZATION AND YOUR SKILLS

What kind of organization appeals to you? Start by considering these factors:
- size
- profit-making or nonprofit
- manufacturing or service
- type of product or service provided
- rate at which it is changing
- well-established or start-up business
- approach to individual career development
- international or domestic.

At the same time, identify your own skills, attitudes and ambitions, and see how these are likely to match any given organization. Ask yourself:
- What are your interests, strengths and weaknesses?
- Who do you want to work with?
- Where do you want to work?
- What kind of organizational context do you want to work in?
- What are the financial implications?
- What do you know about the job market at the moment?
- What more would you like to know?

CHANGING WORK STRUCTURES

Many organizations have moved toward flatter, more open structures. They have cut overheads by employing a relatively small core of employees, with noncore work contracted out. Management layers have been reduced, and remaining staff are often expected to "do more with less." One consequence for career development is that traditional, vertical hierarchies have disappeared. Horizontal development has taken its place: employees must now acquire lateral skills to further their career development.

APPROACHES TO PERSONAL AND MANAGEMENT DEVELOPMENT

Organizations can be considered along a spectrum of development. At one end are those larger companies, which, shaped by scale and multinational scope, have a consistent approach. Their established programs may be complemented by more flexible modules, but essentially management development is structured.

At the other end of the spectrum, more and more companies are practicing self-career management, horizontal skills development, and open learning.

The ideal setup is where learning and development are firmly your own responsibility, but, vitally, the company provides the resources. This is opening the door from within: living up to the adage "If it's to be, it's up to me." The two key questions are:

- does the organization mean it when it says it will introduce self-development programmes, or is it simply jumping on the buzzword bandwagon?
- are real resources available?

CAREER BRIDGES AND REASSIGNMENTS

Able managers usually enjoy a natural progression up the career ladder. But the key need is to find the bridges that enable you to cross from one ladder to another. Career bridges move you into new areas of experience and build on existing skills.

"Secondments" may mean different things in different organizations, but essentially, people leave their main job temporarily, to gain new knowledge, but maintain the "home link." A reassignment may be to another division or function within the organization, perhaps an overseas posting, or even to another organization entirely.

As you cross career bridges and gain valuable experience in reassignments, you may sometimes have to take what seems to be a step downwards. This should be temporary, as you are investing in your long-term career development. Personal growth should never be subservient to the acquisition of job grades and status or short-term rewards.

BALANCING WORK AND LIFE

Employees increasingly expect a good balance between work and life. This can be achieved by hot-desking, flexible hours, contracting out, part-time, telecommuting, sabbaticals, open contracts on self-managed careers, and "school-term" years. These are all practiced by progressive companies that treat their employees like human beings, and get the best out of people as a result.

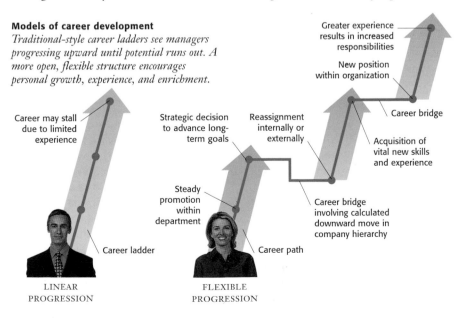

Models of career development
Traditional-style career ladders see managers progressing upward until potential runs out. A more open, flexible structure encourages personal growth, experience, and enrichment.

Greater experience results in increased responsibilities

New position within organization

Career bridge

Acquisition of vital new skills and experience

Career may stall due to limited experience

Strategic decision to advance long-term goals

Reassignment internally or externally

Steady promotion within department

Career bridge involving calculated downward move in company hierarchy

Career ladder

Career path

LINEAR PROGRESSION

FLEXIBLE PROGRESSION

SUCCEEDING IN A NEW JOB

ONCE YOU HAVE TAKEN A NEW JOB, THE HARDEST PART LIES AHEAD. YOU WANT TO MAKE AN IMPACT AND DEMONSTRATE YOUR SKILLS AND VALUE, BUT YOU MUST ALSO ASSESS AND ASSIMILATE THE COMPANY'S "WAY WE DO THINGS AROUND HERE."

GETTING STARTED

Most organizations have some kind of orientation program, which introduces new members of staff to the people and the processes of the company. Orientation is best seen as an ongoing process, separate from starting work in the actual job.

It will be up to you to find out about internal relationships: the politics of the business and the way in which the staff work together. At the same time you will need to familiarize yourself with all the outside links: the people and other organizations that your company serves and is served by.

DEMONSTRATE YOUR UNIQUE VALUE

It is not enough simply to be good at your work. You want key colleagues to recognize and respect your skills, abilities and achievements. You need to:
● make yourself visible
● highlight your contribution to organizational goals.

One useful way of thinking about how other people see you is the "Johari Window." This approach is based on the idea that there are things you know and do not know about yourself; there are also things that other people know and do not know about you. The aim is to increase both self-knowledge and others' knowledge of you. If you can identify and demonstrate those skills that are most useful to the organization (for example, raising sales, motivating staff), you will actively highlight your unique strengths and capability.

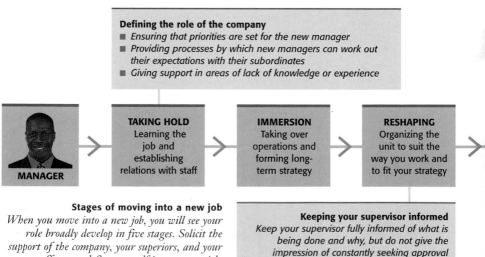

Defining the role of the company
■ Ensuring that priorities are set for the new manager
■ Providing processes by which new managers can work out their expectations with their subordinates
■ Giving support in areas of lack of knowledge or experience

MANAGER

TAKING HOLD
Learning the job and establishing relations with staff

IMMERSION
Taking over operations and forming long-term strategy

RESHAPING
Organizing the unit to suit the way you work and to fit your strategy

Stages of moving into a new job
When you move into a new job, you will see your role broadly develop in five stages. Solicit the support of the company, your superiors, and your staff as you define yourself in your new job.

Keeping your supervisor informed
Keep your supervisor fully informed of what is being done and why, but do not give the impression of constantly seeking approval

Using the Johari Window
The Johari Window expresses the idea of knowledge about ourselves and others. "Public" is the area of ourselves that is seen by others; "Blind" is what we do not know about ourselves; "Hidden" represents the aspects of ourselves that cannot be known to others unless we tell them; "Unknown" is the potential we have.

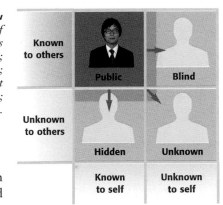

GETTING THE BEST VALUE FROM OTHER PEOPLE

Other people can play a big part in highlighting your effectiveness and getting you the support and recognition that you need. A personal mentor (a senior adviser who follows your career but does not supervise you at all) can:
● be your advocate in the organization
● help you plan and manage your career
● help you learn from experience
● give you guidance on your next steps.
In theory, mentors could be anyone in the organization, but usually they hold a prominent position. If possible, choose someone you enjoy working with, whose style and personality you find compatible.

Ideally, your line manager is your advocate – an unsympathetic boss may try to block your progress. As with all relationships, this one should be actively managed, on an adult-to-adult basis. Keep your boss informed, but also be sensitive to his or her priorities and needs. There is nothing Machiavellian about "managing your manager."

NETWORKING AND "HOTSPOTS"

Building relationships with key people is just as important as doing your current job well. Good social skills are absolutely vital, while networking will bring you a web of valuable contacts.

It is in your interest as well to identify the key jobs in the organization: the so-called "hotspots" that drive the business. Some organizations refer to the "traffic lights" system to highlight key jobs and people. Amber represents those hotspots, the crucial jobs that bring about change in an organization. Red is for people seen as brilliant, while Green is for those with the potential to be brilliant, but who have not yet been in the job long enough. Not surprisingly, companies aim to get Reds or Greens, rather than what are termed "blockers," into the Amber hotspots.

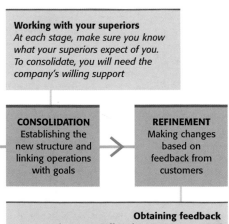

Working with your superiors
At each stage, make sure you know what your superiors expect of you. To consolidate, you will need the company's willing support

CONSOLIDATION
Establishing the new structure and linking operations with goals

REFINEMENT
Making changes based on feedback from customers

Obtaining feedback
Learn what your staff and customers expect of you as you progress from stage to stage, and use their feedback as a major source of ideas

CREATING A PERSONAL DEVELOPMENT PLAN

A PERSONAL DEVELOPMENT PLAN IDENTIFIES WHAT YOU NEED TO LEARN TO PROGRESS IN YOUR CAREER, AND PROVIDES A FRAMEWORK FOR ACHIEVING IT. YOU WILL THEN ADD TO YOUR STRENGTHS IN THE MARKETPLACE.

IDENTIFY YOUR LEARNING NEEDS

Make a concrete analysis of your learning needs by evaluating your current position and establishing what you would like to do next. Work performance can be measured under a number of key result areas, including:

- customers and clients: satisfying internal or external customers
- operations: managing processes or systems
- financial: raising profits or reducing production costs
- technical: applying specific skill sets
- resources: taking responsibility for people, materials, and equipment
- people: organizing, monitoring and motivating others
- teamwork: leading and working effectively with others

- information: interpreting information and translating it into knowledge
- innovation: finding better ways of doing things
- personal effectiveness: demonstrating motivation, organization, and flexibility.

Each key area will require a certain level of skill, acquired by listening, reading, and/or attending seminars and training courses. Skills usually require practice in a "real" situation in order to reach a required level of competence.

SET YOUR LEARNING OBJECTIVES

Having identified your learning needs, you should now set out clear objectives and draw up a plan for achieving them. You need to consider exactly what you want to learn, the desired level of competence, and a means of knowing

The stages of your personal development plan
In working out your plan, be as objective and realistic as possible, with long-term ambitions firmly in mind. Maintain a self-development checklist and monitor your progress in these key areas continually.

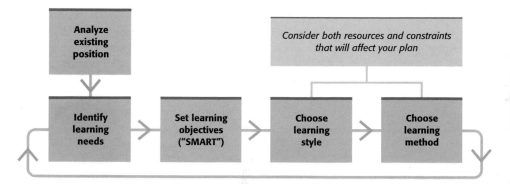

Analyze existing position

Consider both resources and constraints that will affect your plan

Identify learning needs → Set learning objectives ("SMART") → Choose learning style → Choose learning method

COMMITMENT Be honest. How committed are you?	TIME Do you really have time to fit everything in?	MONEY Do you have enough to fund your plan?	SUPPORT Are family and others close to you supportive?

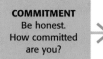

Assess your resources and constraints

For your plan to succeed, you need to assess realistically the resources that will sustain you and the constraints that will hamper you. These will be determined by your circumstances; what is a resource to one person is a constraint to another.

how you have reached that level. A useful acronym to remember is "**SMART**":

- **S**pecific: focus on one defined skill area.
- **M**easurable: set defined targets to assess your performance.
- **A**ttainable: you can reasonably expect to achieve them.
- **R**ealistic: they should be necessary and important enough to motivate you.
- **T**imebound: set a realistic time limit.

CHOOSE YOUR LEARNING STYLE

It is up to you how and where you acquire the information you need. There is a wide range of environments and tools, and you will know which you prefer.

You may like to work alone, at your own speed, in quiet surroundings, or you may prefer teamwork in a lively open-plan environment. Again, you may respond best to a highly organized, step-by-step system of learning, or prefer a looser, more flexible structure.

Learning tools include both the traditional (lectures, seminars, critiques of written work, in-depth discussions, and so on) and those of modern technology (computer-based instruction, interactive multimedia, videos, and so on). Make yourself aware of the available resources, and use them to maximum benefit.

CHOOSE YOUR LEARNING METHODS

When you have established what you need to learn, and your preferred tools and environment, you then have to consider the best way of learning for you. Make the method suit the topic, your personality, and your circumstances.

Qualifications

Courses leading to formal qualifications may be full-time, part-time or modular. They demand a high level of commitment and motivation, especially if combined with paid employment; but academic and professional qualifications will open doors and raise your self-esteem.

Training courses

This method is the one most commonly used for work-related learning. Many, though not all, organizations will provide a range of vocational and skills training courses, free to their employees. Take advantage of these.

On-the-job training

Working alongside skilled, experienced professionals and modeling yourself on what they do has been, and will continue to be, one of the most effective learning routes, particularly for busy people.

Special projects and reassignments

Special projects, or temporary or short-term contracts, may be a good way to prove yourself by turning knowledge and skills into useful experience. Highly relevant for both employed and self-employed people, these opportunities can be taken between jobs as well as within ongoing full-time employment.

Distance learning

This is flexible in terms of time, but very demanding in terms of the self-discipline needed to keep going. Some courses incorporate tutorials at certain times of the year. These enable people to overcome the loneliness of remote learning, meet up with colleagues and their instructor, exchange ideas, and ask questions.

Computer-based training (CBT)

CBT has similarities to distance learning, in terms of both flexibility and self-discipline, but uses IT and the Internet.

Reading

Reading is a quick and familiar way to acquire knowledge, although it does not in itself develop skills.

Coaching and mentoring

A coach or mentor helps motivated and capable people improve the way they work by encouraging and challenging them and by providing feedback.

CHECKING THE PLAN

A plan has limited use unless it is tested and measured. You need to maintain a checklist and monitor your progress on a regular basis. The following techniques are a good basis for self-management:

- specify a clear-cut (not unrealistic) goal that you want to accomplish
- set a target date by which you will achieve it
- quantify the desired output
- measure your hit rate: make a record of your successes and failures
- make a public commitment (tell someone your goals and deadline, and even ask them to check on you).

Be flexible: review your plan from time to time, and be willing to reset its course if necessary. It helps to discuss your self-management project with someone you meet with regularly and formally – a senior manager, colleague, or mentor.

LEAVING A JOB

DECIDING WHEN TO LEAVE A JOB CAN BE EVEN MORE DIFFICULT THAN STARTING A NEW ONE. YOU NEED TO ASSESS YOUR CURRENT SITUATION AND CONSIDER YOUR FUTURE OPTIONS. IT IS A BIG DECISION, AND ONE YOU MUST MAKE WITH CONFIDENCE.

WHAT WOULD MAKE YOU STAY?

Is there anything in your current job that would keep you there? Most people are motivated by the nature of their job, rather than money alone. Money may be important in recruiting staff, but not necessarily in encouraging them to stay. The key attraction seems to be interesting, challenging work, together with variety, autonomy, and good relationships with colleagues.

Other positive factors include the prospect of enhancing one's role – gaining strategic influence regardless of one's position in the hierarchy – and of achieving a significant level of personal development. So ask yourself:

- do you feel valued at work?
- are you adding any value to your organization?
- is your organization adding any value to you?
- is there still a buzz?
- do you look forward to going to work in the morning?

LOOK AHEAD

If your current job is not satisfying, take a longer-term view of your organization, and (given the information available to you) ask some more questions:

- What plans for the future is your organization considering?
- What changes will be needed to make these plans happen?
- Do these plans reveal anything about what the organization will be like as a place to work?
- What role could you then be playing?
- What would you expect to achieve?
- Where will you be working?
- Who will you be reporting to, and who will be reporting to you?
- What opportunities for training and career development will there be?
- Where would you be after another three, five, or 10 years?

If the answers are not inspiring, it probably is time for you to move on. And always remember – the best job does not necessarily pay the most money. If you can find another job that you actively enjoy, then you are much more likely to make a success of it.

WHEN TO MAKE THE RIGHT MOVE

It can be time-consuming to look for a new job while you are busy holding down your current one. While opportunities will always present themselves, it is a good idea to introduce a degree of structure into your search.

You could maximize your choices by "clustering" job applications so that offers crystallize at around the same time. This may involve time and energy during evenings and weekends, plus covert behavior at work. Increasingly, however, people are being up-front.

USING THE INTERNET

The Internet is generating a vast range of opportunities for people to change career direction. Be ready to embrace the unique opportunities that it offers. The explosion of e-commerce and the use of the web as a marketing and information medium have created many new job vacancies. There are few ideal candidates for these positions, however. Many of the required skills are still new and have to be learned, rather than being brought in from previous work.

Even if the Internet means little to you in relation to your specific career, it can be a highly fertile source of information on companies, careers, and job vacancies.

Knowing that they intend to move on, some resign from their existing position before they have a new one. This not only clears the air but, depending on notice periods, could well free up valuable time to make a thorough job search.

TAKING ACTION

Whatever your career move, be decisive. Most decisions are made with a combination of reason and emotion, using the head and heart. Having listed all the options, criteria, and priorities, think them through and then step back. Allow yourself time to see how you feel. You must feel good about your decision – confident that you have based it on the best available information, and with full knowledge of the consequences.

Whatever your decision, remember that it is *your* decision. Have no regrets. The beauty of managing your own career is that you are the one who is always in control, who always has the choice. Armed with this knowledge, approach your future with confidence.

Understanding Organizations

the learning
ORGANIZATION

AS THE INDUSTRIAL AGE GIVES WAY TO THE
INFORMATION AGE, WE NEED TO RADICALLY
RECONSIDER OUR APPROACH TO ORGANIZATIONS:
HOW THEY ARE ENERGIZED AND HOW THEY ARE
STRUCTURED. AS OLD CERTAINTIES AND BOUNDARIES
CRUMBLE, BUSINESS MUST ADAPT OR DIE.

It is increasingly recognized that people, and their rate of
learning, will determine the nature of future organizations.
All managers need to be aware of new developments that
affect their community, the marketplace, and their own
jobs. However, what remains constant is the fundamental
importance of the customer: the key to business success.

Any organization must be able to learn new processes
and create new adaptive structures. This is especially vital
when coping with global conditions of turbulence and
complexity, and their implications. Strategic thinking and
organizational capabilities should be constantly reviewed.
And throughout, the organization's explicit mission should
be guided by its intrinsic vision and values, while the
integrity of its public image and reputation is maintained.

THE IMPETUS TO CHANGE

ORGANIZATIONS HAVE TRADITIONALLY BEEN SEEN AS SIMPLE, RIGID, PYRAMID STRUCTURES, WITH WELL-DEFINED BOUNDARIES BETWEEN THEIR "INSIDE" AND "OUTSIDE" WORLDS. SUCH THINKING IS NOW OUT-OF-DATE. IN TODAY'S WORLD, ORGANIZATIONS MUST LEARN TO RESPOND RAPIDLY TO NEW DYNAMICS THAT ARE FORCING CHANGE ON THEM.

CHANGING VIEWS OF "ORGANIZING"

Many directors and managers no longer see their world as static or slowly evolving. Increasingly, they see it as part of a global entity that is uncertain, turbulent, complex, and fast-changing. This view causes immediate organizational problems for any static structure, and a need to redefine what is meant by "organizing," for the following reasons:

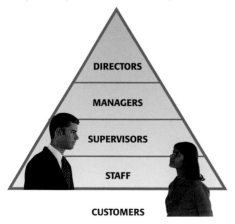

The classic pyramidal hierarchy
This structure of organization was the norm in business for a long time. At the top would be the directors, with power diffusing down successively lower layers of employees. And at the bottom would be the customers: the very people for whom the business existed.

- the previous, hierarchical organizational structures are not designed to cope with this new dynamic world view
- organizations are seen increasingly as a response both to reducing risks and to achieving tasks that small groups and individuals could not do on their own
- much of what has been taught as "management" has not included any serious study of organizing.

There is now a clear need to develop organizational capabilities and processes that will respond effectively to these changes in the external environment. This response must be far-reaching: it must include adapting to both changing customer needs and changes in the political, physical, economic, social, technological, and trade fields.

There is also a need to design organizational nimbleness far beyond anything ever dreamed of in the old bureaucracies. To ensure organizational responsiveness, we must encourage continuous learning by people at all levels of the organization, and across it.

People are the only organizational resource that is capable of learning. They can deal not just with the hard, numerical facts from the managerial control systems, but can also use the "soft facts" of sensing environmental changes and customer responses. Thus equipped, they are able to reach wise judgments based on both values and logic.

Creating a "learning organization" is now the visionary goal of many directors and managers. They see that establishing a "learning climate" would allow much richer and more transparent flows of honest data both within and outside the organization. In this way, people's learning can be turned into better quality information for audit, risk assessment, and decision-making.

HOW NEW LEARNING FLOWS AFFECT POWER

New flows of information have a key part to play in the erosion of traditional organizational boundaries. Today, staff and customers can find themselves simultaneously inside and outside the organization, for example as both employee and customer or citizen, and with a learning role in each position.

Such continuous, two-way flows of information irrevocably change the nature of the power of managers and directors. Traditionally, they had a strong, personal ability to amplify or reduce messages up and down the organization. This ability has now been reduced, allowing the development of new processes for creating and diffusing information across the organization.

As information power becomes more widely distributed across organizations, old hierarchical structures are being flattened. These days, there are often only four to six major organizational levels between the top and the bottom of organizations. The traditional managerial approaches to power, focusing on "top-down" and "command-and-control" positions, are being increasingly seen as valid only in limited conditions.

However, free-flowing information creates new problems. For example, what is the new role of a manager when more and more work groups have access to more and more information that allows them to begin to self-manage? Or, how does a manager plot a career path in a flattened hierarchy? The previous stereotype of continuously upward career progression must give way to more diagonal or tangential career moves, with an increased emphasis on the self-management of careers.

THE IMPLOSION OF MANAGEMENT

The rapid convergence of computing and telecommunications technologies means that information can flow all the way through an organization at the same time. The old notion of employing large numbers of "managers" to control the flows of information seems increasingly to be an indefensible cost.

This is why "management" as a role needs a major redefinition – but not to say that managers will disappear entirely. Some will be crucial to any organization for designing, installing, auditing, maintaining, and learning from the human and technological systems that ensure organizational survival and development.

With fewer managers, we will see the rise of more self-managed work groups. But their inputs and outputs will still need managerial coordination and control throughout the organization.

SOME CONSEQUENCES FOR ORGANIZING

In future, the nature of this key process of organizing is likely to be affected in four major ways.

Encouraging diversity

As people "become their own tools" in the information age, systematic learning is vital for survival in increasingly turbulent and complex global markets.

There will be pressure to seriously reconsider how to unlock and use human diversity in organizations.

Eroding the boundaries

Organizations will become more and more "virtual," forced by cost pressures to downsize and "rightsize." They will outsource more processes, employ more staff on shorter fixed-term contracts, and use single-project contract staff. This will erode the inside/outside boundaries.

Keeping up with change

Learning regularly and rigorously at work will become necessary at all levels of the organization's new hierarchy, to keep up with the rate of change in its external environment.

Freeing systems

Learning systems will be developed to allow for a more open, critical review. This will apply both within each organizational level and between them.

GETTING THE BALANCE RIGHT

An organization needs to balance effectiveness (as perceived by the customer) with efficiency (as perceived by the managers and accountants). This will necessitate more rigorous design and maintenance systems of organizational capabilities, along with regular auditing of them.

The traditional approach to organizing embraces strictly segmented functional disciplines or divisions, which use only short-term, convergent thinking styles for managerial problem-solving. The wider organizational implications are not taken into account, and neither is the external context. This approach is dying rapidly, as are those organizations that insist on staying with it. To be effective, organizations must rise to the challenge of constant external turbulence and create new organizational capabilities.

THE CHANGING ORGANIZATION

TO SURVIVE, AND THRIVE, IN A WORLD OF RAPID CHANGE, AN ORGANIZATION MUST ALWAYS BE READY TO ADAPT. NEW CONCEPTS AND NEW TECHNOLOGIES BRING NEW BOUNDARIES, AND SUCCESS WILL DEPEND ON IDENTIFYING AND RESPONDING TO THEM.

THE ORGANIZATIONAL CONTEXT

Traditional boundaries are being eroded, and not only between the inside and outside of organizations. Computing and telecommunications technologies have converged to blur familiar demarcations between "retail" and "wholesale," for example, or between "companies" and "government." New flows of customer information, new customer demands, and new delivery channels are forcing a fundamental rethink of such concepts.

The challenge now is to identify the key component activities for competitive success in this new world. Then it is necessary to organize effectively and efficiently for this, and so define your new boundaries.

Whether you work in a traditional manufacturing company, or a rapidly developing new service industry, the basis of business, and business analysis, will remain the same: the design, production, sale, and distribution of goods and services. What is changing now is the growing need for new organizational structures and processes to service these demands.

However, these demands will require a significant change of directorial and managerial problem-solving mind-sets and behavior. There needs to be a shift from the present dominant "either/or" (binary) thinking to the more subtle "both...and" (integrative) thinking. Many current managers are not yet prepared for this. The challenge for managers is how to start.

MAINTAINING
ORGANIZATIONAL INTEGRITY

As the ranks of overhyped dot-com entrepreneurs learned to their loss, no one in a democratic society has ever suspended the laws of economics for more than a few months without dire consequences. It is worth remembering two fundamental truths of business and organizing, which have held force over the centuries, even in times of great turbulence and complexity:

- the customer is paramount
- the customer's perception is all.

It is only the customers who matter. No "market" ever bought anything. And customers increasingly have global access to more transparent information through the internet. Logically, this could lead to all products becoming commodified: that is, being seen as so similar that they are sold only at the lowest price quoted.

How can this be avoided? Studies have shown that the key is to create a certain perception in the customer's mind. Your offering must be seen as significantly different and a good value. The customer will then stay loyal (and so reduce your cost of sales), and be willing to pay a small premium price (and so increase your margins).

This differentiated marketing approach, based on core competencies, helps counter the "cost leadership" strategy

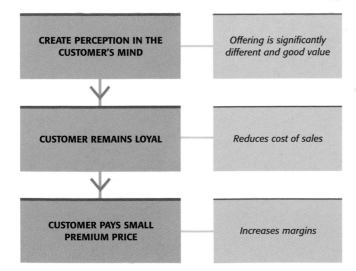

CREATE PERCEPTION IN THE CUSTOMER'S MIND	Offering is significantly different and good value
CUSTOMER REMAINS LOYAL	Reduces cost of sales
CUSTOMER PAYS SMALL PREMIUM PRICE	Increases margins

Building up customer loyalty
Customers want good quality, good service, and good value. A learning organization is aware that through the internet, customers can access a global marketplace where often the only distinction between competing brands is the price. So if you make your offering distinctive, desirable customers will become – and stay – loyal and be willing to pay extra. With customer loyalty comes the opportunity for increased profit.

adopted increasingly by big businesses, which leads to low prices and tiny margins. Inevitably, many companies fail, as they are unable to compete on cost and volume with the few globalized big players. In organizational terms, it is important to note that in the service/profit chain approach, the perception of good value by customers relies highly on simultaneously retaining both customer loyalty and good customer-facing staff.

The customer's perception is based on both logic and emotion. They must be able to "sell" to themselves and to others the idea of buying the product or service from you, in terms of both the logic of its utility and the emotional benefits given by the purchase. A manager needs to install and maintain organizational systems and create an organizational culture that will guarantee delivery of goods and services that meet all the customer needs of quality, budget, and time.

This provides the long-term basis of the customer's logical and emotional attachment to your product or service, which over time creates a "brand image." This is an essential tool if you are to survive by using a differentiation strategy.

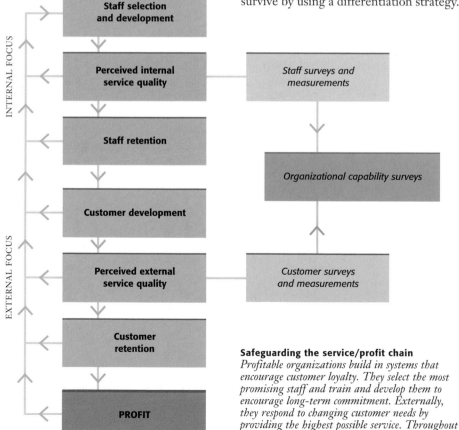

Safeguarding the service/profit chain
Profitable organizations build in systems that encourage customer loyalty. They select the most promising staff and train and develop them to encourage long-term commitment. Externally, they respond to changing customer needs by providing the highest possible service. Throughout the chain the systems are monitored continuously.

COPING WITH TURBULENCE AND COMPLEXITY

IN A FAST-MOVING WORLD, SIMPLY TRAINING PEOPLE FOR A SINGLE JOB IS NOT SUFFICIENT. WHILE TRAINING IN ITSELF IS NECESSARY AND ENSURES THAT A PERSON HAS REACHED A SPECIFIED LEVEL OF COMPETENCY, STAFF MUST BE FURTHER ENCOURAGED TO LEARN CONTINUALLY FROM THEIR WORK.

ENSURING CONTINUOUS CUSTOMER FOCUS

With the development of greater power in computing and telecommunications technologies, even large-scale, automated production processes no longer need make only standardized products. Now, each item can be "customized" on the production line. A good illustration of this phenomenon is what happened after Ford acquired Jaguar Cars. There was a massive surge in both volume and quality, with cars being created to an individual specification for individual customers.

For service industries, whose staff are often face-to-face with the customer at the point of delivery, this use of technology allows them to be seen as more sensitive to customer needs. In turn, this means having to develop staff to become better at both interpersonal and problem-solving skills than had previously been thought necessary. As the outside/inside interface of the organization becomes more sensitive, so customer loyalty can grow.

With many organizations becoming less centralized and more like a series of parallel projects, there is more need for future managers to become skilled project leaders across the whole organization. This means a dual role for directors and managers, who must:

- create a conscious, and continuous, dynamic tension between the task achievement aspects and the social process by which the project is delivered successfully
- ensure the simultaneous development of high-quality, experienced staff throughout centers of excellence in the organization.

DECENTRALIZING THE PROCESS

The operational (day-to-day) power to learn through decision-making in response to customer needs should be delegated to the lowest possible layers of the organization: that is, those staff who have the most face-to-face contact with customers. These staff make the minute-to-minute and hour-to-hour decisions that affect the customer's perception of the organization's effectiveness. This is enhanced if individuals and work groups establish a culture of conscious learning at all levels of the organization.

Typically, this will involve members of staff becoming self-managing as a work group. They then pass on their learning to other related work groups, both horizontally and vertically within the organization, through defined types of agreement.

Finally, they learn how to ensure rigorous and regular critical reviews of their work in relation to the organization as a whole.

ESTABLISHING A CYCLE

Often, the decentralizing process means getting rid of old organizational baggage. For example, the traditional tyranny of 12-month budgeting can be cast out. Few work groups fit a 12-month cycle. Some need only a month or two, while others may need a couple of weeks.

While the 12-month period may be a legal requirement to produce annual financial statements, there is no such legal requirement for producing budgets. This period may be administratively convenient, but it has become a burden in many organizations. Twelve months is usually too long for operational learning, and often too short for strategic thinking. It is preferable for the budget cycle to be adapted to the learning needs of the work group, while the accountants figure out the annual rationalization and presentation of the finances.

DELEGATING POWER

Delegating operational power can be quite an unsettling experience for many directors and managers. It requires them to undergo a process of conscious personal learning, while developing a positive emotional organizational climate in which to share such learning. This whole process can be achieved relatively easily in some small organizations, but in many larger departments or companies, it requires conscious and sustained directorial and managerial effort.

A notable example of such an approach is BP Amoco's introduction of a personalized "home page" on its intranet for every staff member. Over a five-year period, the learning culture changed significantly for the better. Originally, most people would hoard data as a source of power, but with this innovation they moved on to sharing information and learning for the common good.

As a result, if someone has a problem, it is now accepted (and rewarded) behavior to consult others via the intranet. The person with the problem can ask if anyone has faced such a difficulty before and, if so, which solutions worked under what conditions. Whatever the issue in question – which could be anything from viewing a stuck pipe in Alaska via the webcam to coping with a taxation wrangle in Kazakhstan – members of staff are expected to be able to tap the learning of the whole organization, in both technical and organizational terms.

LEARNING TO LEARN

If such learning processes, organizational culture, and corporate strategic intent are encouraged, this will allow the development over time of a corporate value that builds on the famous Revans axiom. This holds that for any organism to survive, its rate of learning (L) must be equal to, or greater than, the rate of change (C) in its environment:

$$L \geq C$$

This attitude becomes the central value for solving organizational issues.

In these times of turbulence and uncertainty, this is a vital attitude to have for all levels of the organization, from the board of directors to the unit managers' meeting, from the out on the road sales team or the maintenance engineers to the workers in the call-center.

This new mind-set is a fundamental requirement for all managers who are trying to organize for the future.

ORGANIZING FOR THE FUTURE

THE MODERN MARKETPLACE DEMANDS A RADICAL CHANGE FROM THE TRADITIONAL PYRAMID STRUCTURE OF ORGANIZATIONS. THESE DAYS, MEMBERS OF STAFF SHOULD BE ENCOURAGED TO LEARN, TO LOOK BEYOND THEIR JOB DESCRIPTIONS, AND ABOVE ALL TO ALWAYS BE CUSTOMER-FRIENDLY.

THE PROBLEM WITH A PYRAMID STRUCTURE

Most people of all cultures around the world still see organizations as pyramids, with authority flowing down from an omnipotent figure at the apex. While all organizations have hierarchies that are based on a mixture of sources of power, strictly pyramidal hierarchies tend to be

The inverted pyramid
Turning the traditional structure of an organization on its head, this model radically changes business priorities. Now the customer is at the top of the pyramid of power, interacting with front-line staff in "moments of truth" that define the customer's relationship with the business.

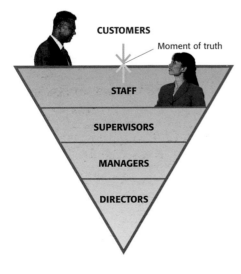

CUSTOMERS

Moment of truth

STAFF

SUPERVISORS

MANAGERS

DIRECTORS

focused only "inside the organization." In a complex and turbulent external environment, such internally oriented organizations will not survive.

Virtually all such pyramidal structures exclude the very reason for their existence: the customer (for the private sector) or consumer or citizen (for the public sector). Typically, these "outsiders" will not appear on an organization chart, or in any statement of organizational competence. Yet these are the very people who pay for the products, or the taxes for the services, and so pay the wages of everyone in the organization.

The mind-sets of all directors and managers must change so that in future they focus on the primary issue that "the customer is paramount." Those who actually pay for the product or service should have their needs listened to sensitively, and responded to seriously, sympathetically, and effectively.

How can such changes in attitude and function be brought about? In short, how do we organize for the future?

INVERTING THE PYRAMID IN FAVOR OF THE CUSTOMER

An effective approach for the operational aspects of organizing is to turn the hierarchical pyramid upside-down in everyone's thinking and behavior. This puts the customer firmly on top.

This idea is quite revolutionary for many organizations. It stresses that whatever we do inside the organization, it must be for the benefit of the customer outside, and not for the managers and staff within. This demonstrates a

THE IMPACT ON MANAGEMENT

In the inverted pyramid style of organizing, the supervisors, or first-line managers, of the customer-facing staff become more important in day-to-day decisions. They need to have more internal discretionary power to ensure the continuing positive motivation and learning of each work group. They also need their own agreed levels of external discretion to cope with each customer's needs, while staying within the managerial control systems. In becoming more sensitized to changing customer needs, these supervisors become a crucial part of the external environmental monitoring process, spanning the inside/outside boundary of the organization.

Middle and senior managers become less involved in the hour-to-hour, day-to-day decisions of the organization. Their job is to design, implement, audit, and maintain the operational risk assessment and control systems. They must be able to see connections across functions, rather than keep their thinking within a single functional discipline. So, whether they come from finance, sales, operations, human resources, design, or marketing, they need to develop an overall, "helicopter view" to ensure that they are functioning as part of the integrated, mutually dependent, whole organization.

As information management systems begin to take over many of the old managerial message-passing roles, and as organizations are progressively flattened to reduce costs, the inverted pyramid style of organization speeds up the implosion of "management" at distinct levels of the organization.

different mind-set from that commonly found in, for example, Japan, China, Russia, and many continental European countries. The inverted pyramid model shows that the customer is indeed "paramount." When this is recognized, the business priorities are highlighted.

INCREASING THE IMPORTANCE OF CUSTOMER-FACING STAFF

Customer-facing staff are key players in the inverted pyramid scenario. Their direct interactions with the customers – their "moments of truth" – determine whether the customers are willing to buy from you again or not.

This is a major change in the attitude of most organizations. It is no longer the brilliance of the directors' vision, values, or mission statements, or the insight of the business strategy that affects the customers' emotions and decision to buy. Customers rarely meet directors or strategists, but they do often come into contact with other members of an organization: sales assistants, for example, or telephonists, check-in clerks, and maintenance crew. These are the true customer-facing staff.

Customer-facing staff are the main creators of a customer's perception of the company and the brand. Unless staff are properly trained they can be very unimpressive and disconcerting, so there is a need to invest in training. Customer-facing staff need to learn and apply simple, robust, problem-solving and interpersonal skills. This improves the quality of their customer contacts, and by using systems of regular feedback from customers, significantly improves the organization's rate of learning.

It is important that customer-facing staff should be given clearly prescribed levels of discretionary power. When required, they need to be flexible to some extent in order to accommodate a customer's individual needs.

DEVELOPING THE LEARNING ORGANIZATION

IN A LEARNING ORGANIZATION, DIRECTORS AND SENIOR MANAGERS ARE ACTIVELY ENGAGED AT THE CENTER OF TWO INTEGRAL CYCLES OF ORGANIZATIONAL LEARNING: THE POLICY-FORMULATING AND THE OPERATIONAL. THIS CENTRAL, BALANCING ACTIVITY DEPENDS CRUCIALLY ON STRATEGIC THINKING.

IDENTIFYING DIRECTORIAL AND MANAGERIAL ROLES

Within an inverted pyramid model of organizing, directors are hardly visible because their role is not operational. They have major duties in the areas of policy and strategy, and these are not addressed by this model.

A model that does address, and integrate, the directorial role as well as the managerial is the increasingly popular idea of the learning organization. This model builds on the operational aspects of the inverted pyramid model, but it represents the whole organization as a series of three continuous learning loops.

One important aspect of this model is that to maintain reasonable stability in the organization, the operations' learning cycle must continue to do the daily, routine work. It must be able to deal with any deviations from plans, and so

Understanding the learning loops
Here the three continuous loops representing the whole organization are split into two parts to show the respective functions of employees and directors. Employees maintain routine operations, while directors address policy and strategy.

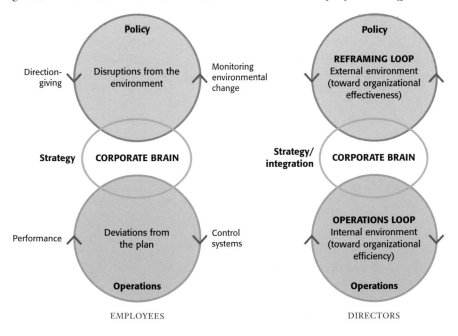

Policy	Policy
Direction-giving — Disruptions from the environment — Monitoring environmental change	REFRAMING LOOP — External environment (toward organizational effectiveness)
Strategy — CORPORATE BRAIN	Strategy/integration — CORPORATE BRAIN
Performance — Deviations from the plan — Control systems	OPERATIONS LOOP — Internal environment (toward organizational efficiency)
Operations	Operations
EMPLOYEES	DIRECTORS

increase organizational efficiency. At the same time, in order for the organization to be healthy, the directors and managers must ensure that a balance is struck between organizational efficiency (as seen by the managers) and organizational effectiveness (as seen by the customer).

Directors affect this balance through their own learning in the policy and strategy cycles. They cope with, and learn from, disruptions caused by the external environment (their policy formulation), and their subsequent positioning of the business in the changing markets (their strategic thinking).

With the responsibility of leading the total organization, the directors must always ensure – as noted earlier – that its rate of learning is equal to, or greater than, the rate of change in the external environment. So, in addition to gaining a better understanding of changing customer needs, they must now increase awareness of competitor intelligence, and also be alert to changes in what is called the PPESTT (Political, Physical, Economic, Social, Technological, and Trade) trend analysis.

THE ROLE OF THE BOARD OF DIRECTORS

The information generated in the policy-generation cycle of learning is taken by what can be called the "learning board" into the strategy learning cycle. This allows much higher quality information (provided especially by customer-facing staff), risk assessment, and debate by board members and senior executives. Then the organization's scarce resources can be positioned in the best possible way for maximum effect in the changing outside environment.

This board-based process of critical review, risk assessment, and debate creates an annual rhythm for the organization's year.

THE NEED FOR CONTINUOUS STRATEGIC THINKING

In this new system, strategic thinking, not strategic planning, is the key skill for the board and senior managers. To help develop this, it is important to understand that strategic thinking revolves around the primary, and continuous, directorial dilemma: "How do we drive the

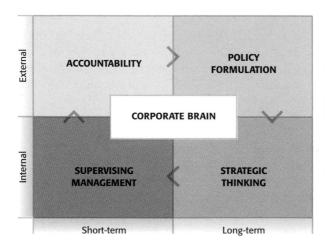

The "Learning Board" model
In this model, the board – or the corporate brain – is now positioned at the center of the organization, and not isolated at the top of a pyramidal hierarchy. It has become what could be called the central processor of the organization, blending information from both internal and external sources. In this way, it learns effectively from the operational and policy worlds before it makes its strategic decisions.

enterprise forward while keeping it under prudent control?"

Board performance is monitored by its ability to implement its strategies, and so learn how best to balance and continually rebalance this fundamental dilemma. Sadly, implementing strategy and learning from the feedback is one of the least preferred thinking styles for many directors and senior managers. They tend to be much happier dealing with the daily micropolitics of the organization (the use of "soft" facts), and then using their strong inclination to logic to rationalize what is occurring.

Such people are often annoyed by the intervention of "hard" facts (being told the consequences of their actions). In an era of overconcentration on the short-term, financial bottom line, there is now a marked tendency to downsize and "rightsize," and then capsize.

THE RISK OF TAKING
SHORT-TERM FIXES

Hacking too deeply into the cost base of an organization may temporarily increase its efficiency, but at the same time it can damage its long-term effectiveness as perceived by the customer. It then cannot become a learning organization.

Similarly, a thoughtless reduction of the "experience base" of an organization weakens its motivation to learn, and leads ultimately to "organizational amnesia." By the time that this stage is reached, few people really know, or care, how the organization works any more. Then everybody is forced to keep relearning, expensively, what had previously been known. This is a hugely debilitating process in terms of time and money, and usually wipes out any efficiency gains.

THE EFFECTS OF ALIENATION

In the service industries, where downsizing has been taken to extremes – in the banks and airline services for example – customers leave, or "churn," by the thousands. This is not because they have anything notably better to go to, but because their emotional bond with the service provider has been broken. They become disenchanted, and finally angry.

The economic consequences for the business of breaking this bond are profound in the medium and long term. First, the cost of sales rises enormously as many new customers must be recruited to maintain anything like the old volumes (so margins are usually substantially reduced). Second, the previously loyal customer base becomes fickle and shops around for each specific need, often via the internet.

The combination of increased sales costs, increased customer "churn," and the push by nondiscriminating customers to commodify products or services through demanding lowest prices, can be crippling for a business. These economic aspects of organizational capability are rarely measured or discussed by directors and senior executives. Many of them believe that finance is the only measure for organizations, and they are shocked to find that more enlightened enterprises are developing more integrated and balanced organizational measures.

ORGANIZATIONAL CAPABILITY

The table on page 49 lists 12 organizational capabilities that could profitably be developed in an organization. A measure for these starts with the idea that work can be broken into two basic components: task focus (with which most of us are comfortable), and emotional process focus (with which many are uncomfortable).

We can achieve our allotted tasks of working with others only if the specified task is clear, and the working process sufficiently socially elastic to allow people to be willing to work together. Where people cannot work together, there will be no development of a "learning culture." Indeed, a "blame culture" will arise, to the detriment of the business. This emotional aspect of work is often not appreciated, yet it is ignored by directors and managers at their peril.

REORGANIZING ORGANIZATIONAL CAPABILITY

THE ORGANIZATIONAL CAPABILITIES OF A BUSINESS ARE CREATED BY THE COMPLEX INTERACTION BETWEEN ITS INTERNAL AND EXTERNAL WORLDS, AND ALSO BETWEEN INDIVIDUALS' FEELINGS ABOUT THEIR WORK AND WORKING RELATIONSHIPS. IT IS THE INDIVIDUAL, AND NOT THE SYSTEM, THAT ULTIMATELY DETERMINES THE QUALITY AND QUANTITY OF THE WORK OUTPUT.

THE TASK ELEMENTS

The task elements of organizing can be classified as internally oriented or externally oriented. The internal can be characterized as:
● clarity of personal responsibility
● organizational clarity
● financial rewards.
The externally oriented task elements can be characterized as:
● work quality perspective
● competitor orientation.

THE SOCIAL–EMOTIONAL PROCESSES

Frustratingly, the crucial "soft" areas of social–emotional processes can be influenced only indirectly by directors and managers. They can create the right conditions, the right emotional climate, and ultimately the right organizational culture. But in the end, these processes are controlled by the individuals in the workplace themselves.

This makes the processes invisible to most managers, yet they are strong enough to determine the final output of work. Internally, these capabilities are:
● personal rewards
● personal performance indicators
● group performance indicators.
Externally, they are:
● organizational adaptiveness
● customer orientation.
Finally, two further capabilities the whole organization is held together and energized by have a crucial role and feed off each other continuously:
● leadership
● learning climate.
Organizational capability should be regularly surveyed. Then the directors, managers, and staff members can be shown, graphically and transparently, the trend on each dimension of organizational capability: from where we are to where

The 12 Organizational Capabilities model
This model focuses on the task elements involved in an organization, and the emotional processes experienced by the members of staff who carry out those tasks. Tasks and emotional processes are viewed from both an internal and external perspective, identifying 10 specific capabilities. The remaining two, leadership orientation and learning climate, are closely linked together and function as the dynamo of the whole organization.

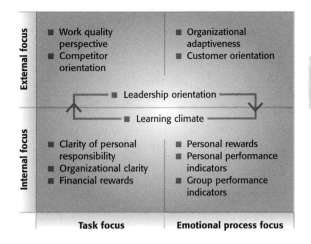

External focus

- Work quality perspective
- Competitor orientation

- Organizational adaptiveness
- Customer orientation

- Leadership orientation
- Learning climate

Internal focus

- Clarity of personal responsibility
- Organizational clarity
- Financial rewards

- Personal rewards
- Personal performance indicators
- Group performance indicators

Task focus | **Emotional process focus**

we need to be. This then forms the agenda for constant adaptation within the organization relating to the changing external environment.

While the inverted pyramid and the learning organization models are becoming popular ways of organizing for the future, the very complexity of that future needs to be understood for any manager aspiring to be a director.

GETTING TO GRIPS WITH COMPLEX ADAPTIVE SYSTEMS

Many data-rational directors and managers, driven by the bottom line, find measuring the "hard" and "soft" aspects of organizing uncomfortable. Their training and subsequent attitudes have not geared them for a world in which turbulence is a given and disruptions are frequent. They grapple with the phenomenon of organizations becoming more "virtual," as they downsize and outsource. They see the whole world as so complex that nothing is totally certain in science or business anymore.

Complexity Theory is being applied to the issues of the governance of an organization. It accepts that the world is so interdependent that nothing is totally predictable. This approach can be characterized by four major assertions.

Chance as cause
You cannot predict what will happen, no matter how familiar the inputs seem to you. Outcomes are created through random choices, or chance, within the system. This does not mean that just anything can happen, because constraints operate as choices. In a Complex Adaptive System (operating both inside and outside the organization), chance, rather than any immutable law, causes the particular outcome.

Winning as losing
Evolution happens when an organization, or ecology, is replaced because it failed to respond to a new challenge. It has not kept up with the rate of change in its environment. But even understanding this will not guarantee "winning" in the new environment. Chaotic instabilities, via feedback and natural selection, may cause current fitness to decrease (contrasting with the usual view that selection always increases fitness).

Organizations as structures and processes

This assertion picks up the argument about organizational capabilities and stresses the interrelationship of both, so that having an effective structure and process mutually determine each other.

Rationality as limitation

You can succeed without overfocusing on rational planning if you can understand your structural position inside and outside the organization, and then learn how best to exploit the stream of opportunities and threats that your position invites.

COPING WITH THE CHALLENGE OF CHANGE

A number of managers and directors may find these assertions of Complexity Theory challenging, and even disturbing. As mentioned earlier, many would have been brought up as professionals on "convergent thinking" problem-solving styles, and the primacy of data-rationality. Accordingly, their mind-sets are not easily geared to cope with an irrational, unpredictable external world and an increasingly "virtual" internal world. In times of increasing uncertainty, most such managers and directors try to become even more rational and more bottom-line oriented – which usually only makes matters worse.

However, learning organizations are designed to cope with such a challenging world, and organizational capability measures help to audit and develop effective organizational responses. They are important human attempts to cope with understanding how to deploy one's scarce organizational resources in the vast scope of a complex world.

MANAGING BOTH INSIDE AND OUTSIDE THE ORGANIZATION

As we progress through the information age, with its emphasis on learning and the consequent acquisition of knowledge assets, then "people become their own tools." This is a fundamentally important concept for all future directors and managers. It demands the need to rethink our approach to organizations, so that they release and readily use the natural learning, commitment, and energies of their people.

A key element of such release is in consciously changing the direction of everybody's problem-solving skills, away from overconcentration on prediction and certainty. This means encouraging the development of organizational competencies that show nimbleness, and the toleration of ambiguity to generate more creativity and a more effective implementation.

ORGANIZATIONAL GOVERNANCE

Some people may ask the question, why should we bother with all of this? Surely organizations will plow through in the same old way, with the weak going to the wall and the strong producing profits or surpluses for their owners? Why not leave strong managers to create their own organizations, within the law, to deliver their goods or services?

Such thinking was acceptable until the end of the twentieth century, but now the sociopolitical tide is turning, and organizations must take heed as the following pressures build:

- for too long organizations have increasingly been seen by their users to have underperformed in terms of effectiveness and efficiency

ADAPTING TO DEVELOPMENT PROCESSES

Altering the way that people think about organizations needs a radical change in the mind-sets of us all. There has to be a shift in the organizational balances and rewards from:

- demanding certainty to accepting and using complexity and diversity
- only "hands-on" managing to more "brain-on" working
- praising logical reductionism to rewarding "both … and" creative thinking
- overemphasizing the importance of organizational structure to acceptance of the importance of organizational process
- thinking of organizations as purely mechanical structures to seeing them as interrelated, mutually dependent, living human systems
- seeing organizations as fixed, rigid hierarchies to seeing them as complex adaptive learning systems
- always accepting the need for a large "management" level to accepting more self-managed work groups that can function without top-down management
- focusing on distinct, functional groups to accepting integrative working and thinking
- staff feeling helpless, trapped in a psychic prison to their becoming active, valued members of a learning organization.

disregard of customers, shareholders, and stakeholders has changed the external political climate to a point where the cries of "Something must be done" are growing fast.

Both nationally and internationally, politicians are forcing organizational changes, through new laws on liabilities, responsibilities, and accountabilities, and an increasing range of tough, honest, and transparent audits. Organizations used to be able to get away with just an annual financial report. This is increasingly considered insufficient. In future we shall see the development of "triple bottom-line" reporting, at least annually, on:

- financial performance
- physical environmental performance
- social performance.

This may sound like a fantasy land to many current directors and managers. It is not. It needs to be taken seriously by anyone organizing for the twenty-first century. A number of multinational organizations, led by Shell International, have already started to report in this way. They have agreed tight measures in each of the three performance areas, and have appointed separate and independent external auditors to ensure the credibility of their figures. These reflect clearly changed mind-sets and show that the inside/outside organizational boundaries are becoming increasingly blurred.

The rise of such accountabilities to prominence brings into sharper focus the growing pressure from "stakeholders" for better organizational performance. The term "stakeholders" includes not only shareholders but also customers, staff members, suppliers, the physical environment, and local communities.

Whereas shareholders have a direct say over the ownership, values, priorities, and control of the organization, the other stakeholders usually have indirect powers to influence the outcome of the business through law and community pressures. These pressures will not go away: quite the reverse. They will have an increasing influence on what a future organization can, and cannot, do.

Looking back on recorded history, the essence of good corporate governance in a civil society is based on the fundamental values of accountability, probity, and transparency. These values work at both the governmental and corporate levels. They are the values on which we need to build our future organizations so that they become beneficial, mutually dependent, and vital elements of our society. Organizations can no longer be comfortably isolated. Indeed, looking at the new techniques and processes that have been brought in, it is now possible to see that future organizations will be more democratic.

STATING THE VISION AND MISSION

WHAT DISTINGUISHES ANY ORGANIZATION FROM ANOTHER IS ITS ESSENTIAL PURPOSE, AND THE WAY IN WHICH THAT PURPOSE IS CARRIED OUT. IF THE PURPOSE AND THE CONSEQUENT ACTION ARE BOTH MADE EXPLICIT, THE ORGANIZATION HAS A MUCH GREATER CHANCE OF SUCCESS.

IDENTIFYING THE PURPOSE, VISION, AND MISSION

The "purpose" is the fundamental reason for the organization's existence. This may be "to create shareholder value," or "to improve health services for this region." The "vision" is a long-term aspiration of how the company aims to develop in relation to its world; it may be "to be the world's first 'green' pharmaceutical company," for instance. Finally, the "mission" is the objective or set of objectives that will allow the vision to become reality.

Writing down a vision and compiling a mission statement are not enough, although many companies have wrongly concluded that they are. A vision has value only if it conveys explicitly what the organization intends to become. The more concise, realistic, meaningful and widely accepted it is by staff and shareholders, then the greater its worth.

Most vision statements fail abysmally on a number of counts. While they should be a conscious challenge for all staff over the long term, too often they are generated by the top person alone, or by a small top group. The words in the vision statement are often interchangeable with those of countless other organizations' statements. This is partly because the wording is vague and the message unfocused, so it cannot be readily understood or easily memorized.

CHECKLIST

✔ Should be the work of many hands, not imposed by top management

✔ Should have consensus support

✔ Should be unique to the organization, not equally applicable to many others

✔ Should be concentrated and specific, not generalized and rambling

✔ Should be easy to understand as well as memorable.

A GOOD VISION STATEMENT

TradeCom® will become the premier global supplier of website services, by achieving unbeatable standards of quality, productivity, and innovation.

Making the vision statement work
The vision statement should be short and to the point. As in this example, it should say simply what the goal of the organization is – making it superlative – and specify the positive steps of achieving that goal.

Making the mission statement work
The mission statement builds on the vision statement, but the two are distinct. The mission statement sets out the objectives whereby the particular vision will be realized. These objectives should be specific and positive, and convey a dynamic commitment to success. They must be grounded in reality: the organization must have the infrastructure and resources to carry them out.

A GOOD MISSION STATEMENT

TradeCom® will seek to be rated "the best" by customers on those attributes of our products and services that they value most.

We will monitor all key operating efficiencies and aim to improve them by at least 10 percent every year.

We will work to earn half of our revenues and profits in three years' time from new products and services.

MASTERING THE VISION

A truly valuable vision starts with a task force. Its first task is to establish just where the organization is now, and how it is perceived by its constituencies: customers, employees, suppliers, opinion-formers, and the public at large.

The next task is to establish what progress the organization intends to make: that is, what it wishes to become. A notable illustration of progression is the rise of Honda, which, under its founder Soichiro Honda, was world-famous for motorcycles. Honda's vision was to achieve an equal reputation and global success with cars and become a premier automobile manufacturer.

The vision, while it can and should be expressed in words only, must (like Honda's) translate readily into tangibles. A "premier position" implies a certain scale, range of models, mastery of technologies, cash flow, market share,

and profitability. Also, the vision should define the company's activities: what it will specifically do. Another car firm, Daimler-Benz, defined its vision too broadly (as a transportation firm rather than an automobile maker) and created great difficulties for itself by doing so.

VISION INTO MISSION

A vision that translates readily into concrete, measurable ambitions thereby generates a mission statement of equal power. This statement sets out the broad, dynamic objectives for the organization.

Neither the vision statement nor the mission statement is itself a strategy, but together, they establish a strategic framework. They should, however, be quite distinct. Many mission statements read like visions under another name. If the vision is to become "the largest, most profitable, and most respected supplier of microwidgets, leading the industry on all key factors valued by the customers," the mission task force must establish:

● how largest is defined
● what profitability targets are required
● how respect will be achieved and measured
● which key factors customers value
● how far short the organization falls on the above four counts.

Once such demanding questions are answered, the mission statement can be drafted, concentrating on clear objectives that people can pursue in their own working lives. Drafts of both vision and mission statements should be widely circulated, and objections and suggestions taken into account before the task force produces its final work. Part of

that is to hone down the text to the shortest length but maintaining clarity and purpose.

Finally, remember that circumstances change, and organizations should not become complacent. The statements must be revisited each year, studied again in detail, revised as necessary, and then resold to the organization.

When another great Japanese manager, Ryuzaburo Kaku of Canon, achieved his vision of "climbing Mount Fuji" by becoming a "premier Japanese company," he moved on to "climbing Mount Everest" and becoming a "premier world company." There are always new mountains to climb, but the vision and values do not change.

MAINTAINING IMAGE AND REPUTATION

HOW AN ORGANIZATION IS VIEWED AND RATED BY ITS CUSTOMERS DETERMINES ITS SUCCESS IN MANY WAYS. IT IS CRUCIAL TO UNDERSTAND THAT PERCEPTIONS ARE IN THE EYES OF THE BEHOLDERS, NOT IN THOSE OF MANAGEMENT, AND THAT ACTIONS SPEAK MUCH LOUDER THAN WORDS.

MEASURING PERCEPTIONS
Many companies try to measure the reactions of their target audiences. Market research, whether confined to the firm itself or conducted among a group of competitors, is valuable in itself, but it is not enough.

So-called quantitative research, based on questionnaires and large samples, needs to be supplemented by qualitative

work on smaller samples (digging deeper to understand customer attitudes), and by employee surveys. How employees regard the organization and its management has a profound impact on its performance, including the vital matter of customer satisfaction.

Here, too, the investigation should be both quantitative and qualitative. Inevitably, some of the findings (perhaps many) will be unwelcome. Resist the temptation to deny the bad news. You may think that customers, employees, financial analysts, and so on are wrong in their critical opinions. But perception is reality. Either the criticisms are justified, in which case you must seek to rectify the faults; or they are unjustified, in which case you must seek to alter the adverse perceptions by using effective public relations techniques.

SETTING TARGETS

Quantitative research is valuable in setting bench marks against which progress can be measured. You should always be careful, though, to look at any given measure in the right way.

A rating of "good" for quality of service may sound fine. But good is not good enough. People rating your service as "excellent" are six times more likely to buy from you again. The percentages of long-lasting customers (and employees) and repeat purchases are meaningful and difficult to distort.

LIVING THE VALUES

Image-building is not an exact science. Companies that have enjoyed the best of reputations can run into bad trouble. When this happens, remedial action must be taken as soon as possible.

One of the worst experiences was that of Johnson & Johnson, when a criminal poisoned a batch of its best-selling painkiller. Disasters befell Ford Motors, too, when its Pinto car (and later its Firestone tires) became linked with fatalities. Ford's efforts at denial and blame-shifting became a byword for counterproductive public relations. In contrast, Johnson & Johnson became a model of quick and sensitive acceptance of the disaster, and its correction.

The right reaction can be greatly helped by having a set of written values that embody the organization's basic beliefs and rules of conduct. These should be worked out in consultation with staff and circulated to everybody

GETTING EXPERT ADVICE

You will need expert help to conduct both quantitative and qualitative research, to interpret the findings, and to install and monitor programs designed to improve perceptions. Outside agencies are almost always the best choice. A good public relations company, for example, can bring wide experience and broad contacts to bear on your company's image and reputation. Many PR companies will do excellent work for clients who are willing to listen and who understand that the product (in this case, the organization and all its works) must support the promise.

The accessibility of top management plays an important part in helping PR advisors deliver an improved image of the organization and raise its reputation. Training in media relations and giving TV interviews can help, but only marginally. The greatest persuader is the truth: if the truth is told in an honest way, then PR professionals have an excellent chance of delivering their promises.

concerned. A good example of this is the UK retailer Marks & Spencer's policy of automatically accepting returned goods and repaying the purchase price. The implicit underlying values here are "The Customer Is Always Right" and "Trust the Customer."

Figuring out the values is one thing: living them is another, and is far more problematic. The actions and words of managers and other members of staff in support of the values must be encouraged and rewarded continuously. By the same token, any behavior that contradicts the values should be penalized immediately, otherwise the company's image and reputation are certain to suffer, and customers will rapidly leave for a more capable learning organization.

financial
MANAGEMENT

EVERY MANAGER, WHATEVER HIS OR HER SPECIALIZATION, NEEDS TO BE FAMILIAR WITH THE PRINCIPLES AND DOCUMENTS OF FINANCIAL MANAGEMENT. SUCH KNOWLEDGE IS NECESSARY TO ENSURE FINANCE IS AVAILABLE TO COVER THE NEEDS OF AN ORGANIZATION AND STILL YIELD A PROFIT – OR AT LEAST PAY ITS WAY.

Most people invest in a business to make money. Owners wish to see their money "grow," or look for a financial return as a reward for their investment. As a manager, you need to understand the methods used in the control of money, the measurement of profit, and the monitoring of financial performance. You should also learn to recognize the content and layout of relevant documents.

You first need to know about the various sources of finance, and then how to control cash flow. You must know how to create and control the budget in relation to the forecast, and become familiar with the systems to establish costing and pricing parameters. You should be aware of the ways in which owners are rewarded, and how the ever-present risk in business can be managed and minimized.

FINANCING THE BUSINESS

WHEN MANAGING A COMPANY OR A PROJECT, IT IS VITAL TO ENSURE THAT IT DOES NOT RUN OUT OF MONEY BEFORE IT HAS TIME TO SELL ITS PRODUCT OR SERVICE AND RECEIVE PAYMENT. HOW AND WHERE TO RAISE ADEQUATE FINANCING IS THE FIRST MAJOR CONSIDERATION.

THE NEED FOR ADEQUATE FINANCING

A business needs the tools with which it is to work, such as plant and machinery, vehicles, computers, and buildings in which to work. These are known as capital items (that is, the business intends to keep them for longer than 12 months), and a decision has to be made whether to purchase or lease them.

The cost of stock (the inventory), that is parts needed for manufacture, work in progress, and finished goods to sell, needs to be calculated, along with the running costs of the business, for the days or weeks before its customers pay.

If customers are given credit, or shelves are stocked with manufacturing parts or finished goods to sell, then financing is needed to cover the period before payment is made by credit customers. Expenditure to cover these items is called working capital.

To finance a business, it is usual to look at how much cash the owners can put into the venture, how much they can borrow from banks or other suppliers of

UNDERSTANDING KEY TERMS

KEY TERM	DEFINITION
Asset	Something the business owns that has a monetary value.
Audit	An inspection of the books of account, either by an accountant working for the business (internal audit) or by an independent accountant (external audit). A report is usually produced by the auditor, verifying the accuracy (or lack of it) of the accounts.
Depreciation	The reduction in value of an asset caused by wear and tear.
Equity	The value of the business to its shareholders. It should include the value of the issued share capital, plus reserves. It thus equates to the net asset value of the business.
Fixed asset	Something the business owns that has a monetary value and that it intends to keep for longer than 12 months.
Liability	Something that the business owes that has a monetary value.
Reserves	Increased value of the business that has not been paid out as cash to its owners (e.g. retained profits, revalued land and buildings, etc.)
Working capital	The value of the capital (cash) that is tied up in the day-to-day management of the business (e.g stock, money owed by customers, petty cash, cash at bank, less cash owed to suppliers, IRS, etc.)

financing, and what the benefits and costs are for leasing or buying.

As a general rule, businesses try to finance long-term investments with long-term financing, and use short-term financing such as overdrafts to "top-up" their working capital requirements. Thus buildings will often be purchased via a mortgage; plant and machinery with a long-term loan; vehicles through a loan or lease for the length of the vehicle's life, and so on.

SOURCES OF MONEY

Banks are not the only source of financing, and anyone managing a new project is advised to shop throughout the financial markets. Credit unions will advance you financing if the terms and the security are attractive to them, while investment banks and venture capitalists are also on the lookout for investments and can put together an attractive financial package.

Many people avoid venture capitalists because they often require a large percentage of the company's shares in return for financing. However, 60 percent (or whatever proportion is left over) of something valuable is worth more than 100 percent ownership of an idea that is never implemented.

We seldom get something for nothing in this world, and the "advisers" or representatives of the source of financing you use will wish to maximize their own profit from their relationship with you and your company. If you go to the bank for money, then the bank employees you deal with may be dressed in customer-friendly titles such as manager, business adviser, and market executive, but they are employed to maximize the bank's income, not your company's.

SECURING A LOAN

Security (often called collateral) taken by the lenders of financing usually comprises a charge over the venture's or company's assets (things owned or partly owned) and/or your personal possessions. The lenders would like the company to bear the greatest part of the risk, therefore they take a charge over the assets. Usually, the company is prevented from disposing of the assets without first discharging the debt. This allows the lenders to sell the assets to recover the debt if the company fails to make the repayments or if they are unable to pay the interest on time.

The terms under which financing is secured are fully negotiable, so the skills of the company's negotiator can considerably reduce the debt burden of a new company or project.

SHARING THE COST

One way to completely avoid the debt burden is to go out to your shareholders (the owners of an incorporated company) and ask them to finance the new project. This often looks very attractive to the manager, but very few people invest money in a company without wishing for a return on that investment. Shareholders usually require that their company is worth a lot more as a result of completing the new project; or they are looking for a substantial increase in dividends (the payment they receive each year for holding shares) – or of course both.

OTHER METHODS

There are many financial instruments (ways of raising financing); in fact, the key to success is in your negotiating skills. These can be put to work to arrange a convertible loan. Providers of financing will sometimes lend the money at a very low or zero interest, in return for the ability to convert their loan at repayment time (or earlier) into shares in the company at their current value or at a stated value.

The attraction of this method to financiers is that they get the opportunity to share in the success of a venture (if that has been achieved), by converting their loan into shares that should be worth a great deal more than their loan. If the project fails to achieve its forecasted returns, then at least the financiers will get their money back, and possibly they may get a small interest payment along the way as well.

Whatever form of financing is negotiated, there is always a cost and often a repayment to be made. The most profitable, cost-effective, and satisfying method is to self-finance growth through performance, but that is a specialized subject in itself.

Before going ahead with any project, go over the details thoroughly to make sure that your closeness to the venture has not made you over-optimistic. Whether it be a multimillion-dollar business decision you are taking as part of a huge organization or a simple investment of your own, if you think the risk is worth taking, then good luck with the venture. All the above principles are sound, and they apply to both levels of investment.

CONTROLLING THE CASH

CASH IN THE BANK OR AN AGREED OVERDRAFT IS NEEDED TO PAY WAGES, SALARIES, AND SUPPLIERS, AND TO PURCHASE NECESSARY CAPITAL ITEMS. ORGANIZATIONS MUST ACCOUNT FOR CASH AND CHECKS RECEIVED FROM THEIR CUSTOMERS OR PAID TO THEIR SUPPLIERS.

UNDERSTAND THE CASH FLOW
In large businesses, controlling the cash is usually left to the accountant, but this can be effective only if every manager in the organization is involved.

Apart from the methods of financing described earlier, cash comes into the business or organization via sales (or rather when customers pay for the goods or services they have bought) or, in the case of many charities and nonprofit organizations, from collections and donations.

There is often a considerable time lag between an organization making a sale and it receiving the cash for it. A similar delay is present when it purchases goods. Most businesses "add value" and sell goods for more than they paid for them, so they are usually owed far more money by their customers than they owe to their suppliers.

The difference in the amount owed from the amount owing fluctuates each day and needs careful managing. If one or two major customers delay their payments, the business might find it does not have sufficient cash to pay its suppliers. If it has too little to pay wages and salaries, then it is in serious trouble and may face liquidation, however profitably it is operating.

Many companies have realized that delaying payments to suppliers provides a cheap form of financing. In theory, suppliers put their prices up to compensate them for late payment. In practice, the market decides the selling price of a product. The larger the buying power of the customer, the less likely it is that the supplier will try to increase the price to compensate for the late receipt of the amount due.

THE FINANCIAL INSTRUMENTS

A great number of financial arrangements have sprung up to help companies who are having trouble getting prompt payment from their customers. It pays to search the financial markets if your company is in need of this service. Two of the most popular seem to be a fluctuating overdraft from a bank and debt factoring.

The fluctuating overdraft allows you to withdraw the funds you need; but bankers put a limit on the maximum overdraft they will allow, and in difficult times or rapidly increasing business a company can run up against that barrier very quickly.

Debt factoring is where the amount of cash owed to the company by its customers is factored to a third party, which will advance you a percentage of the sum immediately after you issue the invoice for the sale of the goods. The third party (usually a financial institution) then effectively takes ownership of the debt, and will often collect the sum from your customer. If they fail to collect any or all of the outstanding amount, due to disputes or payment refusal, they will reduce your next advance by the amount they have failed to collect on this one.

Any system you use is going to cost money, and the cost needs to be taken

The cash book
This contains the accounts that document all the bank transactions, checks paid and received, loans, and so forth, used by the organization. This also contains the cash account, which tracks the movements of the actual money.

BANK ACCOUNT FOR XYZ INC.

Receipts		Payments	
Jan 1 from Shareholders	20,000.00	Jan 3 to Equipment Supplier	12,000.00
		Jan 5 to Goods Supplier	5,000.00
		Jan 7 to Wages	3,000.00
		Jan 9 to Expenses	2,000.00
Jan 10 from Customer A	4,000.00	Jan 10 to Goods Supplier	5,000.00
Jan 10 balance c/fwd	3,000.00		
TOTALS	27,000.00		27,000.00
		Jan 11 balance c/fwd	3,000.00
	(Debits)		(Credits)

This side of the cash book lists the money received by the company

This side of the cash book lists payments made by the company

The difference between income and expenditure is balanced here account of when you are costing your product and budgeting for profit. Most companies attempt to minimize the amount of working capital. Many employ credit controllers to phone the customers and persuade them to pay. Some even go so far as to use specialized debt collectors. Many have regular purges of the debtors' list (a list showing the amount owed to the company by every customer).

RECORDING THE CASH

To record the movements of cash, the accountant keeps a cash account and a bank account in the Cash Book. In their simplest form, these accounts list all the cash received on the left side of a page and note all the cash paid out on the right. Account books title the column on the left as Debits and the column on the right as Credits. Payments into the bank are debits, while drawings from the bank are credits. This is the reverse of the bank's statement, and causes great confusion to many people starting out in book-keeping and accounting.

The account would usually be totaled at month-end or at the end of each week (or daily if the lack of cash was becoming critical). The balance brought forward above reveals that the company has paid out $3,000 more than it has received.

BUDGETS AND FORECASTS

A BUDGET IS THE FINANCIAL EVALUATION OF A PLAN OF ACTION FOR A PERIOD OF TIME IN THE FUTURE. A FORECAST IS THE LATEST ESTIMATE OF THE ACTUAL RESULTS THAT WILL BE ACHIEVED OVER A PERIOD OF TIME IN THE FUTURE.

THE BUDGET

No modern business can leave its performance to chance. Its board of directors should decide upon a strategy that, if achieved, would yield at least the level of return required by the shareholders. That strategy should then be dissected into constituent action plans for each division and department within the business, so that when the financial evaluations of the plans are consolidated the result will achieve or exceed the shareholders' requirements.

The consolidated plan – the budget – is then used as a "measuring stick" to check progress throughout that year. A year is a long time to await the outcome of the plans, so it is typical for companies to subdivide the departmental or constituent budgets into monthly or four-weekly periods throughout the year based on seasonal trends in sales and production.

By recording and monitoring the actual sales and expenditures and comparing the actual results with the budget, the company can obtain early evidence of areas of the business that are not performing as expected and those that are. The managers can then concentrate their skills and energy in the areas of greatest need. Early remedial action can be taken in poorly performing areas of the business, while the managers are given the opportunity to enhance the business areas that are working better than budget.

BUDGET STATEMENT FOR XYZ INC.

Accounting period: Day, Month, Year

	Actual	Budget	Variance
Sales Revenue	11,000	12,000	(1,000)
Cost of Sales	7,800	8,000	200
GROSS PROFIT	3,200	4,000	(800)
Overhead			
Wages & Salaries	780	800	20
Expenses	220	220	0
Sales & Marketing	600	460	(140)
Delivery	330	300	(30)
Administration	290	200	(90)
Premises Costs	500	50	0
TOTAL OVERHEAD	2,720	2,480	(240)
OPERATING (TRADING) PROFIT	480	1,520	(1,040)
Interest Paid	220	200	(20)
Taxation	78	400	322
AFTER-TAX PROFITS	182	920	(738)

Sales that have been made in budget period — Sales Revenue

Costs incurred in making products for sale — Cost of Sales

Sales Revenue less Cost of Sales — GROSS PROFIT

Non-product costs and ongoing expenses — Expenses

The profit of the company's operation. Here it shows the company performing below budget — OPERATING (TRADING) PROFIT

The budget balance, here showing a loss against budget — AFTER-TAX PROFITS

The budget statement

This measures performance against budget, allowing differences to be investigated and corrected. It is the company's principal financial control document. The budget defines the financial effects of the strategy of the company.

By monitoring the actual results and comparing them against the budget, you will have an ongoing financial performance measurement itemized on a departmental, divisional, or company basis.

THE BUDGET STATEMENT

It is typical to display the results with the individual month (or accounting period) compared with the budget in the columns to the left of the page, and the year-to-date Actual, Budget, and Variance results in the columns to the right of the page.

From the trend of the figures each month, the management should be getting a reasonably accurate feeling for the effect of the remaining months' results. This will enable them to produce a similar document to the one above except that it will forecast the year-end position based on their estimates. A forecast can be for any period ahead and may affect the whole of the budget, a part of the budget, or the results of a project or action over the coming months.

ACCOUNTING FOR MANAGEMENT

SHAREHOLDERS REQUIRE A RETURN ON THEIR INVESTMENT. THEY LOOK TO THE DIRECTORS OF THE COMPANY TO ENSURE IT PRODUCES THAT RETURN. THE TASK OF ACHIEVING THAT RETURN IS DELEGATED TO THE MANAGERS VIA THE BUDGET, FORECASTS, AND THE ACCOUNTING DOCUMENTS.

PRODUCING THE RETURN

If you put money on deposit at a bank, you will receive interest and you can still get back your original sum. When shareholders buy shares in a company, their money is locked in. The only way they can get it back is to sell their shares to someone else, or to liquidate (close) the company.

Shareholders tend therefore to require a higher return than the interest available from a bank. They need to see their shares increasing in value so that they have the option of selling them and making a profit, or they expect substantial dividends paid to them as cash, or they want both.

Finance plays a crucial role in the management of a business, and every aspiring manager needs to understand at least the basic elements of financial management documents. The actual entries into the accounts can be left to the accounting specialists, but managers need to ensure that they understand the contents of accounting statements.

Accounting conventions throughout the world have divided costs and revenues into three main documents – the balance sheet, the profit and loss account (earnings statement), and the cash flow document.

THE BALANCE SHEET

This displays everything the business owns (assets) and subtracts all it owes (liabilities), providing a snapshot of the total net assets of the business. Generally, the first part lists the assets of the business, split between fixed (long-term) assets and short-term assets. The second part lists the long- and short-term liabilities. The third part shows shareholder's funds and long-, medium-, and short-term borrowings, reflecting how the business is financed.

The assets can be shown at cost, realization, or their depreciated value. A note should be attached to the balance sheet defining which value has been used.

Shareholders' funds contain the nominal value of the issued shares (the number of issued shares multiplied by the value written on the face of the share certificates). The nominal value does not therefore reflect the current market value (the value the share is trading at on the stock market), or the value at which the company may be able to issue new shares, for this will be closer to the market value.

Shareholder's funds therefore contain the nominal value of the issued shares plus any of the reserves that might reflect the value the shareholders have in the business. (A share with a nominal value of 25¢ might be issued to a new or

BALANCE SHEET FOR XYZ INC.

As of Day, Month, Year

These are the things the business owns, i.e. the items it intends to keep for longer than 12 months (capital items) ——

Fixed (long-term) Assets		
Land & Buildings	10,000	
Plant & Machinery	16,500	
Vehicles	6,500	33,000

Things owned by the business that have a monetary value, which it uses on a day-to-day basis (i.e. part of working capital)

Short-term Assets		
Stocks (Inventory)		
Debtors or Accounts Receivable	16,500	
Short-term Deposits	1,000	
Cash and money at bank	500	18,000

These are the things the business owes, i.e. the amounts that should be paid back within the next 12 months (part of working capital)

Short-term Liabilities		
Creditors or Accounts Payable (suppliers)	(6,000)	
Bank Overdraft	(4,000)	
Unpaid Taxation	(450)	
Unpaid Dividends	(150)	10,600

Short-term Assets less Short-term Liabilities

NET WORKING CAPITAL	7,400	

Fixed assets plus working capital ——

CAPITAL EMPLOYED		40,400

The amount the business owes that is due to be paid back in the longer term

Shareholders' Funds		
Nominal Capital (issued)	8,000	
Reserves	5,500	13,500

This is the total shareholders' funds, plus the total long-term borrowings

Long-term Borrowings		
Bond Holders	10,000	
Finance Institutions	7,500	
Banks	9,400	26,900

TOTAL FINANCING		40,400

CAPITAL EMPLOYED		40,400
Long-term Borrowings		
Bond Holders	10,000	
Finance Institutions	7,500	
Banks	9,400	26,900
NET ASSET VALUE		13,500
Shareholders' Funds		
Nominal Capital (issued)	8,000	
Reserves	5,500	
TOTAL SHAREHOLDERS' FUNDS		13,500

The balance sheet
Above: The balance sheet shows the net worth of a business at one point in time.
Left: Many versions show long-term borrowings deducted from the capital employed, giving the net asset value. In both cases, the net asset value is always equal to the total shareholder funds.

existing shareholder at a price of 75¢. The value shown under nominal capital – the nominal value of the shares – will increase by 25¢ for each share sold, and the value shown under reserves will increase by 50¢.)

Retained profits from previous years and a revaluation of the property and assets are also included as reserves.

The value of the shares in the financial markets varies on a daily or even minute-by-minute basis. The market value (sometimes called market capitalization) of the company is the total of nominal shares that have been issued, multiplied by the price that they were quoted at on the financial markets when the valuation was made. This is not shown on the balance sheet.

THE PROFIT AND LOSS ACCOUNT

This is also called the income, revenue, or earnings statement.

A business should plan that the difference in the amount it is due to receive from the supply of goods and services exceeds the costs it will bear in providing them. If the income is greater than costs (subject to certain restraints and conventions), the business will make a profit. If it is not (subject to similar restraints), the business will suffer a loss.

The profit and loss account (P&L) usually starts with the source of income called sales, turnover, revenue, or, simply, income. The cost of making the product (materials, labor, and factory costs) is then deducted, and the resultant remainder is called the gross profit or loss (the gross margin).

The rest of the costs of running the business, called overhead, expenses, and burden (such as rents, heat, light and power, distribution, and administration), are then deducted. The resultant amount is known as the operating (or trading) profit (loss), sometimes called PBIT (Profit Before Interest and Tax).

The interest paid or interest received are deducted or added, and the taxation deducted to show the after-tax profits or loss (the profits or loss that belong to the shareholders of the company).

The dividend (the amount of profits that are to be paid out to the shareholders) is then displayed.

The balance that remains (retained profits) will be used in the company and is added to the reserves, which are shown as part of the shareholders' funds on the balance sheet.

The above headings may be altered to fit the type of business, but the principle will stay the same.

Material costs are adjusted by adding any opening stock at the start of the period to the purchases of materials that were made throughout the period and then deducting the closing stock. The resultant cost should reflect the usage of materials to satisfy the sales throughout the year and not be distorted by increased or reduced stockholdings.

The direct costs, such as labor, materials, and factory expenses, of manufacturing the product or of providing the service is deducted from sales to reveal the gross profit.

The indirect costs (such as admin) are then deducted to reveal the operating profit (the profit management made from the operation of the company).

After accounting for interest and taxation, the after-tax profits is the amount that remains to be divided among the shareholders.

PROFIT AND LOSS ACCOUNT FOR XYZ INC.

For the year ending Day, Month, Year

Sales Revenue		100,000
Cost of Goods Sold		
Materials	27,000	
Labor	22,000	
Factory Costs	15,000	64,000
GROSS PROFIT (MARGIN)		36,000
Overhead (Expenses)		
Administration	8,000	
Selling Costs	7,000	
Delivery Costs	5,500	
Telecomm	1,500	
Premises Costs	3,300	
Management Costs	2,400	
Other	1,300	29,000
OPERATING (TRADING) PROFIT (PBIT)		7,000
Interest Paid/Received	2,600	
Taxation	1,400	4,000
AFTER-TAX PROFITS		3,000
Dividends Paid	400	
Dividends Proposed	600	1,000
RETAINED PROFITS		2,000

Invoices and cash sales included — Sales Revenue

This is goods sold, not goods purchased. Stock fluctuations will not change this cost

The profit is maximized at this stage

The nonprofit costs involved in running the business

This is the critical measure of management and worker performance

These are the profits that belong to the shareholders

This is the amount of profit that is retained by the company after the shareholders have received their dividends

The profit and loss account
This covers income and expenditure for a period of time, usually a month or year to date. It lists the Gross Profit made from sales, less the costs for Overhead to reveal PBIT, an important measure of managerial performance.

THE CASH FLOW

Profit is not cash. Profit is having a business or organization that (prior to the payment of any dividends) is worth more at the end of the period than it was at the beginning. The profit and loss account might show a profit but the company can still run out of cash. Cash is actual money in the cash box, bank, or anywhere else the business prefers to keep it.

If a business kept its stock at a constant value, all its customers pay in cash, every supplier and employee is paid cash, and nothing is depreciated, then the operating (trading) profit could represent an increase in cash. That is, cash will come in on every sale and go out on every purchase. As businesses (hopefully) sell at a higher price than they buy, then the extra cash at the end of the year would equate to profit.

The cash flow statement
This is perhaps the most vital document – and the most neglected. It is the cash that pays the bills and wages. This is the document that records the cash coming in and going out over a period of time.

In most businesses, the value of stock fluctuates, as does the time customers take to pay, as well as the time the business takes to pay suppliers. The adjustments in these values need to be taken into account before a company can define whether it has received an increase in its cash (positive cash flow) or a decrease (negative cash flow).

In the profit and loss account, a charge for the depreciation of vehicles, plant and machinery, or any other asset, should be included. For example, when you purchase a car, you pay out the cash value

CASH FLOW STATEMENT FOR XYZ INC.

For the year ending Day, Month, Year

The PBIT shown on the Profit and Loss Account — Operating (Trading) Profit		7,000
Adjustments for Noncash Items		
(e.g. Depreciation)	1,700	
Adjustments to reflect cash movements — **Adjustments for Changes in Working Capital**		
- Increase/+ Decrease in Total Debtors	(750)	
+ Increase/ - Decrease in Total Creditors	440	
- Increase/+ Decrease in Total Stocks (Inventory)	(300)	
- Outflow of cash from reorganization.	(1,200)	(110)
The actual cash acquired from the operation of the business — **NET CASH INFLOW FROM OPERATING ACTIVITIES**		6,890
Interest Received and Paid	(2,600)	
Dividends Received and Paid	(400)	(3000)
NET CASH INFLOW/OUTFLOW ON INVESTMENTS AND SERVICING OF FINANCE		3,890
This figure is based on the previous year's profits — Taxation	(800)	
Net Cash Inflow/Outflow from Investing Activities	(4,600)	(5400)
NET CASH INFLOW/OUTFLOW BEFORE FINANCING		(1,510)
Issue of Bonds	5,000	
This should reflect the difference between cash in the bank from the beginning of the year — Redemption of Loan	(3,000)	2000
INCREASE/DECREASE IN CASH AND EQUIVALENTS		490

at the time you purchase it (or you owe the finance company the value of the car less your deposit). A year later the car is worth less money since it has depreciated in value and cannot be sold for the same amount of money as you paid when you bought it. Companies need to show the reduction in value of such assets due to the wear and tear of usage.

The company does not actually pay out any more money; it merely reduces the value of the vehicle or other reducing asset on its balance sheet and shows the reduction in value under the heading of depreciation in its expenses on the profit and loss account.

In the cash flow statement, the company therefore needs to add back those items under the depreciation column to the profit column if it is to find out whether it has had a positive cash flow or suffered a negative cash flow in that accounting period.

In the year or the financial period being reported, the company may have bought new assets or sold off old ones. The value that the business has spent or received will not be shown on the profit and loss account. Only the profit or loss on the sale that the company has suffered will be recorded.

A company may also have borrowed more money during the year, or repaid some loans that it took out earlier.

To understand its cash position, the company needs to produce a cash flow statement that starts from the operating (trading) profit that was reported in the profit and loss account and then adjust for all the above factors.

COSTING AND PRICING

TYPICALLY, THE SALES PRICE OF A PRODUCT OR SERVICE IS SET BY MARKET FORCES. THE COSTING SYSTEM IS USED NOT TO ESTABLISH A SELLING PRICE, BUT TO ENSURE THAT THE PRODUCT CAN BE PRODUCED AT A COST THAT IS SUFFICIENTLY BELOW THE MARKET PRICE TO LEAVE AN ACCEPTABLE PROFIT.

COSTING FOR PROFIT

Most customers need to believe there is some intrinsic value in a product or service if they are to pay a high price or one that is higher than that charged by competitors. It is the perception of the customer that is important rather than the actual intrinsic value of the product, and this is one of the major reasons for the vast amounts spent on marketing a product. The volume of sales you are going to make and the price you can charge are usually intrinsically tied into the customer's evaluation of the worth of your product.

The objective of all costing systems is to identify where and why costs arise, to help control them, and to help maximize the profits available to the owners to compensate them for the risk they took when investing in the business.

The budgetary control system attempts to control costs on a global, divisional, departmental, or cost center basis. The costing system attempts to break these costs down and allocate them to each product that is produced or each service that is provided.

Some costs are relatively easy to define for a particular product. The amount of material used in an item can be measured and allocated to a particular product and, if necessary, divided by the number of units produced from that batch of material to give a material cost per unit produced or sold. The time it takes to make the product will help to define the direct labor costs (the costs of the people who actually produce or work on the product) to each unit that is produced.

But there are a great number of other costs where the exact cost allocation to a product is either impossible or too costly to record and calculate. For example:

- How much of a supervisor's time is spent on a particular product?
- What proportion of the factory overhead should be allocated to that particular product or service?
- How long did a salesperson spend selling that particular product and how much of his/her travel costs should be absorbed by it?
- How much of the accountant's costs should be allocated to that particular product?
- How much of the administration costs or the directors' costs should be spent on the product?

In these instances the accountant gives a best estimate, but it can be very inaccurate, with dangerous consequences.

ABSORPTION COSTING

Absorption costing is a costing system where every cost is absorbed by a product or batch of products.

Unit cost is the analysis of the costs to each individual unit of production in a given period of time.

Using the methods outlined at the start of this section, a unit costing of a product using the absorption costing system might look something like the product costing shown (*see* opposite).

Direct costs are those that can be attributed directly to the unit that is being produced.

Indirect costs are those that cannot be directly attributed to the unit being produced or sold, or where the cost of attributing that element to a unit is greater than any savings that can be made by so identifying them. A degree of inaccuracy is therefore inevitable.

MARGINAL COSTING

Marginal costing details the costs that vary with volume (variable costs) and calculates a contribution that the product makes toward the payment of the indirect costs (called fixed costs in a pure marginal costing system) and to a profit.

Variable costs vary with sales and/or production. The more you produce, the higher the cost in an almost direct ratio.

Fixed costs are those that vary in some way other than the variation of volumes produced and sold. They are often described as time costs, as their behavior is more closely related to time than volume. Rent is payable for a period of time irrespective of the volume produced, salaries are often paid on a monthly basis with little or no connection with volume, and so on. In this system, no attempt is made to allocate or absorb fixed costs to the products.

Semivariable costs are sometimes included for the type of cost that has some volume and time in its makeup.

Most companies operate a hybrid costing system

PRODUCT COSTING FOR SUPER WIDGETS

		per Unit
The accounting period — Year		
The price at which the — Sales Price		<u>60.00</u>
product or service is sold		
Direct Costs		
Costs that can be — Materials	12.00	
directly attributed to Labor	16.00	
the product or service Expenses	<u>4.00</u>	
TOTAL DIRECT COSTS	32.00	
Factory Overhead	<u>10.00</u>	
EX-FACTORY COSTS		<u>42.00</u>
The difference between — FACTORY MARGIN		<u>18.00</u>
Ex-factory Costs and		
Sales Price		
Indirect Costs		
Delivery	1.70	
Selling	1.50	
Costs that cannot be Marketing	3.60	
directly attributed to Administration	1.40	
the product or service Depreciation of Premises & Vehicles	1.00	
Finance	1.50	
Management	<u>0.30</u>	
TOTAL INDIRECT COSTS		<u>11.00</u>
The Sales Price — OPERATING (TRADING) PROFIT		<u>7.00</u>
minus Direct and		
Indirect Costs is the		
Operating Profit		

Absorption costing

The costing system shown above is a useful way of estimating the operating profit of a particular product or service on a unit basis. In this example, direct and indirect costs leave an operating profit of just $7 from a sale price of $60.

OTHER COSTING SYSTEMS

Over the years, many costing systems have been developed. The Activity-Based Costing (also known as ABC) still has some loyal supporters. This method has the advantage of allocating costs from fixed costs cost centers to production units on a beneficiary, rather than a unit, basis.

In a unit-based system, the costs are allocated according to the number of units produced. On a beneficiary-based system, investigation is made to discover precisely what benefits arise from the operation of a cost center and who are the beneficiaries. The costs are then allocated in proportion to the benefits.

PRODUCT COSTING FOR SUPER WIDGETS

Year	Super Widgets	Standard Widgets	Low-grade Widgets	Totals
Forecast Volume Units	1,000	5,000	8,000	14,000
Unit Values				
Sales Price	60.00	50.00	40.00	
Variable Costs				
Materials	12.00	10.00	9.00	
Labor	16.00	15.00	14.50	
Expenses	4.00	4.00	3.50	
TOTAL VARIABLE COSTS	32.00	29.00	27.00	
Contribution	28.00	21.00	13.00	
TOTAL CONTRIBUTION	28,000	105,000	104,000	237,000
Fixed Costs				
Factory Overhead				105,000
Delivery				16,000
Selling				18,000
Marketing				23,000
Administration				13,000
Depreciation of Premises & Vehicles				10,000
Finance				22,000
Management				10,000
TOTAL FIXED COSTS				217,000
OPERATING (TRADING) PROFIT				20,000

Side annotations:

- Forecasts for the volume of sales
- Costs that increase in relation to increased production
- The contribution that each product makes to cover the fixed costs of the company
- Total profit contribution
- Costs that cannot be directly attributed to the product; they are usually more related to time than the number of items produced
- The operating profit or Loss is listed here

ABC and the many hybrids using beneficiary costing can help identify costly or wasteful operations within a company. If the cost center that receives the allocated cost feels it is much higher than they want to pay, or can buy elsewhere, then a cost constraint is immediately passed to the in-house supplier to improve their operation or face competition from outsourced parts or services.

Marginal costing
This separates the costs that can be directly attributed to the product or services provided from those that vary with time. The changes in operating profit caused by variations in quantity can be rapidly calculated.

WATCHING THE RATIOS

WITHIN THE FORMAL DOCUMENTS THERE ARE A NUMBER OF ACCOUNTS WHICH, WHEN COMPARED WITH EACH OTHER, WILL PROVIDE VALUABLE INFORMATION FOR MANAGERS. SELECTING THE CORRECT COMBINATION OF THESE COMPARISONS (RATIOS) ALLOWS THEM TO BECOME THE "INSTRUMENT PANEL" OF A BUSINESS.

CASH MANAGEMENT RATIOS

How long are the account customers – known as debtors but sometimes called accounts receivables (A/Rs) – actually taking to pay their bills? A working ratio for debtor days is:

$$\frac{\text{Trade debtors (A/Rs)}}{\text{Sales turnover in period}} \quad \text{x business days}$$

Most customers pay late if they are allowed to!

The debtor days should be continuously monitored on a monthly basis. Remedial action should be taken, if necessary. In this way, the company can save a large amount of cash that has been needlessly tied up in customers' accounts and save all the interest charges that would otherwise be incurred.

The suppliers to the company can be similarly monitored. If you compare the creditors' value shown on the balance sheet (suppliers' accounts – creditors – are often called accounts payable or A/P) with the total amount shown against outside suppliers on the profit and loss account, you can get a feel for the length of time the company takes to pay the bills received from suppliers. A formula for creditor days is as follows: trade creditors (suppliers) multiplied by the number of days in the business period, divided by the trade purchases for that period.

Debtor (customers or A/R) days, creditor (supplier or A/P) days, and stock (inventory) days are vital controls in the management of cash. They can dramatically affect the financial well-being of a business.

SHAREHOLDERS' RATIOS

The vast majority of company shareholders invest their money in the business in the hope or determination of enjoying a reward. A critical ratio therefore is the return the owners are getting on the investment they have made.

The after-tax profit is the value that is left for the owners after all sales and costs have been accounted for and an allowance made for interest received and paid and for taxation.

The total shareholders' funds (that is, the value of the issued shares plus the reserves) is the value the owners have in the company.

After-tax profits as a percentage of the total shareholders' funds gives a feeling for the return the owners are enjoying from the business – the Return on Investment (ROI). A formula for ROI is as follows:

$$\frac{\text{After-tax profits}}{\text{Total shareholders' funds}} \quad \text{x 100}$$

Using this formula, after-tax profits of, say, \$13,400 on total shareholders' funds of \$80,000 would give an ROI of 16.75 percent, which many businesses look for.

Earnings per share is another ratio that is of concern to shareholders. It reveals what value each share is earning. Here is a formula for figuring this out:

$$\frac{\text{After-tax profits}}{\text{Number of ordinary shares issued}}$$

A formula to figure out dividends per share is as follows:

$$\frac{\text{Dividends}}{\text{Number of ordinary shares issued}}$$

These two ratios are normally expressed in cents.

The formula for working out the P/E (price/earnings) ratio is as follows:

$$\frac{\text{Market price per share}}{\text{Earnings per share}}$$

Earnings are based on the previous year's reported profits, whereas the market price is based on future expectations. The higher the P/E ratio, the more confident the shareholders can be of higher returns on their shares.

PROFIT MANAGEMENT RATIOS

The most important Profit Management Ratio is underutilized by many company managements: the Return on Capital Employed (ROCE). The business owners need an adequate Return on Investment

CALCULATING THE RATIOS

Debtor days =	$\frac{\text{Trade debtors}}{\text{Sales turnover}}$	x no. of days in business period
Creditor days =	$\frac{\text{Trade creditors}}{\text{Trade purchases}}$	x no. of days in business period
ROI (Return on Investment) =	$\frac{\text{After-tax Profits}}{\text{Total Shareholders' Funds}}$	x 100
Earnings per share =	$\frac{\text{After-tax Profits}}{\text{No. of ordinary shares issued}}$	
Dividends per share =	$\frac{\text{Dividends}}{\text{No. of ordinary shares issued}}$	
P/E (price/earnings) ratio =	$\frac{\text{Market price per share}}{\text{Earnings per share}}$	
ROCE (Return on Capital Employed) =	$\frac{\text{Operating Profits (PBIT)}}{\text{Capital Employed}}$	x 100
ROS (Return on Sales) =	$\frac{\text{Operating Profits (PBIT)}}{\text{Total Sales Revenue}}$	x 100

(ROI), but the business managers often enjoy the funding from borrowed capital as well as the shareholders' funds.

The capital employed (shareholders' funds plus long-term borrowings) is the value that is effectively in the hands of the managers of the business. The managers must make a high return (PBIT – profit before interest and tax) on the capital employed to allow for the payment of interest and tax and still leave enough to meet the owners' required return.

The formula for Return on Capital Employed (ROCE) is:

$$\frac{\text{Operating profits (PBIT)} \times 100}{\text{Capital employed}}$$

A frequent profit ratio you find in companies is the Return on Sales (ROS). The problem with ROS is that it depends upon volume, and the figure for volume is not expressed alongside it or as part of this ratio. Volume can suffer while the ROS improves, thus negating any benefit to the business.

This does not invalidate the use of ROS as a control ratio, but it should be handled with care and always coupled with the sales volume.

The formula for return on sales (ROS) is:

$$\frac{\text{Operating profits (PBIT)} \times 100}{\text{Total sales revenue}}$$

REWARDING THE OWNERS

MOST INVESTORS WANT THE MAXIMUM RETURN POSSIBLE, BUT AS A MINIMUM THEY NEED ONE THAT IS COMMENSURATE WITH RISK. IF THEY BORROW TO MAKE THE INVESTMENT, THEN MOST REQUIRE A RETURN THAT IS FAR ABOVE THE COST OF BORROWED MONEY.

DISTRIBUTION OF PROFITS

Profits are not always distributed to the shareholders. Managers often require more investment in their part of the business (and an increase in salary commensurate with the increase in profits achieved or forecast).

When these same managers are asked what they require from any shares that they hold in a company, the answer is invariably "money" or "increased wealth." Increased wealth can perhaps be achieved by a low dividend policy (keeping most of the profit in the company for future growth) but, as a wise old British investor once said, "Beware of the offer of jam tomorrow." Take your rewards today!

DIVIDENDS

Dividends are a distribution of profits to the owners of a company and are thus the most direct way of rewarding them for their investment. However, in most companies there is a certain amount of "jam tomorrow" in that much of the profit is retained in the company and only a proportion is paid as a dividend.

When dividend distribution is low, the only way the owners can cash in on that success is to sell their shares or borrow money against the strengthening price of their shares.

In all cases the shareholder will hope that the market (in other words, the stock exchange where the shares are traded) will recognize the potential to grow the retained profits, and as a result, the shares will increase in value. However, the market's approval should not be taken for granted.

For those needing additional income, a successful company with a high dividend policy (distributing most of its profits as dividends) would be an attractive proposition.

CAPITAL GROWTH

Some shareholders (particularly those in higher tax brackets who do not need access to immediate cash) might be more interested in watching their investment grow so that it can be enjoyed at some time in the future.

Provided the company can ensure that retained earnings grow at the same or a better profit ratio (ROCE) as the rest of the business, they might be content with a low-dividend policy.

If the shares are increasing in value, then the shareholders can sell them at some time in the future – when they need the money, for instance, or when they believe the shares have reached their peak price.

A company's market capitalization is calculated by multiplying the number of issued ordinary shares by the current share price.

PUBLIC OFFERING

Many company startups are created with a view to "going public" as soon as their business results or creditability allows. "Going public" is the term given to the initial public offering of the company whereby its shares may be openly traded on the stock exchange or bought and sold by members of the public.

If you have a successful company that is providing high earnings per share and offering excellent returns on investment, institutions and the public become interested in investing in that company. The usual result is that the share price tends to go up. If a great number of people are trying to buy a commodity, then its price will generally rise quite significantly. On the other hand, if significant numbers of them are trying to sell, then its price will generally start to fall. So it is with shares.

A successful company being offered on the stock markets can gain a great deal of cash from the issue of shares at a price that is above the nominal value shown on the face of the share (for example, their existing 25¢ per share sold at $2 per share). The extra cash generated can be used by the business to expand and continue to grow its profits, while all the existing shares in the company get rated at the higher price of $2 (or the price at which they are traded).

OVERSUBSCRIPTION OF SHARES

If a shareholder had purchased 40,000 shares of Widget Inc. at the startup of the company for the nominal value shown on the shares of 25¢, it would have cost $10,000 (40,000 multiplied by 25¢ per share). Four years later, Widget.com Inc. goes to market and issues many more shares at a price of $2 each. It is oversubscribed (more people bid for the shares than there are shares available). The shareholder's 40,000 shares are now worth $80,000 at the offering price, or more if the increased demand pushes the price up.

The shareholder may have also rewarded him or herself for all the hard work put into the company in its formative years with either the issue of shares or a share option plan.

Invariably, most share option plans are based on the value of what the shares cost at the date of the option. All the new shares acquired will now be worth the "market" price.

It is easy to see the attractions of a public offering for a successful company.

Whichever way the owners of a business are rewarded, remember that very few people would start or own a company without the reward of an adequate return, and most people want their own return to be as high as possible.

MANAGING RISK

VIRTUALLY EVERY IMPORTANT BUSINESS DECISION INVOLVES RISK. A PROBABILITY MODEL SHOULD BE MADE PRIOR TO AN INVESTMENT TO HELP MEASURE AND MINIMIZE THAT RISK. NEW PROJECTS SHOULD BE FINANCIALLY MODELED ON BOTH AN OPTIMISTIC AND A PESSIMISTIC PLAN, AND THEN MONITORED CLOSELY.

THE BUDGET

The budget method is probably the largest risk management system used by a company on a regular basis.

By measuring actual sales revenue, along with production, support, and administration costs, the company is able to measure variations from the budget plan each month and build a forecast of the end-of-year position.

If the forecast position produces an after-tax profit that is below the required reward to the owners of the business, then remedial actions can be taken during the year.

PROJECT RISKS

During the course of the financial year, an opportunity may arise to become involved in a new project. The more significant the project, the greater the

risk that it can severely damage the company if it goes wrong. It is therefore vital to accurately model the financial implications of any project before the decision to proceed is made.

In all projects there are two key issues:
- How accurate are the estimates of costs and revenue?
- How accurate are estimates of time?

If you keep your eye on major projects currently under construction in your country, you will continue to see a multitude of examples of vast cost and time overruns and/or income shortfalls. The excuses for poor performance will not be new; we will have heard them many times over.

Despite the lessons available from the economic disasters of the Concorde, the European Fighter Aircraft, the Millennium Dome in London, and the "Star Wars" project in the US for example, on the majority of projects that are put before management for approval, most of the major defense contracts of the last 30 years and most of the "international construction projects" in the developing world continue to underestimate costs and time and overestimate expected revenue.

ASSESSING PROBABILITY

Each manager should supply two or three answers on a proposed project, along the lines of:

- At $500 a unit we are 60 percent certain we will sell 45,000 of these in year one.
- 30 per cent of us think we will sell 35,000 in year one.
- 10 percent of us think we might sell 50,000 in year one.

And over three years:

- 40 percent of us think we will sell 180,000 in the first three years.
- 30 percent think we will sell 160,000 in the first three years.
- 20 percent think we will sell 150,000 in the first three years.
- 10 percent think we will sell 200,000 in the first three years.

And so on for all expenditures and, most importantly, for the time of each part of the project. Once the project has been reviewed by all involved, a probability tree can be built:

First year:

- 45,000 is favored by 60 percent of experts (45,000 x 60 percent) = 27,000.
- 35,000 is favored by 30 percent of experts (35,000 x 30 percent) = 10,500.
- 50,000 is favored by 10 percent of experts (50,000 x 10 percent) = 5,000.

Therefore, on average our experts give us a high probability that 42,500 (the total arrived at if you add up all the numbers: 27,000 + 10,500 + 5,000) will be sold in the first year. Similar calculations for the first three years give a figure of 170,000.

In virtually every case: "Managers overestimate the expected revenue, underestimate its cost, and are hopelessly optimistic with time."

REDUCING THE RISK

A way of reducing the company's exposure to risk is to ask every key department to estimate the quantity the company will sell over the first 12 months and over three years, along with their estimate of the price. A similar approach can be made on the time of each construction stage and costs. The probability function can narrow errors in estimates and possibly prevent the project's champions from altering their estimates to fit criteria that they know will be accepted. However, it still does not guarantee success.

TIMING

Trying to obtain accurate timings for developments can be a frustrating task. Some major projects, upon which millions of dollars have been invested, are so late that by the time they are delivered they have already become obsolete.

Some projects are destined never to work in the way they were envisaged when the go-ahead for the plan was given. And some have bankrupted the company long before they could deliver any payback for the vast expenditure they have incurred.

Carrying out a probability exercise may well narrow errors in estimates of time, but your business plan needs to be produced in three versions in order to measure risk under the alternative situations that the company might face. These are as follows:

- the most probable
- the most pessimistic
- the most optimistic.

For example, the most probable scenario is that the project will be completed in X amount of time; the most pessimistic scenario is that it will run over significantly and cost much more than was originally estimated. The optimistic view is that it will be completed earlier and under budget. The budgets for such estimated profits and losses will deviate significantly from each other but the personnel will at least know how to focus their efforts.

The effect of time on a project can be illustrated by the following example:

"If I owed you $1,000 with no interest payable, would you rather have it now or $1,000 in five years' time?"

Most people would prefer to have the money now. Some point out that if they had it now they could put the money in their bank or credit union account and watch it grow to $1,276 (if growth is at 5 percent per annum) over the next five years. Thus, $1,000 received now is worth $1,276 in five years' time because it will accrue compound interest.

Looked at from another angle, the $1,276 received in five years' time has the same worth as the $1,000 received now, provided the rate in inflation/interest remains constant at 5 percent per annum.

Money received or paid out later is therefore effectively worth less than that same amount received or paid out now. A system of discounted cash flow has sprung up to express this when costing any project that involves future cash flows. This system effectively discounts future cash flow back to today's money.

None of the systems in use can guarantee a future without risk, but they can help to measure and maybe also mitigate that risk.

OTHER RISKS

There are multitudes of other risks that need to be managed. Liabilities arise from health and safety issues, the defective supply of components, services, and products, the negligent actions of a company's employees, negligent advice, and so on. Often, the cost of completely negating a risk is greater then the cost of that risk.

At all times the risk should be measured not only in financial terms but also in terms of its effect on the legality and moral standing of the company.

All of the above should give you an insight and a guide to the ways you can manage finance more effectively and mitigate risk.

However, ultimately, business is all about people and their ability to make accurate assessments and judge the best course that needs to be navigated for a successful future. If they possess these outstanding virtues, they still have to learn how to manage and guide people, organizations, and financial results successfully forward.

To give the owners the return on investment that they are looking for, managers must understand the financial implication of all their actions.

Financial management cannot guarantee success but it can be of tremendous assistance in measuring progress and performance. It is also a great help in achieving the company owners' goals.

managing
RESOURCES

THE TASK OF THE MANAGER IS TO ALLOCATE AND USE ALL THE RESOURCES UNDER HIS OR HER CONTROL TO MEET THE PURPOSES OF THE ORGANIZATION. THE KEY RESOURCES ARE NOT ONLY INTELLECTUAL CAPITAL AND FINANCING, THE FACILITY AND MACHINERY, BUT, ABOVE ALL, THE PEOPLE WHO PUT LIFE INTO THESE ASSETS.

The successful management of all resources depends on effective planning. You must understand the essentials: first the strategy, then the action plans that follow. An introduction of the discipline of Total Quality Management (or an alternative program for continuous improvement) will help you optimize the use of resources, while a good system of monitoring the implementation of your plan will give accurate feedback and allow you to react dynamically.

As people are the key business resource, it follows that to be effective an organization needs to recruit the right people and provide a reward package that will both attract and retain them. Plan carefully for the numbers and categories of workers required to meet current demands and future goals.

THE ESSENTIALS OF PLANNING

THE BASIC TRUTH OF PLANNING IS THAT IF YOU DO NOT KNOW WHERE YOU ARE GOING YOU WILL NOT GET THERE. ALL EFFECTIVE PLANNING BEGINS WITH A STRATEGY: SETTING OUT WHAT THE ORGANIZATION HAS DECIDED IT INTENDS TO ACHIEVE.

DECIDING ON THE DESTINATION

The strategy needs to be clear, concise, and communicated to everybody who will be involved in executing the plan. A crucial word in the strategy's context is "objective." This is easily confused with "goal" or "target." Strategy is about deciding on the destination. The goals are the landmarks that must be passed if the planned journey is to succeed. The targets are the outcomes toward which the strategy aims. The targets must all be measurable; if they are not, you cannot answer two essential questions:

- How will people know what is expected of them?
- How will the planners know that it has been delivered?

As strategies are devolved downward into subobjectives, so the involvement of those affected by the plan becomes increasingly important. All planned outcomes begin with analysis and forecasts, but hinge on execution.

It is foolish in the extreme to conduct planning as a top-down exercise, with no input from the company's middle and lower management, or other affected employees. These very people are the ones who carry out the required tasks. Their knowledge of which factors will determine the outcome is vital in enabling planners to square their forecasts with the known facts of the "business case" – the document setting out the economic justification of the plan.

ANALYZING THE PLAN

A common trap is to produce an over-optimistic business case by working backward from the required outcome. If sales of x units are needed to justify the budgeted expenditure, the requirement becomes a forecast, and failure almost always follows. Proper analysis of the plan must answer, coolly and calmly, a vital set of questions:

- Are the assumptions that underlie this plan feasible?
- What would invalidate them?
- How likely/unlikely is it for an invalidating event to happen?

No plan should be adopted until all the assumptions have been identified and tested for their validity. It is impossible to be 100 percent certain – you are, after all, making predictions. But it is perfectly possible to reduce the area of doubt to comfortable proportions.

The analytical process will determine the "limiting factors" that govern the structure and operations of the plan. An obvious example is plant capacity. There is no point in proceeding with a plan that depends on doubling output if the plant is already operating at full capacity. The plan cannot proceed without a provision either to increase plant capacity or to find outside suppliers.

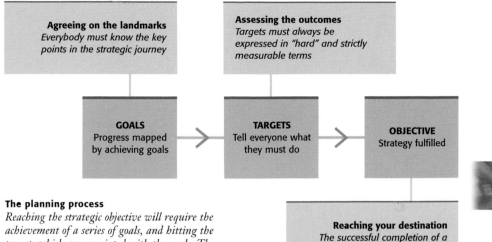

Agreeing on the landmarks *Everybody must know the key points in the strategic journey*	**Assessing the outcomes** *Targets must always be expressed in "hard" and strictly measurable terms*

GOALS
Progress mapped by achieving goals

TARGETS
Tell everyone what they must do

OBJECTIVE
Strategy fulfilled

Reaching your destination
The successful completion of a plan sets the stage for the next one

The planning process
Reaching the strategic objective will require the achievement of a series of goals, and hitting the targets which are associated with the goals. The targets motivate individuals and teams and bind them into achievement of the overall plan.

The limiting factors common to all plans are as follows:
- time
- money
- people.

The plan must spell out what is proposed for all three factors, and specify what action is being, or must be, taken to cover any deficiencies. It is obviously preferable to build in margins of safety, especially for time, but that luxury is becoming harder to afford in an age in which speed of execution crucially affects the quality of the plan.

STRUCTURING THE PLAN

Delegation is vital to successful planning, but it means more than simply delegating tasks to others. Rather, it means dividing the task into distinct components that can be handled separately by specified teams or individuals. The plan must be broken down in this way, with each element properly delegated. When completed, the parts should add up to a coherent whole.

This process of divide and conquer, or separate and win, can very easily be neglected. The results of such neglect are confusion, loss of control, and greater vulnerability to slippages of all kinds. Remember, a plan is only as good as the sum of its parts. It is also only as good as the quality of the thought that has gone into making the plan.

Planning should be done with a scientific rigor, even though it is not rigorously scientific. Much depends on good ideas, creativity, and enthusiasm – qualities that are difficult to quantify. The argument for wider involvement in planning is that it increases the vital flow of ideas and commitment.

However, the results should always be presented scientifically. As a model, the plan can be tested by computer simulation, which may be no more complicated than running a spreadsheet to establish strengths and weaknesses. Only unwise managers omit this final reality check before they take the plunge.

PLANNING FOR ACTION

A PLAN WILL SUCCEED OR FAIL THROUGH THE ACTIONS THAT FLOW FROM IT. ONCE THE STRATEGIC PLAN HAS IDENTIFIED THE OBJECTIVE – THE DESTINATION – AN ACTION PLAN SHOULD MAP OUT THE MEANS OF GETTING THERE.

DEFINING RESPONSIBILITIES

An action plan is needed for each component of the overall plan, and for each individual involved in the various teams. These plans are critical and must be clearly defined.

Everybody must know what is required of them and the rest of the team, as well as the why, when, and how. It is not enough simply to give people a document detailing their part in the plan. Two-way, face-to-face briefings are also essential so that roles can be specified and a clear understanding on both sides of the planning relationship can be established.

Deadlines are an indispensable part of the action plan, and a key pressure point. They should be realistic and fully agreed upon, otherwise the plan will be jeopardized. Deadlines will also need to be reviewed regularly: first, to establish that they are still likely to be met, and second, as a fundamental means of control.

EFFECTIVE CONTROL

The better the action plan, the less the need for invasive controls. Overtight monitoring and excessive intervention can be counterproductive. Inadequate controls, on the other hand, can be fatal. A well-established set of actions and associated metrics (used to evaluate and optimize performance) will provide a degree of semiautomatic checks that enable the leadership to ensure, without constant interference, that the plan is on schedule, rather than falling seriously behind or failing in any key dimension.

Such controls depend on a continuous flow of information, built around carefully selected key statistics (such as spending against budget) that will provide a real-time, effective check on progress and will validate or challenge the plan's assumptions. Key data should be made available as widely as possible (an intranet is invaluable for this purpose). In this way, everybody can be fully aware of what is happening and fully equipped to contribute to the plan's progress – and ultimate success.

However, it should be remembered that the action plan is not set in stone. On the contrary, since reality never goes according to plan, revisiting and possible revision of the basic assumptions will be essential for success. Every action plan is a test-bed for the planners.

Acting on the answers means that, in effect, the action plan is a series of plans,

CHECKLIST

✔ *Establish which underlying assumptions have to be modified or even abandoned.*

✔ *Discover which goals have proved to be unrealistic.*

✔ *See where significant shortages of resources occurred.*

✔ *Find out what revisions of the plan are needed in consequence.*

incorporating the new decisions that have to be made as events unfold.

ANTICIPATING EVENTS

The action plan must take into account all eventualities. That includes the worst-case scenario, when severe deviations give rise to an absolutely critical decision: whether to abort, revamp, or continue. "Go–No Go" points – when you decide whether to proceed with the plan or to abandon it – should always be built into the planning schedule. When making Go–No Go decisions, it is essential to restart the action planning with a blank slate. You will hear the argument that "We've come so far/spent so much that it would be foolish to stop." Ignore it. Reexamine the plan from scratch, and always answer this question:

● "if we had known then what we know now, would we have proceeded in the first place?"

Even if the answer is "no," abandoning the plan may still not be the correct response. There is a further, potentially more valuable line of enquiry:

● "Knowing what we know now, can an alternative, viable plan be developed that will meet or posssibly surpass the same objectives?"

Success can often be snatched from failure in this way. Giving up too soon and blindly persisting with failure are two mistaken sides of the same coin. The excellent action planner seeks a compromise between the two extremes.

That is not the only necessary compromise. Never forget that small errors may have devastatingly large effects, so scrupulous attention to detail is vital to action plans. But it is by no means everything. The art of the action planner is to focus on both the trees and the wood, not to bog people down in unnecessarily precise specifications of their duties.

Remember that action plans are not mere documents, but living human experiences. To be successful, they depend on personal relationships and talents, among which leadership is appropriately the leading attribute.

STARTING AGAIN

Turning a failing plan into success is a stern test of leadership and analytical ability. The first analysis is a ruthless post-mortem. What has gone wrong and why? Do not seek to apportion blame. This is a dispassionate search for truths.

The answers may leave no logical alternative to closure. However, other options are likely to exist. The second analysis examines these alternatives and estimates their financial outturns. If the failing plan is a new product, for example, what are probable sales and profits (or losses) if revamped for a different market?

You need financial analysis again to compare the options: continue, hoping that the plan will "come good"; closure; change to the new strategy. The figures must cover a three-year period. If the new approach gives the lowest first-year cost, no further losses in the second, and a reasonable profit in the third, the business case supports the change.

Leadership is required to drive the analysis forward, rally support behind the chosen strategy, and replan the project. The forecasts, like all forecasts, may be wrong. But attend particularly to the first-year results after starting anew. If they are on forecast, you have reason for confidence in the rest of the plan.

PURSUING TOTAL QUALITY

TOTAL QUALITY MANAGEMENT (TQM) EMBODIES ALL THE ESSENTIALS OF PLANNING. TQM COMPRISES A CONTINUOUS SET OF ACTION PLANS, INVOLVING ALL ACTIVITIES, ALL UNITS AND SUBUNITS, AND ALL INDIVIDUALS IN THE ORGANIZATION. SUCH A DISCIPLINE OPTIMIZES THE USE OF ALL RESOURCES.

STRATEGIC INTENTION

Total Quality Management must start with an overall strategic aim. This aim can be revised and reoriented regularly (for example, every year), but within an unchanged context: that is, to achieve a continuous improvement in processes and products (including services) until the organization is the leader in every aspect considered to be of importance to customers.

The program never ends, so improvement is always possible, both in the planning of the value chain and in its operation. The value chain links all the activities, inside and outside the organization, which culminate in the delivery of value to the end-user. The end-point of the chain (a more than satisfied user) is also the beginning. The planner designs the chain in the light of the user's needs.

It follows that "customer satisfaction" is one of the key total quality management metrics to evaluate and optimize performance. This response is usually rated by quantitative surveys, which should, however, be supplemented by qualitative interviews that enable the company to probe more deeply into user reactions.

TQM also involves seeking metrics for all other activities, since what goes unmeasured cannot be demonstrably improved. The use of metrics is an essential part of technical training, which, in turn, is indispensable to a successful TQM program.

EMPLOYEE SATISFACTION

Good training and planning processes contribute powerfully to employee satisfaction, which in turn has been shown to play a vital role in satisfying the end user. It should be noted that the term "end user" does not only apply to the external customer. Internal users, for example, the units served by the finance function, must also have their needs demonstrably met by a constantly rising standard of service.

THE SIX SIGMA PROCESS

In order to achieve an enhanced level of employee satisfaction, there needs to be full involvement in selecting quality projects, planning implementation, carrying out the quality plan, and achieving the targeted results. This principle of total mobilization of the labor force – from the board of directors to the shop floor – is fundamental to TQM, but it also represents the biggest single stumbling block to its adoption.

It demands a whole new way of life for the organization, and establishes extremely demanding objectives like the "Six Sigma," requiring a highly disciplined process that helps focus on developing and delivering the highest quality products and services.

IDENTIFYING THE PROBLEM
Make sure that you have correctly identified the
problem – or else the solution will fail

ANALYZING THE PROBLEM
Quality of analysis is essential to ensure that you
possess and understand the key facts

GENERATING POTENTIAL SOLUTIONS
Develop alternative solutions to provide a
complete picture of the possibilities

SELECTING AND PLANNING SOLUTIONS
Work for everybody's agreement that the chosen
solution is the best option

IMPLEMENTING SOLUTIONS
Give people and teams clear responsibilities

EVALUATING OUTCOMES
Check results carefully against what was
expected when the solution was agreed upon

Using a Total Quality Management process
*Total Quality Management (TQM) aims to
achieve continuous improvement in processes
and products by empowering teams (and even
individuals) to tackle problems methodically,
by analyzing and measuring processes to
devise better working methods.*

The Six Sigma process aims to achieve
no more than 3.4 defects per million parts
or operations, a goal that cannot be
achieved without rigorous, sustained, all-
around effort.

UNDERSTANDING STATISTICAL TOOLS
Production environments that use
modern quality control methods are
dependent upon statistical information.
Some common tools used are called the
Seven Statistical Tools.
They come under four headings:
- generation of ideas and collection
  of information
- planning actions
- reaching consensus
- analyzing and displaying data.

The tools range from the familiar, such
as check sheets, pie charts, and line
graphs, to those that have to be taught,
such as cause-and-effect diagrams, which
form a "fishbone" pattern, histograms,
which chart the frequencies of different
outcomes, Pareto analysis (*see* p.121),
which separates the significant few factors
from the insignificant many, scatter
diagrams which plot variables against
each other, and process control charts.

THE BENEVOLENT CYCLE
All tools and techniques are subordinate
to the basic PDCA cycle – Plan, Do,
Check, and Act. The cycle may involve
the whole organization, a large or small
group, or even an individual (individuals
are encouraged to propose their own
projects, as well as belonging to QITs –
Quality Improvement Teams). If the TQM
system is not adopted by the company,
three of its basic principles are still
essential for effective use of resources.
These are the three Ms: Map, Mobilize,

Measure. Plan what you want to achieve, engage all in the pursuit of those goals, and constantly and accurately measure your success in reaching those goals.

The PDCA cycle
The PDCA cycle (or Shewart Cycle) is a basic process in TQM. Each plan for improvement leads to implementation: monitoring for deviations is followed by their correction.

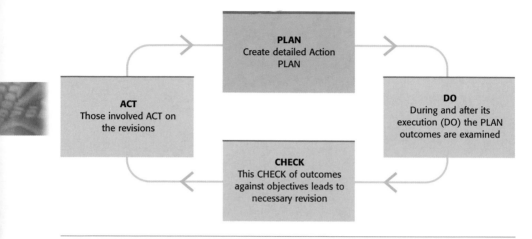

IMPLEMENTING FEEDBACK

AS PLANS ARE PUT INTO ACTION, INEVITABLY THINGS GO WRONG. DEVIATIONS MAY BE MAJOR OR MINOR, BUT THE REQUIREMENT IS THE SAME: YOU MUST RECEIVE ACCURATE FEEDBACK THAT WILL GENERATE ACTION TO RESOLVE OR RESCUE THE SITUATION.

RAPID RESPONSE
When a plan goes wrong, it needs to be put back on course or revised to meet the unforeseen circumstances. The action must be fast or the most common deviation, time slippage, will follow or intensify. Contingency planning, which aims to anticipate potential problems, should allow for a speedy response. Remember, though, that contingency plans may also be affected by events and must then be revised themselves. There must therefore be a reliable, real-time

system to consider information on progress and problems, and to adopt fact-based solutions for any new contingencies. Schedule a regular meeting (at least weekly) for the key executives at which reports are reviewed and the way forward is discussed. It helps if the reports follow a planned format, establishing:
● What are the critical data?
● How will the information be delivered and checked?
● What form will the presentation take?

THE CRITICAL PATH AND VARIATIONS FROM IT
A basic planning tool is critical path analysis. It generates a diagram setting out the sequence of operations, and shows where one activity must be complete before another can proceed. Checking

progress against the critical path will highlight variations and deviations.

Good plans always build in leeway to allow for such accidents, but this can rapidly disappear when events distort the original plan. Variation analysis will establish what went wrong, and why. The analysis must dig deep until it uncovers the root causes of the failure. These could be anything from faults in the original plan to inept execution.

You must go on asking "Why?" until you are satisfied with the answer. You can then make a critical decision. You must discover whether the fault is systemic or specific. Even if the latter is the case (a bad employee appointment, say) deeper questions still have to be answered: Why was the bad appointment made? A thorough variation analysis will lead to improvements that should make it less likely for faults to recur.

It is very important to make the widest possible use of this fault-finding, as people outside a particular project can learn from the feedback you receive, drawing on your information to improve their own operations.

TROUBLESHOOTING

If the deviation is severe, you will need the services of expert troubleshooters, whose special skills include cutting through the difficulties to the essentials. They will need a clear and precise brief on what is required from them, and by when. Their leader(s) will also require:

- the authority to pick their own team
- adequate resources to tackle the task
- a clear reporting relationship to their superiors.

The relationship should be one of advice and consent, not command and control. Troubleshooters are more likely to be given a free hand, because the situation is likely to be urgent: action will not unfold on paper, but in the real world. It is all too common and easy, however, for superiors to weaken and muddy the execution of a good action plan by unnecessary interference.

SUSTAINING THE MOMENTUM

Successful implementation of the plan depends heavily on sustaining the motivation of team members at all levels – above all, the leader. If the leaders and the led are not allowed to exercise their responsibilities, and are not involved in the planning as well as the execution, problems are more than likely to follow. Motivation does not depend only on success. While that should always be celebrated, tackling problems and overcoming them can be deeply satisfying in themselves. People must, however, feel that the problems and the plans "belong" to them if motivation is to remain high.

If the plan involves a project, rather than the year-to-year work of the organization, the leader must plan for what happens when implementation is complete:

- Will the team be disbanded?
- Is there a program beyond the immediate project, for which all or some of the team will be required?
- If so, is it a fresh project, or one that will build on the completed plan?

This issue of continuity is just as important when the plan involves the whole organization. Failing to plan for further advance is one of the most common faults, and one that is easily avoided. Remember that the organization's resources should be improving all the time and in every respect.

STAFFING AND RECRUITMENT

AS AN ORGANIZATION GROWS, IT WILL NEED NEW PEOPLE TO FILL NEW ROLES AND TO REPLACE STAFF WHO LEAVE. MAKE SURE YOUR PLANNING IS SUCH THAT YOU ARE ABLE TO HAVE THE RIGHT PEOPLE IN THE RIGHT PLACE AT THE RIGHT TIME.

REVIEW YOUR BUSINESS GOALS

Start by reviewing exactly what your short- and medium-term business goals are. For example, if you plan to increase sales, it will have implications for sales resources. The exact implications will depend on how those sales will be achieved. An increase in home retail sales may mean finding another salesperson, while foreign sales might call for language skills that are not required in the home market.

DEFINE THE JOB

You need to set out the scope and responsibilities of the job before you start the process of recruitment. The job description should include the measurable outcomes that you expect, as well as listing the tasks. So, for a salesperson you need to spell out what the sales target is, how many calls should be made, what the customer retention target is, and so on.

PROFILE THE PERSON

With the job description done, you can begin to put some flesh onto the kind of person who could do it well. If you are looking, again, for a salesperson, then communications skills and appearance will be important factors to consider, along with their personal circumstances: for example, they may have to stay away from home frequently.

ADVERTISE THE JOB

You need to give as much thought to your job advertisement as you would to your latest new product. Include a job description covering such aspects as the job title, who the person will report to, what their responsibilities will be, what their tasks will be, and details of the terms, including pay, conditions, work

RECRUITING FROM WITHIN

ADVANTAGES	DISADVANTAGES
■ You know the strengths and weaknesses of the candidate.	■ Other people who work for you may be upset if a fellow worker is promoted.
■ You know the candidate can fit in with your style and culture.	■ If the candidate fails in the new job, he or she may be unhappy or unable to return to their previous job.
■ The candidate will be available for interview at times convenient for you.	■ If the candidate fails, you will have double the amount of recruiting to do.
■ The candidate should know enough about your business to get off to a flying start.	■ You miss an opportunity to bring in new blood and new ideas.
■ It will show other people who work for you that they too can aspire to a better job with you.	■ You miss a chance to let the outside world know you are successful and need new staff.

hours, and so on. Also list key personal attributes that you are looking for, such as education, experience, and special skills such as foreign languages.

Remember, the goal of a job ad is not only to generate responses from suitably qualified applicants, but also to screen out those who are unsuitable.

You can advertise both internally and externally. Do not overlook your existing staff if they could be promoted into the job, even if they will need some additional training. While there are also disadvantages to recruiting from within, there are distinct advantages.

The type of external advertising will depend on the type of vacancy. The internet is a major force in the recruitment market, and may be right for, say, design engineers, or for desirable applicants who are working elsewhere in the world. However, if you are looking for temporary assembly line workers, going through an employment agency would probably be more productive.

Press advertising is the most popular way of recruiting staff externally, though you should choose the publication with care. The local press may well work well for attracting people in your area, but trade and business publications may be better if you want people with industry knowledge.

You could also use a recruitment consultant or headhunter to fill key posts. This has the advantages of confidentiality and access to skills and processes you may need to help in your selection, such as psychometric testing.

MAKE YOUR SELECTION

If you have more good applicants than you have time to interview, you need to

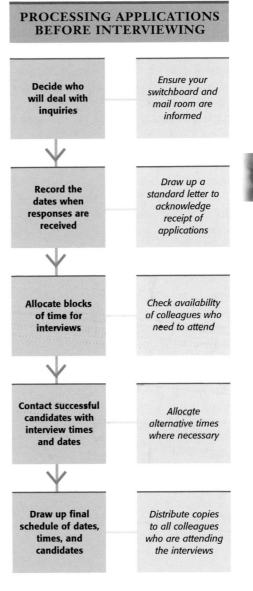

PROCESSING APPLICATIONS BEFORE INTERVIEWING

Decide who will deal with inquiries
Ensure your switchboard and mail room are informed

Record the dates when responses are received
Draw up a standard letter to acknowledge receipt of applications

Allocate blocks of time for interviews
Check availability of colleagues who need to attend

Contact successful candidates with interview times and dates
Allocate alternative times where necessary

Draw up final schedule of dates, times, and candidates
Distribute copies to all colleagues who are attending the interviews

evaluate them against some cutoff criteria. The cutoff point should be where applicants below a certain standard would not be offered a job under any circumstances. If this still leaves too large a list of candidates, raise the bar higher.

Assuming that the response to the vacancy is satisfactory, you should have at least three applicants on your shortlist. But, as interviewing is time-consuming, you should aim to have no more than about eight. When you draw up the shortlist, arrange the interviews.

CONDUCTING AN INTERVIEW
Conducting a job interview can seem a lot easier than it is, and a lot of the success is down to investing the time and effort that effective job interviews need. Plan the interview thoroughly: reread the application form before you see the candidate to clarify what questions you will ask, and ensure that all the relevant information is on hand for all the interviewers during an interview. Where possible, include either a skills test or psychometric test in the process.

The starting point for your questions will be to test the validity of the candidate's resumé. While not necessarily untruthful, applicants may exaggerate their achievements. It is also probable that their understanding of certain terms is not exactly the same as yours. For example, sales administrators may believe they have successfully landed big contracts when in fact they have only handled them once these have been landed by someone else.

You also need to ensure that all the possible candidates are not made to feel uncomfortable and therefore unable to demonstrate their true worth.

Ideally, everyone who will work directly with the applicant should have the chance to meet them and form their own opinion.

Offer the job to the best candidate, but keep one or two others in reserve.

You must have a reserve in case your first choice turns you down. Always take up references, preferably on the phone. Do not take "testimonials" at face value.

Having made an offer that is accepted, stay in touch with applicants until they arrive. Keep them posted about any developments, put them on the memo/email list and invite them to social events.

MAKE THEM WELCOME
Having gotten the right people to join you, make sure they become productive quickly and stay for a long time. The best way to do this is to have a comprehensive orientation program showing them where everything is and the way things are done in your business. Set them short-term objectives and monitor their job performance on a weekly basis, perhaps even daily at first, giving praise or help as seems to be required.

An orientation program should be designed to:
● make the trainee feel at home and a necessary part of the team
● provide basic local knowledge
● start the process of building networks
● initiate the basis of a balanced appropriate work program, based on an assessment of training needs
● establish "ground rules" for the working relationship between the trainee and supervisor.

It should normally include:
● a preliminary meeting to carry out an assessment of training needs and to set goals and targets
● an information pack giving details of the organization and its products, services, and staff
● an introduction to key people
● a meeting schedule.

SALARY AND REWARD PACKAGES

YOU SHOULD REWARD MEMBERS OF STAFF FAIRLY AND COMPETITIVELY, AND GIVE INCENTIVES TO IMPROVE PERFORMANCE. AN EFFECTIVE SYSTEM OF SALARY AND REWARD WILL HELP RETAIN STAFF AND MOTIVATE THEM TO GIVE THEIR BEST.

JOB EVALUATION AND THE "GOING RATE"

To evaluate a job, look at each position and assess it against a range of factors such as complexity, qualifications, skills, experience required, any dangers or hazards involved, and the value of the job's contribution to your business.

You also need to find out the going rate for key jobs in similar businesses. This is the pay rate that normally applies to a particular job in a particular geographical area. Inevitably, not all jobs are identical and certain aspects will involve differences in employment conditions that affect the going rate. Working hours, employment conditions, security of tenure, pension rights, and so on vary from firm to firm. You need to have a procedure in place to routinely monitor local going rates, and a system to correct for variations in employment conditions between your firm and other similar firms.

If you are too far out of line with the going rate, your staff turnover will rise.

REWARD BY RESULTS

Different types of work have different measurable outcomes. Those outcomes have to be identified and a scale arrived at showing the base rate of pay and payment above that base for achieving objectives. Different types of "payment by results" plans are commonly used in organizations, including commission, profit-sharing, share option schemes, and output-related bonuses. The conditions that most favor these types of reward need to be carefully examined to ensure that you pick the right mix of goals and rewards, to ensure that people are encouraged to deliver the required results.

Skill or competence awards can be made when an employee reaches a certain level of ability. They are not directly tied to an output (such as improved performance), but you must believe that raising a particular skill or competence will lead to better results.

Whichever method you choose to reward employees, it should meet some basic criteria. First, everyone must be able to understand how the reward system works and how it is calculated. Where possible, stick to measurable results: for example, a certain level of sales or profits, or attaining a specific level of competence that can be certified.

The reward has to be worth achieving, relate to the amount of effort involved, and be attainable. If no one ever reaches the standards you set for your rewards, the message will soon get out and people will stop trying. Worse than that, they may come to see themselves as failures and their performance level may actually drop. Try to give rewards soon after the results have been achieved.

CHECKLIST

✔ *Make the rules clear so that everyone knows how the reward system will work.*

✔ *Make the goals specific and, if possible, quantifiable.*

✔ *Make the reward visible, so that everyone knows what each person or team gets.*

✔ *Make it matter: the reward has to be worthwhile and commensurate with the effort involved.*

✔ *Make it fair, so that people believe their reward is correctly calculated.*

✔ *Make it realistic: if targets are set too high, no one will try to achieve them.*

✔ *Make it happen quickly: reward results as soon as possible.*

REWARDING EXCEPTIONAL RESULTS

The objectives you want people to achieve in order to be rewarded beyond their basic pay need to be challenging but also achievable, which is something of a contradiction in terms.

The targets have to be achieved, so it makes sense to pitch on the conservative side. However, exceptional performance will be attainable only with breakthrough thinking and performance. The question may not be, how can we grow the business by 20 percent a year, but how can we grow it by 20 percent a month?

A way to get the best of both worlds is to have a performance range, rather than just one finite goal. So, instead of saying, "Sell 10,000 books" you say, "Sell between 9,000 and 12,000 books." The reward for achieving a really great result should be equally great.

If this high goal is missed slightly, to avoid demotivating an eager employee reward should be given as if the goal had been set slightly lower. This technique can provide an "inspiration dividend." Teams can be persuaded to set higher goals than they might otherwise have set and, even when they miss them, the year-on-year improvements can be stunning.

BUILD IN BENEFITS

A benefit is defined as any form of compensation that is not part of an employee's basic pay and that is not tied directly to performance.

These nonsalary benefits, such as noncontributory pensions, enhanced working conditions, free private medical insurance, and so forth, can also play a part in keeping people loyal.

In addition, personal development training, company product discounts, flexible hours, telecommuting, and fitness facilities are all on the list of benefits that people can expect in certain jobs, alongside a company car and extra paid vacation days.

NONFINANCIAL REWARDS

Financial awards are not the full story. In fact, it is often the nonsalary-based rewards that are most likely to create lasting results. These include recognition and words ranging from a simple thank you through to individual, team, and company award ceremonies at which their successes are celebrated. Prizes such as vacations and theater trips, as well as certificates and engraved trophies, are also valued rewards.

Making employees' work interesting and varied, as well as providing opportunities for responsibility, job growth, and advancement should all play their part in your reward package.

EVALUATING SALARY AND REWARD PACKAGES

If you raise the qualifying limits of your salary and reward package too far, employees will become demotivated, their achievements will decline, and ultimately they may leave for other more rewarding positions.

Track the numbers of people leaving the company each year to ensure that they are not rising. In any event, you should ask them before they leave what part, if any, your salary and reward package has to play in their decision.

In developing a salary plan, there are several questions to be answered:

- What is the goal of the compensation system? Is there an intent to reward employees for good performance?
- Will you pay market rates?
- How will you communicate the compensation plan to employees?
- How will decisions regarding pay be made? Who will be involved?
- What is the desired mix between benefits and cash?
- Does the organization pay for performance or seniority or both?
- What is the role of performance appraisal in the organization?
- How will the compensation plan be managed once it has been developed?

MANPOWER PLANNING

MANPOWER PLANNING GENERALLY MATCHES HUMAN RESOURCES TO BUSINESS NEEDS. YOU NEED TO BE ABLE TO DO THIS EFFICIENTLY FROM A LONGER-TERM PERSPECTIVE, WHILE ALSO BEING ABLE TO ADAPT TO SHORTER-TERM REQUIREMENTS AND FORESEEABLE PEAKS AND TROUGHS.

ANALYZING MANPOWER

Manpower planning addresses needs in both quantitative and qualitative terms, which means having the answers to these fundamental questions:

- How many people does the organization require?
- What kind of people, and with what skills and attributes, are needed?

Manpower planning is not just a numbers game. It may also take in other issues such as the way people are employed and developed in order to improve organizational effectiveness.

WHAT TO PLAN FOR

The business plan sets out the projected scale of business activity in terms of key outputs, sales, production, operations, and so on. It also defines the types of activities to be undertaken, determining which are to be discontinued and which new ones are to be started up.

The end result of this process should set out the number of people required in each skill set and by which date. The longer it takes to find and train staff for your business, the further ahead you need to plan. For example, it might take just a month to recruit a production operative, a further month for the potential employee to work out their notice period and then additional time will be required for you to train them.

Within two months they could be working at their optimal level, able to play their part in achieving business

PLANNING MANPOWER LEVELS

Employees	Have now	Extra needed	Possible wastage	Total new staff	
Sales	10	5	1	6	Present sales person unsatisfactory so may have to go
Operatives	30	10	5	15	
Admin	5	1	1	2	One staff member is looking for new job nearer home
TOTAL	45	16 +	7 =	23	Total staffing gap

Planning manpower levels
This organization needs to recruit 16 people to meet its goals for next year. Past experience shows that they can expect to lose seven of their current staff, so they should plan to recruit 23 new people.

goals. A field sales person might take four months to recruit, select, and work out their notice period. It could take a further three months to train them in your methods, to fully understand your products and services, and to be earning their keep. Unless you are looking ahead at least a year or two, it is unlikely that you will have skilled people in place to meet planned growth.

In arriving at the number of people you need, you must also allow for a number of people leaving your employment, voluntarily or otherwise. There are two ways to calculate this: using the turnover index and/or the skill stability index.

Turnover index
This is sometimes called the "wastage" rate and it is the traditional formula used by human resources experts to estimate turnover in staffing levels. The formula is the number of leavers in the year, divided by the average number of employees that

year, multiplied by 100. This gives you a percentage. So, for example, if a department employing an average of 80 people over the year loses 10 people, its wastage rate is 12.5 percent.

Skill stability index
Although the wastage formula is simple to use, it can be misleading. It does not tell you anything about the type of people who are leaving. The skill stability index takes the number of people who have been with you for one or more years in each key skill area as a proportion of the number of people you employ in those skills. You then multiply that by 100 to get a percentage. This gives you a feel as to whether your longer-serving employees or newer staff are causing the greatest wastage, and from which skill areas.

Using the department in the above example, and for simplicity assuming they are all similarly skilled, then: if 50 of the 80 employees have been with the firm over one year, the skill stability index is:

$$\frac{50}{80} \times 100 = 62.5\%$$

If the stability index last year was, say, 75 percent, then it is clear that the longer serving employees are leaving in growing (and worrying) numbers.

Once you have the business goals and an estimate of the likely wastage rate, you can start to plan manpower levels for the period in question.

OUTSOURCING

Almost every part of the work you do can probably be outsourced. Websites can be designed and hosted, and technology can be rented. There are e-wholesalers and packers and internet-only delivery groups. Customer services can be handled by third-party call centers, while online banks compete with traditional banks to offer online payment processing. Almost every other aspect of business, from recruitment to accounting, to payroll and human resources services, can be outsourced.

Clearly, if you can buy something from outside the company less expensively than your internal cost, it makes sense to do so. You might also consider outsourcing in areas that may not be cheaper, but could save scarce cash or unnecessary upheaval. You will of course have to satisfy yourself that your outsource firm can meet your quality and reliability standards. In any event, take up references and have a trial period before handing over.

PART-TIME AND TEMPORARY STAFF

If some of your staffing requirement is temporary or seasonal in nature, you could consider using part-time staff or job sharers.

Using part-timers can open up whole new markets of job applicants, sometimes

of a higher quality than you might expect on the general job market. Highly skilled and experienced retired workers, or mothers who have given up successful careers to have a family, can be tempted back into temporary or part-time work. It can sometimes make sense to have two part-time staff sharing one job. This tactic can also be used to retain key staff who want to leave full-time employment. This makes for continuity in the work, allows people to fit work around their personal circumstances, and brings to the business talents that might have been lost if full-time work had been insisted upon.

When part-time or temporary workers arrive, make them feel welcome and part of the team, provide an orientation program and assign mentors from your full-time staff. Do not just give them the "grunt work," and do let them participate

CHECKLIST

✔ *Decide upon long-term business plan.*

✔ *Gather objective data on how many employees leave each year and why they leave.*

✔ *Know the likely impact of training, motivation or capital investment on the output and efficiency of each section of the business.*

✔ *Build into the plan the time needed to recruit and train new staff.*

✔ *Make those responsible for achieving key results also responsible for planning their own manpower needs.*

✔ *Support line managers with the advice and data needed to make sound manpower decisions.*

✔ *Build contingencies for seasonal fluctuations in demand, or any other short-term factors that could affect manpower requirements.*

fully in projects and follow them through to completion. Be sure part-timers are recognized and praised for their efforts, and are invited to company events.

WHO SHOULD PREPARE THE PLAN?

The individual responsible for achieving key business goals should be responsible for planning the manpower required to achieve those goals. In practice, this means line managers. They alone have access to vital information, such as the achievable efficiency improvements that can be gained by training, motivation, or capital investment. They need to be coached and trained to give them the knowledge and skills to carry out the manpower planning tasks effectively.

MEASURING PERFORMANCE

WHAT IS NOT MEASURED CANNOT BE EVALUATED; NOR CAN IT BE IMPROVED. GOOD MEASURES OF PERFORMANCE AND HIGH BUT APPROPRIATE STANDARDS MUST BE SET, IF THE ORGANIZATION IS TO BE MORE EFFICIENT.

CHOOSING MEASURES

Every individual or team effort contains some elements that can be measured by performance. Make sure those measures have the capacity to deliver real economic benefits to the organization. Too narrow a measure, or the wrong measure, can deliver undesired results.

For example, if salespeople are measured only by the number of calls made or by the number of customers they have secured, they may spend most of their time chasing poor quality leads while also neglecting their existing customers. Setting a quota based on gross profit and customer retention, as well as call rate, will be a better way of raising performance.

WHAT SHOULD BE MEASURED?

Anything that impacts on business performance should properly fall within the scope of performance measurement.

Typical areas include:
- production or output levels
- sales results
- net profit and gross profit (both amounts and percentages)
- attendance levels, absences, and timekeeping
- accident levels
- staff turnover levels
- meeting deadlines
- achieving personal and team development targets
- new product, market successes
- customer retention rates
- new account acquisition rates.

SETTING THE RIGHT OBJECTIVES

The starting point for measuring performance is setting an objective. Objectives can be related to the results to be attained or the contribution to be made to achieving organizational, functional, and individual or team goals. They can take the form of personal development or learning objectives designed to improve performance in specified areas.

The common mnemonic **SMART** may help you set the right performance measures. This is as follows:

- **S**pecific: clear and unambiguous (also Stretching: taking people beyond their present level of achievement)
- **M**easurable: in terms of time, quality, quantity, money, and standards
- **A**chievable: within the reach of a competent and committed person, although still challenging (also Agreed upon: explicitly, by manager and employee)
- **R**elevant: to the overall corporate goals (also Resourced: appropriate resources must be made available)
- **T**imed: all objectives need a start and end date and ideally should have intermediate review points built in.

MEASURING TEAM PERFORMANCE

Since there are many types of teams with different measurement challenges, this process is not simple. You need a clear understanding of your destination to find the most efficient path to your goal. This is often difficult for at least three reasons:

- It is not always obvious what results should be measured. Most teams will use the obvious measures without asking what results they should be producing and how they will know they have done a good job
- It is not often clear how the measurement should be carried out. Not everything can be measured with numbers, for example "creativity"
- Measurement must be done both at team and individual levels, avoiding conflict, doubling the size of the task.

CHECKING OBJECTIVES

Here are seven questions to check out the state of your objectives:

1 Does everyone in the organization have some measurable objectives that impact directly on the fundamental performance of the business?

2 Do you have objectives for your part of the organization?

3 What happens if people meet, exceed, or miss those objectives?

4 How are those objectives arrived at?

5 How frequently are objectives and targets revised and reviewed?

6 Why have you chosen that time period?

7 How do you know that people are committed to achieving their targets?

ASSESSING RESULTS

Performance measures should provide evidence of whether or not the intended result has been achieved, and the extent to which the employee has produced that result. Make sure the data you use to measure performance is accurate, reliable, relevant, free of bias, and available in a timely manner. Check that those concerned also have confidence in the reliability of the information.

If necessary – and this is particularly important with financial measures – make sure that those concerned actually understand what the information means and how it has been constructed. They may need specific training in this aspect.

Here are some guidelines for assessing the results:

- Measures should relate to results, not efforts.
- The results should be within the employee's control.
- Measures should be objective and observable.
- Data must be available for assessing results
- Results should be reviewed frequently, and in any case soon after the event concerned.

operations
MANAGEMENT

TO MANAGE OPERATIONS EFFECTIVELY, YOU NEED TO CONCENTRATE ON THE CRITICAL COST, QUALITY, AND DELIVERY REQUIREMENTS THAT WILL ACHIEVE OPERATIONAL EXCELLENCE. FOR A HEALTHY, EXTERNALIZED VIEW OF OPERATIONS MANAGEMENT, IT IS ESSENTIAL TO FOCUS ON ALL RELEVANT CUSTOMER NEEDS.

You must know how all the core operational requirements should be managed, and how the key measures for individual disciplines should be implemented. You need to understand how the value chain works, and be aware of the demands of purchasing and supply. It is essential to have a sound plan for production, balancing forecasts against demand, inventory against capacity. Underlying everything is the need for lean manufacturing: maximizing efficiency and minimizing waste. You can also consider how to make the most profitable use of research and development, while understanding new technology and how best to exploit it.

It is vital to have an excellent communications system throughout the whole company. All staff, from top to bottom, should have access to relevant information.

IN THIS CHAPTER

MANAGING THE VALUE CHAIN

TO MANAGE THE VALUE CHAIN, YOU MUST UNDERSTAND THE TOTAL CUSTOMER SUPPLY CHAIN, AND THE INTERNAL SERVICE LEVEL AGREEMENTS USED ALONG IT. YOU SHOULD KNOW THE ADDED VALUE AT EACH STAGE OF THE CHAIN, WHILE SETTING TARGETS AND IMPLEMENTING MEASURES, AND BE ALERT TO REENGINEERING POSSIBILITIES.

UNDERSTANDING THE VALUE CHAIN

The value chain is the series of linked processes that make the company's money (*see* opposite). The processes are the responsibility of the management team, using internal service level agreements, and provide the key inputs into the total customer supply chain. The value to be added at each stage must be identified.

DESCRIBING THE PROCESS TEAM

As a starting point, the team handling each process and its objectives must be clearly described. Inputs to the supply chain always have specifications for quality and delivery, and you need to have agreed on measures for both with your internal supplier. By the same token, your output measures, again for quality and delivery, need to be agreed on with your internal customer.

DEFINITIONS

Internal service level agreements: *these govern quality, delivery, and cost of the processes along the value chain.*

Total customer supply chain: *the series of processes by which the needs of the customer are met, involving people both inside and outside the organization.*

It is important to understand the role played by production teams in internal processes. But what do they do for the external customer? In other words, why are they there?

You should also understand the key competencies and skills required for the entire task of meeting customer needs. Problem-solving methods (*see page 115*) and improvement targets are necessary, too. These should always be agreed in line with the company's overall needs for speedy production, shorter cycle times, and continuous improvement in quality.

Process teams for a typical company will represent most of its functions. The crucial requirement is that all process teams must have key measures for quality and delivery. This is how the team actually adds value in the supply chain.

SUPPORTING THE PROCESSES

Process support teams, as their name states, support the actual process teams in the supply chain: finance, human resources, and so on. Their internal customers are the people working in the supply teams. The same requirement for internal service level agreements on quality and delivery operates here, too. The agreements can apply specifically to personnel, finance, and technical functions. Agreement of service levels should be reached through team purpose charts, and through detailed checklists for the quality and delivery requirements. Always refer to these controls in terms of the total management of the supply chain.

The process team approach should also be applied outside the walls of the organization. This means having a flat structure, in which teams are organized around processes to meet customer needs. The approach has to include key suppliers, the distribution chain, and outlets serving the customer.

This inclusive concept holds the key to achieving both distribution deals and supplier purchase agreements. The value chain is therefore properly described as starting with the end-user customer, going back through the distribution chain, back into the organization, and back out again into the suppliers, and also into the research and development area.

Remember, too, to treat subcontractors like process teams that have their own quality and delivery parameters.

MAINTAINING CUSTOMER FOCUS

Creating an organization in this manner will ensure customer focus at all stages of the chain. All process teams must be able to describe what they do, why they do it, and for which internal customers. They must also be able to demonstrate the quality and delivery parameters to which they work. Furthermore, they must work toward improving quality and delivery through problem-solving.

In applying these policies, you should be sure to make no distinction between people inside the organization and those outside it. That principle applies to the supply chain: at the purchase end as well as the distribution and sales end.

The organization's policy must run throughout. Everybody must have team purpose charts; everybody must have checklists agreed; and everybody must be working to improve their unit's ability to perform in relation to the agreed quality and delivery measures.

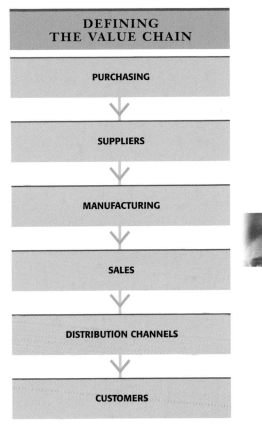

DEFINING THE VALUE CHAIN

PURCHASING

SUPPLIERS

MANUFACTURING

SALES

DISTRIBUTION CHANNELS

CUSTOMERS

REENGINEERING PROCESSES

Business process reengineering (BPR) involves redesigning the customer supply chain, taking out all activities that do not add value. Existing processes are mapped for each functional team, specifying inputs and outputs, as well as controls over resources. As in the customer supply chain, the mapping must run all the way back from the end-user customer.

In all cases, value must be added within each function in terms of quality or delivery for that customer. If a process does nothing for the end-user, it should be removed from the chain. In that way, process after process can be streamlined.

PURCHASING AND SUPPLY

TO MANAGE PURCHASING, YOU MUST HAVE STRATEGIC SUPPLIER AGREEMENTS IN PLACE. YOU NEED TO KNOW HOW TO HANDLE LONG LEAD-TIME ITEMS, AND TO ALLOW FOR R&D. TO MANAGE SUPPLY, YOU MUST KNOW HOW TO TRACK FORECASTS, HANDLE CUSTOMER SERVICE, AND MINIMIZE INVENTORY.

AGREEING ON THE POLICY

Strategic purchasing agreements must consider all suppliers as a fundamental part of the business.

The first necessity is to embark on a long-term supplier relationship, based on performance, not on price. This is achieved by understanding each other's processes and requirements and by a joint commitment to quality improvement. Thus two-way communication is opened from the start. The supplier must:

- have an outline product requirement
- fill in a supplier questionnaire
- seek technical assistance
- agree to regular reviews.

The second phase is to obtain an agreed set of product and supply requirements. Purchase specifications must be agreed on, purchase agreements put in place, and the quality introduction plan agreed between the parties. The plan identifies what actions to take regarding product quality at all stages.

The third phase covers the final acceptance of the supplier and product by the company. This requires the supplier to have a quality control process that is in line with your company's requirements. The customary and best requirement is the internationally recognized ISO 9000 standard. The company needs to validate the product under selection through agreed tests and supplier assessment. If necessary, depending on the scale of the business and technology involved, they will audit all the quality processes. The next step is to monitor progress. Finally, reliability trials should be continuous.

Agreeing on the supplier policy
It is essential to view suppliers as an integral part of the organization. For best performance, a healthy, mutual understanding must be reached, which will encourage confidence and confirm the supplier's long-term suitability.

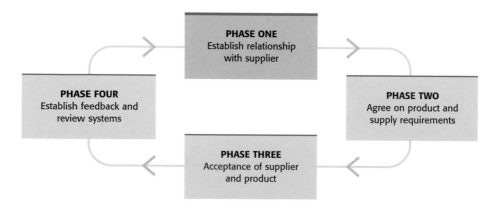

PHASE ONE
Establish relationship
with supplier

PHASE TWO
Agree on product and
supply requirements

PHASE THREE
Acceptance of supplier
and product

PHASE FOUR
Establish feedback and
review systems

The fourth phase is to establish feedback and follow-up systems. Specific failed item systems and failure analysis track back to the overall quality improvement plan. The key to supplier control is, clearly, to provide a mutually beneficial long-term partnership, using the methods outlined. There are a number of benefits to the supplier:

- independent proof of its internal quality systems
- rapid feedback of any problems
- exchange of field information on products installed at customer sites
- improvement in product quality
- independent review of the product's workmanship standards.

Finally, when all the criteria in the supplier agreement and the quality and production plan have been met, the company should recognize the supplier by awarding ship-to-stock status (that is, acceptance without inspection). This provides obvious advantages, both to the supplier and the company, by reducing the cost of procurement.

IDENTIFYING THE KEY MEASURES

The key purchasing measures for the organization relate to the availability of the correct stock and the management of material at the raw material stage. Strategic supplier agreements are important for long lead-time items where an element of risk must be agreed between both parties, who must work together to meet the specific product need, especially if the component is new.

For research and development, it is vital to have a supplier agreement. The design and development team can never be sure that the product being developed is correct until it is implemented in the larger system. Therefore, the purchasing department must set up flexible, mutually beneficial supply agreements.

The key requirements for distribution are the ability to: track and control forecasts against delivery requirements; handle customer service after delivery; and minimize worldwide inventory.

The key supply measures are inventory and delivery performance for the end-user customer. Even if you supply to distribution outlets, and so do not usually see the end-user, it is crucial to understand that the key measure is customer perception. This understanding will require close contact with the distribution chain.

The key is to agree on forecasts with distributors and to develop the ability to deliver within short lead times. Strategic agreements with distributors must be formulated in the same way as supplier purchasing agreements. There is no point in having distribution outlets unless they add value; so all distributors should provide an element of fast and efficient customer service. Strategic agreements with distributors must reflect this requirement. A tracking system is also needed to match the forecast requirements against actual delivery.

All communications throughout the purchasing and supply chains should be available via the internet. This enables tracking of information to be done in real time with relative speed and cheapness.

DEFINITION

ISO 9000 standard: *internationally recognized standard for excellent quality systems. Many large firms insist that suppliers be ISO-certified.*

PLANNING PRODUCTION

PLANNING PRODUCTION DEMANDS ACCURATE FORECASTING. IT IS ESSENTIAL TO DEVELOP AND IMPLEMENT A MASTER PRODUCTION SCHEDULE, AND UNDERSTAND HOW TO PLAN MATERIALS AND MAINTAIN STOCK INTEGRITY. INVENTORY MUST BE MINIMIZED, CAPACITY PLANNED, AND MEASURES APPLIED.

CREATING THE MASTER PRODUCTION SCHEDULE

The master production schedule (MPS) matches the forecast against short-term demand, and identifies exactly what everybody must do in the period covered by the schedule. It offers significant advantages over the usual incompletely planned situation.

First, since material will be allocated in line with the MPS, it is consumed in the correct sequence, with assembly taking place as required by the system.

A sample master production schedule
This production schedule shows a typical sequence for the preparation and manufacture of a product, building in systems of regular monitoring and review (both short and long term).

Second, because account will be taken of capacity when the MPS is created, the build planned for week 1 does not exceed available critical supplies of labor and/or equipment. Third, once the MPS program has been drawn up, internal customers (Service/Design/Sales) should receive delivery of products, assemblies, and stock by the planned date.

RECOGNIZING KEY FACTORS

In addition to these advantages, an MPS meets two key objectives. First, it ensures that kits (sets of components required for assembly of the whole) for build purposes are not affected by shortages. Second, it ensures adequate capacity for week 1 (next week's) production.

The relevant measures are the percentage of required shortage-free kits that were not available for week 1 production; and the percentage of planned week 1 production not completed. The MPS system should be implemented more or less successfully, depending on a number of factors, as follows:

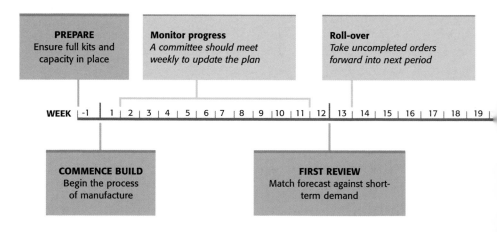

Effective forecasting

To ensure that delivery timescales meet the market requirements, meaningful forecasts must be included, stretching as far forward as possible. Forecasts for all product types can be produced, as long as there is enough information to give the forecasts substance. Forecasts must be reviewed and updated regularly, so the company can react to market changes in good time, and avoid excessive material stock or unacceptable delivery dates.

Products without forecasts

Products with no forecast are those whose delivery period is outside that covered by the MPS. That is, their maximum buy/lead-time plus build time overruns the MPS period. Orders must be placed on the system so that the materials needed can be resourced.

Also, the delivery date stated on the acknowledgment sent to the customer should be realistic. When the product rolls onto the MPS, this ship date will be the maximum target date that the MPS can use while still meeting the delivery promise to the customer.

To ensure that your acknowledgments of deliveries by suppliers are objective,

analyze product material lead times (using "query reports" when problems arise). Include those products whose lead times are outside the MPS window in a long-term plan that looks no further than 30 weeks. Monitor this long-term plan to ensure that requirements for future changes in capacity necessary to meet customer expectations are made visible to management as soon as possible. The necessary resources can then be put in place in time to support the MPS program.

Also, adjust the long-term plan, where possible, to maintain a degree of continuity, avoiding large swings in projected weekly output (if allowed, these would cause inefficiencies in the manufacturing process).

Finally, where appropriate, prioritize purchase of long lead-time components and ensure that it takes place right away. Also, if market expectations are not being satisfied by the delivery timescales in the long-term plan, consider whether it is appropriate to hold certain long lead time components in stock.

Obviously, as products/forecasts on the long-term plan roll into the MPS timeframe, they are entered into the MPS program. This is an important review point for forecasts. Once MPS entry is made, you have decided to build the forecast product to a finished state, thus costing money but (you hope) creating significant value.

When products are ordered that have no forecast in place and their maximum component buy/lead time plus build time falls within the MPS timeframe, the orders may be included in the MPS program, providing that capacity is available, or can be made available.

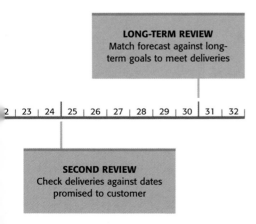

LONG-TERM REVIEW
Match forecast against long-term goals to meet deliveries

| 2 | 23 | 24 | 25 | 26 | 27 | 28 | 29 | 30 | 31 | 32 |

SECOND REVIEW
Check deliveries against dates promised to customer

Planning capacity

You need to understand capacity levels, so that the MPS does not inadvertently build in critical resource conflicts. The main capacity conflicts are likely to affect labor, suppliers, and (to a lesser extent) test equipment. Capacity can be roughly gauged by levels of weekly shipments in previous months, although more detailed data will be useful.

Note that planned capacity conflicts are allowable, provided that the conflict is resolved before week 1. Remove any capacity issues (except for short-term ones) that limit the company's ability to respond to customer expectations.

Kitting

Construct a "kit-marshal" storage area, so that kits can be worked on (to relieve shortages and monitor the situation) and released in the required time/order to meet the MPS program requirements. It is very important to focus on kits required for weeks 1 and 2 production, with any shortage issues on week 1 kits tackled aggressively by the purchasing department. Put the kit-marshal storage area in place before the planned return to storage of stock held by the line. This allows allocated parts to be easily placed in the appropriate kits before remaining unallocated parts are placed in the general stock area. Note: kit-marshal storage areas are not a long-term solution. Once shortage issues are reduced to low levels, the need for the areas will disappear.

Data integrity

You may find that various data integrity issues appear, including stock and lead time accuracy. Implementing the MPS on a reasonable timescale means that checking and/or correcting all these data issues will not be possible. The key area that must be "clean" is stock accuracy. Other areas can be cleaned up on a regular basis, according to an agreed procedure.

MAINTAINING AND UPDATING THE MPS

The MPS must be reviewed and updated weekly, and a committee should be formed to carry this out. Its membership needs to be agreed on. The MPS should be configured to ensure that as far as possible:

- external customer orders are shipped by the acknowledged delivery date
- internal customer requirements are supplied by the promised delivery date (sales stock, service assemblies, design unit assemblies)
- resources are operated at their maximum efficiency levels, avoiding underutilization.

The ideal situation is this: to have no rollover into week 1 from the previous week; all forecasts consumed by customer orders and sales stock requirements (at week 1); and no urgent customer orders requiring unpredicted shortfalls in deliveries. Furthermore, there is infinite capacity. All material supplies are delivered by their promised dates. There are no component scrap/quality issues.

In real life, as opposed to Utopia, there will be problems in all the above areas, to a greater or lesser extent. Therefore, the committee will have to make compromises.

It should be possible to maintain the MPS absolutely at week 1, with zero or very little change at week 2. However, the amount of enforced adjustment allowable will increase as the MPS program stretches further out. A forced adjustment of up to 20 percent may be necessary at the furthest point in the MPS.

The committee should ensure that hard copies of the updated MPS are circulated weekly to relevant areas of the company, including the kit marshal, production, dispatch, purchasing, sales, design, and planning.

LEAN MANUFACTURING

TWO CRITICAL QUESTIONS APPLY TO LEAN MANUFACTURING: FIRST, HOW TO MEASURE AND REDUCE THE COST OF WASTE IN TERMS OF MATERIALS AND TIME; SECOND, HOW TO ESTABLISH BEST-PRACTICE BENCHMARK MEASURES FOR THE OPERATIONS.

THE IMPORTANCE OF QUALITY COSTING

Quality costing is a powerful technique for monitoring the real effect of failing to achieve requirements. If a requirement is not achieved "right the first time," the full cost impact of this nonconformance must be measured – in money, not in statistics or percentages. The money measure provides effective prioritization and justification for corrective action.

Typically, examination of rework involving over 20 products will show that only two need attention, but that these carry almost 80 percent of the total cost involved. Experience has also shown that there is no "economic quality level," meaning an acceptable trade-off between quality and cost. It is always cheaper to get it right the first time. Two measures of cost of quality should be monitored:

- cost of conformance (COC): the money invested in prevention to ensure that you meet requirements the first time
- cost of nonconformance (CONC): the cost of failing to do so.

THE SIZE OF THE PROBLEM

A typical manufacturing organization wastes 20–25 percent of its total revenue through nonconformance. A service organization can waste up to as much as 40 percent. Careful corrective action, investing in COC, can lead to dramatic reductions. One myth that should be dispelled is that quality costing applies just to the product: the item that the customer sees. This is only part of the story. Quality costing applies to every single activity within the organization. Anything that is not performed right the first time – for example, poorly organized meetings, managers chasing other people's progress, unanswered telephone calls – incurs quality costs.

These CONC costs are multiplied when several processes link together, because a mistake in an early process will require much larger costs when rectified later on. For example, a clerical mistake in a customer quotation can be rectified quite cheaply if picked up immediately. However, if the mistake is processed, this will involve more departments, more people, and more systems involved in work that will need redoing. The costs escalate quite dramatically.

The above are examples of actual expenditure. In addition, there are lost opportunity costs. For example, how much business is lost as a result of slow responses, errors, the poor image presented? These costs are difficult to quantify, but they certainly exist.

Be aware of such costs, but do not try to evaluate them. It is more advisable to spend your efforts on remedying every visible mistake, every nonconformance. If these defects are removed, the opportunity loss is automatically reduced. The right approach is to focus on the visible, tangible aspects.

THE COST-OF-QUALITY METHOD

Data collection identifies the key cost measures for the business. A team will have to be educated and a pilot approach to cost measurement developed. Once the approach has been accepted, it should be repeated for the entire company. At the end of this phase, the cost of quality will have been determined.

The first cost model will probably not identify all the costs. This is because the understanding and identification of conformances and nonconformances have to involve the entire workforce in education and awareness, down through the organization, from top to bottom.

Demonstrable support from management will eventually achieve the necessary breakthrough. Nobody readily admits to nonconformances until they feel the culture is supportive.

MAKING ANALYSES

Modern quality tools and techniques are used to identify root causes from the cost of quality analysis. Once root causes have been identified, problem-solving teams are set up to follow through with the improvement process. The teams are drawn from the entire workforce, and trained and supported in solving identified and prioritized problems.

MAKING RESEARCH AND DEVELOPMENT PAY

TO PROFIT FROM R&D, A COMPANY MUST FIRST INTEGRATE PRODUCT DEVELOPMENT INTO THE OPERATIONAL PROCESSES, AND THEN DEVELOP THE TOTAL PRODUCT. THERE IS A CRUCIAL DIFFERENCE BETWEEN DEVELOPING TECHNOLOGY AND APPLYING TECHNOLOGY TO SPECIFIC PRODUCTS AND SERVICES, AND MANAGERS MUST UNDERSTAND THIS.

INTEGRATING
PRODUCT DEVELOPMENT

Integrating product development into operational processes is largely a matter of policy laid down by senior management. The policy can be judged by one question: Who is responsible for new product development? If the answer is "engineering" or "the R&D team," something is fundamentally wrong. The right answer is, of course: "everyone."

The whole point of integration is to ensure that the structure and processes for implementing products and services do involve every single person. To that end, the right structure sets up a product manager or champion who works with representatives from each function in a team that coordinates product introduction. Everybody in the operation can thus feed back to the development team the exact requirements derived from their customer experience, and from operating with existing products in their day-to-day business.

This approach fundamentally rewrites the traditional rules of product introduction, which follow a sequence of handover from design to manufacturing, and so on. Instead, new products become as fundamental a part of the business as

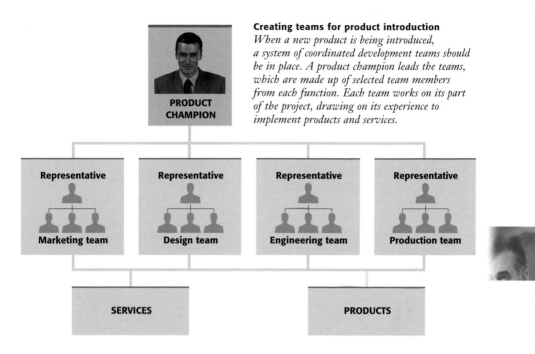

Creating teams for product introduction
When a new product is being introduced, a system of coordinated development teams should be in place. A product champion leads the teams, which are made up of selected team members from each function. Each team works on its part of the project, drawing on its experience to implement products and services.

existing ones. The only difference is that much more effort is required at the front end to test the product, while strict quality checks ensure that it is ready for production. In this new approach, all information is shared with strategic suppliers and also, where appropriate, distributors and customers. Sharing depends on the actual business, but the general rule is that the closer you are to customers, the better the product will be.

USING CHECKLISTS

Ensure that every single function has a product introduction checklist defining exactly what its inputs and outputs are, in terms of technical specifications, quality, cost, and delivery. These checklists must then be applied by a team that operates across the organization. There is no point in having phase reviews. The product champion should simply review

the requirements in terms of time, quality, and functionality, see where they are failing, and ensure that sufficient resources are applied at the appropriate place to meet the quality standards.

DEMONSTRATING TEAM PURPOSE

All parts of the organization must complete a team purpose chart, which identifies their precise roles in the introduction of a new product, and is where they must look to improve performance continuously against agreed standards. This obligation applies to personnel, training, finance, and all the other functions not normally associated with the introduction of a new product.

If, for instance, personnel fails in recruitment for engineering, the critical human resources will not be available and the product will not get off the ground. If finance does not pay suppliers on time, life becomes extremely difficult for engineers. If training does not put the necessary investment into people, engineering quality will suffer – and so will the overall quality of products and services offered to the customer.

UNDERSTANDING THE TOTAL PRODUCT

The key to understanding everybody's contribution to new products is the total product, which is what the customer sees. This comprises:

- the core product (functional capability, service quality, everything the customer sees around delivery, performance, and customer service)
- the added value (the benefit the customer gains from having the product, which hinges on everybody understanding their customer needs)
- the relationship factor (building strong bonds with customers to help in serving their needs as easily as possible).

One common problem in business is misunderstanding the difference between technology development and product introduction. Technology development is concerned with core technology requirements where the company must excel to sustain its business. This demands people whose responsibility is technological, but who are not focused specifically on product introduction, program management, or products.

Strategic direction from the top is vital. Before the development of technology can be focused, top management needs a thorough understanding of the business: who the customers are, and what the products are. Technology can be developed through third parties and

MEASURING PERFORMANCE

The key measures for performance are first: delivery performance on time, related directly to revenues projected from the sales forecasts; and second: quality with regard to first-time fit and "plug and play" (that is, there are no problems and it is easy for the customer to use the product).

Both these measures depend on the specific business, but they are a subset of either delivery or quality. This subset can be contained within the definition of the total product. Reports from the customer should be made available and totally visible to everybody in the organization at all times, so that all staff understand exactly what must be done to correct any problems, and to feed that back into continuous improvement for new products and services.

Again, the total product and the team purpose charts are used to ensure that all members of staff know where corrective action needs to be applied and what their role is in that process.

research organizations, but the basic requirement is to create technology building blocks that can be moved into a product or service as fast as possible.

This can relate to whatever business the company has – mechanical or electronic design, or basic semiconductor design, for example. The need is ready understanding of how to apply the technology to the specific customer requirement for a particular product or service. Achieving this requires people who focus mainly on developing the technology concerned and can support the product teams at the appropriate time. They do not, however, have responsibility for time or for the total product, where responsibility lies with the whole organization.

EXPLOITING NEW TECHNOLOGY

TO EXPLOIT NEW TECHNOLOGY PROFITABLY, IT IS NECESSARY TO UNDERSTAND HOW TO APPLY IT FROM A STRATEGIC AND BUSINESS STANDPOINT. IT IS ALSO ESSENTIAL TO DISTINGUISH BETWEEN PRODUCT-BASED AND PROCESS-BASED TECHNOLOGY, AND HOW EACH OF THEM IS APPLIED.

APPLYING TECHNOLOGY

From a strategic and business viewpoint, the application of technology is essential. Technology must be used to help the business, which means that the business must drive technology, not the other way around. Being good at technology is simply not enough; a company should match the high quality of its ideas with effective commercial exploitation.

There are four dimensions in which technology should be applied, each of which demands clear understanding:

- the strategic direction and vision of the business
- products and markets over the next three years
- where revenues and margins will be generated from those products or markets
- the objectives for the product.

PRODUCT-BASED TECHNOLOGY

The product objectives are established through interaction with customers. You must know the strategic applications of technology to existing and new customers, and to the products and processes serving those customers. Furthermore, there must be a strategy for ensuring that everybody who is responsible for developing and implementing all products and processes is committed to achieving the objectives.

In applying product technology, the first need is to separate the development of the technology from the project management of specific products. The best people for developing technology are not necessarily the best people for driving projects through the system.

Most businesses feel they must have a core team whose sole responsibility is to develop the basic technological building blocks that are essential for meeting the needs of the business – certainly over a three-year period, and possibly beyond. Technology development must be built on the product needs by engineers who can develop new technologies, either on their own or with strategic partners.

PROCESS-BASED TECHNOLOGY

Process technology – innovating with computers and systems rather than engineering – is based entirely on customer needs. There is only one process that matters in a company, and that is the supply chain.

Automation and systems are applied to meet market needs through agreements on service levels with internal customers. The best method is to employ very flexible master production scheduling and other people-based systems on top. Heavy reliance on so-called custom systems is simply not good enough to meet the flexible demands of twenty-first century end-user customers. To meet their demands, it is essential to implement internet-based systems – the only way to ensure that people get the information they need, when they need it, and in the form that they want it. The internet enables you to achieve a speed and flexibility that will transform the economics of information systems throughout the organization.

APPLYING KEY MEASURES
The key measures for technology development are speed and effectiveness. Ask yourself: How quickly are new web-based systems implemented, and how easily are they modified in line with what the customer needs? How smoothly and efficiently are the technological building blocks assimilated into new products?

INFORMING AND COMMUNICATING

FOR SUCCESSFUL OPERATIONS, INFORMATION MUST BE TOTALLY VISIBLE. A CUSTOMER-FOCUSED, KNOWLEDGE-SHARING, TEAM-BASED ORGANIZATION IS THEN CREATED. STRATEGIC ACTION PLANS MUST BE DEPLOYED INTO THE OPERATIONS, AND INTERNET SERVICES FULLY EXPLOITED, WHILE PROGRESS IS CONTINUOUSLY MONITORED.

DEPLOYING THE STRATEGIC ACTION PLAN
First, the management team must reach agreement on the strategic action plan. This will cover the three dimensions of customers, processes, and people. After the key strategic actions have been established, it is essential to ensure that every functional manager and team can clearly identify the key measures of team output. Functional activities can affect only quality, delivery, and cost, so all measures should be related to these activities. The key measures also cover three dimensions:
- customer measures for delivery
- customer measures for quality
- the cost of the operation.

The outputs from the strategic action plan are identified through the key measures for each operation, using a team purpose chart. You then reach service level agreements with the internal customers in the supply chain. This is just as important for personnel, training, and the other support organizations that back up the customer supply chain.

Service level agreements concentrate on quality and delivery, while cost is established through "cost of waste," measured in terms of materials and time. Measures must have total visibility to ensure rapid improvement where action is required. To this end, all team purpose charts or service level agreements are posted on an intranet (internal) website. Everyone in the company has access to how each functional team is doing, so that there is no excuse for internal misunderstanding. Also, the management team can access the key results that must be achieved to meet strategic action plans.

Inevitably, there will be shortfalls on the target measures for customer delivery and quality. This is where the operation-wide problem-solving system is so important. Each functional team must meet regularly to brainstorm all problems that are stopping them from achieving cost, quality, or delivery targets. These items fall into three categories:

- totally under the control of the team (Type T)
- partially under the control of the team (Type P)
- not at all under the control of the team (Type N).

The system should be very strict. All functional teams are expected to work on the T-type problems and to improve their performance continuously with work that is completely under their control.

There must also be a structure for resolving P-type problems that go outside the functional teams: every individual is responsible for helping everyone else. However, if the problem is multifaceted and multifunctional, then a "corrective action team" is needed. This should meet regularly to resolve those problems that cut across functions and processes.

Finally, N-type problems go to the management team, which is responsible for helping other people to achieve their objectives, using problem-solving tools and techniques. All senior managers should have their own intranet websites. They can then communicate their thoughts and ideas to everyone in the company, and ensure that everyone knows exactly what is going on at any time.

SHARING KNOWLEDGE THROUGHOUT THE ORGANIZATION

To ensure commitment to improvement, everybody must know:

- the strategy
- the product and market requirements
- the progress being made on orders
- how the company is doing financially
- what is required to improve performance.

Traditionally, these areas were mostly matters reserved for management alone. Modern evidence shows unequivocally that if the people who are involved in the work are kept fully informed on these issues, then organizational efficiency and employee satisfaction are both increased. Sharing knowledge generates a win–win outcome for all, including the customer.

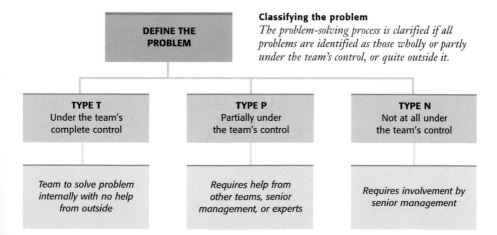

DEFINE THE PROBLEM

Classifying the problem
The problem-solving process is clarified if all problems are identified as those wholly or partly under the team's control, or quite outside it.

TYPE T
Under the team's complete control

TYPE P
Partially under the team's control

TYPE N
Not at all under the team's control

Team to solve problem internally with no help from outside

Requires help from other teams, senior management, or experts

Requires involvement by senior management

marketing
AND SALES

MARKETING IS THE BRAIN OF BUSINESS GROWTH, THE NERVE CENTER OF MARKET SENSITIVITY AND COMMERCIAL PRODUCTIVITY. ALONG WITH SALES, IT RESIDES FIRMLY AT THE CORE OF COMPETITIVE BUSINESS ACTIVITY, DRIVEN BY THE BASIC TRUTH THAT IT IS CUSTOMERS, NOT PRODUCTS OR SERVICES, THAT MAKE PROFITS.

To succeed in the marketplace, an organization must not only identify and respond to customer needs, but also ensure that its response is seen as superior to that of its competitors. Customers are the key to competitive advantage. It is the function of marketing and sales to take the lead in demonstrating and maximizing this customer value.

To be effective in marketing and sales, managers must understand the role of marketing in the organization, and the importance of marketing information. This information enhances marketing strategy and improves planning and implementation. High-performance marketing operations are founded on strong marketing relationships and market position, but ultimately business success lies in the complex task of organizing for marketing and sales: that is, achieving the correct balance within the marketing mix.

THE ROLE OF MARKETING IN BUSINESS

MARKETING IN BUSINESS MUST BE BOTH ENTREPRENEURIAL AND EFFECTIVE. IT HARNESSES THE FIRM'S RESOURCES, AND FOCUSES THEM ON THE MOST PROMISING OPPORTUNITIES. IT IS ALSO CONCERNED, CRUCIALLY, WITH CUSTOMER SATISFACTION AND IDENTIFYING MARKET OPPORTUNITIES.

MATCHING SUPPLY AND DEMAND IN THE MARKETPLACE

At its simplest, marketing may be defined as a business process that seeks to match an organization's resources – the human, financial, and physical – with the wants and needs of its customers. This takes place within the context of its overall competitive strategy. It follows that if your company offers customers a closer match than that of its competitors, then you will have the advantage.

The matching process is complex and challenging, since it involves the skillful management of numerous variables. While some of these variables will be within the control of your organization, such as availability, affordability, and suitability, others will be beyond its control: for example, interest rates, new laws, and fashion trends. A successful match between what the customer wants and what you supply therefore requires a deliberate and organized activity.

This matching activity involves the manipulation and management of the marketing mix, and the monitoring and evaluation of the marketing environment. The marketing mix is the offer that you control: that is, the bundle of benefits and/or solutions offered to the customer, which extends beyond mere product features. The marketing environment is the set of uncontrollable variables within which the marketing process takes place.

MANAGING THE MARKETING MIX

The crucial role of marketing is to ensure that the marketing mix is successfully managed, within the context of the marketing environment. A successful match is achieved when the customer has been satisfied, and your organization's resources have been effectively deployed to that end.

The marketing mix is usually classified as aspects of four elements: product (including services), price, promotion, and place – the "4Ps". The importance of the mix is that successful matching depends on a number of criteria:
- customers must be aware of the product (or service) on offer
- customers must find the product readily available
- customers must judge the product attractive in terms of both price and performance.

If one of these criteria is missing, or wrong from the customer's perspective, it is unlikely that a sale or a long-term relationship will result. Highly effective marketing management welds the elements of product, price, promotion, and place into a coordinated whole in the marketplace, in exactly the right combination and at the right time for the targeted customer. The challenge of

PRODUCT (OR SERVICE) Can be varied in terms of quality, size, functionality, and so on	**PRICE** Can be high or low, involve a discount, or be affected by credit terms
PLACE The channels through which you can distribute a product, plus the service element	**PROMOTION** Can utilize television advertising, salespeople, and other communication methods

The marketing mix
To achieve a successful match between what you are offering and what the customer wants, you need to get the marketing mix right. This means the optimal combination of product (or service), price, promotion, and place: the 4Ps.

achieving the right marketing mix is compounded by the complex set of variables that constitute the marketing environment. These include social or cultural factors, government activities, sources of competition, and technological developments. There is also the influence of institutional evolution, such as the way in which food is increasingly distributed through large out-of-town supermarkets rather than small local outlets.

It is crucially important to perceive and predict these environmental trends, as they determine the relevance of your organization's market presence, and also the reality of its market position.

In today's global trading arena, "open access" means twenty-four hours a day, seven days a week, as well as relatively open entry for market newcomers. No organization can afford to ignore the fickleness of customer loyalty or the ferocity of competitive forces. Prosperous organizations have become so by being good at matching: both in terms of the ways they manage the 4Ps (the offer), and in terms of the ways they relate the offer to the needs of customers.

THE RELATIONSHIP BETWEEN MARKETING AND SALES

The ultimate test of the efficiency of any marketing strategy has to be sales. These are not just measured against volume targets, but rather in terms of profit. Those companies that strive for market share, but measure it in terms of volume only, may be deluding themselves that volume can be bought at the expense of profit. Therefore, it really makes sense to measure the revenue share of the market as well.

Marketing and sales are clearly linked, yet require separate attention. It is essential that the development of a sales strategy should be closely integrated with the marketing strategy, and that market strategy must in turn take account of the role of the sales force.

Good companies set themselves overall objectives, which in turn generate specific marketing objectives. These marketing objectives are then broken down into actual sales targets. This approach gives a number of significant benefits to sales force management. First, corporate and marketing objectives can be coordinated with the actual sales effort. Second, a circular relationship can be established between customer needs and corporate objectives. Third, an understanding of the corporate and marketing implications of sales decisions can improve sales effectiveness.

Managing relationships with customers is recognized as increasingly important in a world of more and more choice. This is emphasized by the growth of customer relationship management and relationship marketing. As a result, the role of sales has been heightened. Usually, sales is considered part of the promotional element of the marketing mix, since it involves communicating with customers, both current and potential. But it is not the only element of promotion. Guidance on the promotional mix can be obtained through the gathering, analysis, and interpretation of marketing information.

MARKETING INFORMATION

RATIONAL DECISIONS NEED RELEVANT DATA. A KEY ROLE OF MARKETING PROFESSIONALS IS SUPPLYING INFORMATION ABOUT MARKET AND MARKETING PERFORMANCE. THIS WILL ENABLE THE REST OF THE ORGANIZATION TO MAKE DECISIONS ABOUT THE MARKET-RELATED AREAS OF THEIR RESPONSIBILITIES.

INFORMATION AND APPLICATION

Marketing knowledge contributes to many managerial or policy decisions. Corporate or strategic managers need reliable information about market environments and competitors to be able to set the overall strategic direction of the organization. Operations managers need to understand the critical success factors associated with the delivery of their product or service, since these should form the basis for the design of their operating systems.

Given its importance, marketing information needs to be collected, collated, and reported in ways appropriate to the decisions it will support. When you request marketing information and research you must, therefore, understand clearly what you need to know in order to make the judgments for which you are responsible. This is often one of the biggest problems in drafting a market research brief or specifying a marketing information system: distinguishing "nice to know" from "need to know."

Research topics can cover both internal and external areas. With the aim of enhancing marketing performance, you should consider:
- market-share analysis
- market potential
- market characteristics
- sales performance
- business trends
- economic forecasting
- competitor products
- pricing studies
- product testing
- information systems.

Integrated as it is with marketing action, marketing information is viewed as a resource, but one that is perishable and has a limited shelf life. Like other resources, it has a value in use. The less a manager knows about a marketing

MAIN AREAS OF MARKET RESEARCH

AREA	ASPECT
Customers	■ Behavior ■ Needs ■ Responses ■ Beliefs ■ Characteristics
Markets	■ Size ■ Structure ■ Dynamics ■ Relationships ■ Trends
Competition	■ Share ■ Positioning ■ Aims ■ Strengths/weaknesses
Environment	■ PEST (Political, Economic, Social, and Technological factors) ■ Institutions ■ Trends
Your impact	■ Share ■ Penetration ■ Coverage ■ Image ■ Service levels

This information can be augmented with proactive research: using questionnaires, in-depth interviews, field experiments, test marketing, and so on.

When you are considering marketing research, it is useful to distinguish between marketing data, information, and intelligence. Data can best be thought of as the raw facts, figures, or descriptions of the topic that is being researched. Information is ordered data, or data that has been selected to describe a particular market or performance feature. Intelligence can be regarded as information from which conclusions have been drawn. As an example, an 80:20, or Pareto, analysis of an industrial company's customers based on sales invoices (the data) would yield a list of the best customers in revenue terms (the information), which could then be interpreted and/or explained to provide intelligence. Thus, an organization might conclude that its best customers are financial services companies from northern regions of the country.

BUILDING AN INFORMATION SYSTEM

Often the information that constitutes the organization's "market intelligence" already exists within the organization, but in a fragmented and uncoordinated form. The construction of a marketing information (or intelligence) system

problem, and the greater the risk attached to a wrong decision, the more valuable the information becomes. The key task of the market researcher is to understand what kind of decisions require what kind of information, and then the best means of obtaining it.

A FRAMEWORK FOR MARKETING RESEARCH

Logically, the starting point for any marketing research program should be investigating sources of existing information, both internal and external. There is no need to "reinvent the wheel."

DEFINITION

Pareto's law: *states that in any activities a small proportion ("the significant few") accounts for the lion's share of outcomes. So 80 percent of profits will come from 20 percent of products; and 80 percent of sales from 20 percent of customers.*

(MIS), comprised of a data bank and analytical and reporting tools, provides management with a resource designed to meet clearly specified information needs.

A sophisticated MIS works not only to ensure that information is complete, valid, and relevant, but also that it is disseminated through the supply chain to partners who would benefit. Integrating disparate data via vast data warehouses enables the sharing of data, and the building of customer profiles and predictive modeling capability. Such activities have become known as CRM (Customer Relationship Management), supported by specialized software.

The use of data mining tools to discover significant patterns in buying behavior or market trends can enhance marketing planning and the development of proactive strategies. On-line search facilities allow even the smallest or most remote company to access commercial databases covering every aspect of information. The internet also provides a phenomenal channel for gathering as well as giving information.

The critical issue when building an MIS is that it is not self-contained within marketing. It requires interface programs that will alter the systems used by finance, sales, and other internal departments so that information can be produced which is user-specific. Also, it will need to capture appropriate datafeeds from external sources to provide other supporting information.

IMPLEMENTING THE SYSTEM

A comprehensive, integrated marketing information system possesses four fundamental functions:

Monitoring performance

This checks the critical aspects of an organization's performance effectiveness. Performance monitoring relies very heavily on information drawn from internal sources, such as sales volumes, profitability analyses, product returns, and registered complaints.

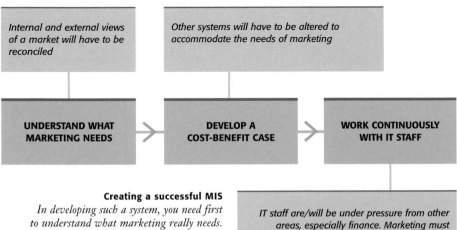

Internal and external views of a market will have to be reconciled

Other systems will have to be altered to accommodate the needs of marketing

UNDERSTAND WHAT MARKETING NEEDS → DEVELOP A COST-BENEFIT CASE → WORK CONTINUOUSLY WITH IT STAFF

Creating a successful MIS
In developing such a system, you need first to understand what marketing really needs. Then you must justify the funding for development, and ensure you have IT support in the face of competing demands.

IT staff are/will be under pressure from other areas, especially finance. Marketing must maintain momentum and direction, or vital information will not be available

TYPICAL BUSINESS OBJECTIVES AND INFORMATION

BUSINESS OBJECTIVE	SEGMENTATION METHOD	INFORMATION SOURCE
Market extension ■ new locations ■ new channels ■ new segments	■ Geodemographics ■ Prospect profiles ■ Survey analysis	■ Electoral roll (consumer) ■ Chamber of Commerce (business) ■ Prospect lists and surveys
Market development	■ Customer profiling ■ Behavioral scoring	■ Sales ledger and added profile data ■ Models from internal data sources and market research
Product development	■ Factor analysis ■ Surveys ■ Qualitative methods ■ Panels/discussion groups	■ Customers and consumers

Monitoring the market

This gains insights into developments in the marketing environment, referring to published materials generated externally. These may be held by an organization's library, by an outside agency, or by individuals in marketing or associated roles. Topics for market monitoring might include competitor reconnaissance, legislative activities, standards bodies, technological advances, interest group campaigns, and fashion trends.

Market investigation facility

This is for specific questions or ad hoc projects. It involves expert researchers administering questionnaires, conducting interviews, or engaging in desk research. The process of problem definition, from which the research plan is developed, is critical. The plan will focus mainly on the population to be researched, and the methodology to be employed.

Decision support systems

This enables marketing personnel to manipulate information and intelligence. They will use such analytical tools as correlation, cluster, or conjoint analysis; customer profiling, predictive modeling, and portfolio modeling; or complete planning systems.

Marketing information is a key source of competitive power and attracts considerable investment. However, you must never forget three simple truths:

● systems cannot be substitutes for personal judgment and the creativity required to develop innovative marketing

● data, information, or intelligence is only ever as good as the specifications from which it was produced

● any market research or marketing information system will generate more questions than it answers.

DEFINITIONS

Correlation: *a significant statistical relationship between one or more variables.*

Conjoint analysis: *a technique for trading off one variable against another.*

Predictive modeling: *a multidimensional model for forecasting the future.*

MARKETING PLANNING

MARKETING PLANNING HAS AN INTEGRAL ROLE IN IDENTIFYING AND CLARIFYING THE PRIORITIES FOR THE BUSINESS. AS SUCH, IT IS AN EFFECTIVE AID TO MANAGEMENT. WITHOUT A CLEAR STATEMENT OF PRIORITIES, THE COMPANY IS VULNERABLE TO INTERNAL CONFUSION AND LOST OPPORTUNITIES.

DEFINING MARKETING PLANNING

Marketing planning is the process of determining and formally writing down the competitive stance the organization plans to take. This ensures that everyone in the organization is pulling in the same strategic direction. Marketing planning is a more sophisticated approach than budgeting and forecasting, and should not be confused with those two activities. It identifies what, and to whom, sales are going to be made in the longer term to give revenue budgets and forecasts any chance of being achieved.

In essence, marketing planning is a managerial process, the output of which is a marketing plan. It is conducted in a

Preparing a marketing plan
To have the best chance of success in practice, a marketing plan should be carefully structured. The 10 steps shown here are refined as necessary by monitoring and feedback.

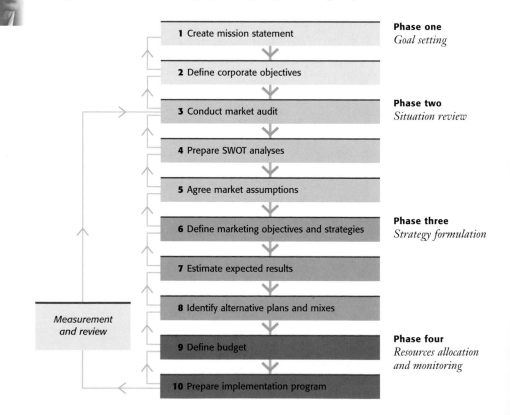

1 Create mission statement

Phase one
Goal setting

2 Define corporate objectives

3 Conduct market audit

Phase two
Situation review

4 Prepare SWOT analyses

5 Agree market assumptions

6 Define marketing objectives and strategies

Phase three
Strategy formulation

7 Estimate expected results

8 Identify alternative plans and mixes

Measurement and review

9 Define budget

Phase four
Resources allocation and monitoring

10 Prepare implementation program

KEY CONTENTS OF A STRATEGIC MARKETING PLAN

ACTIVITY	DETAILS
Mission statement	This sets out the *raison d'être* of the organization and covers its role, business definition, distinctive competence, and future indications.
Financial summary	This summarizes the financial implications over the full planning period, and sometimes uses gap analysis (which measures the revenue and profit gap between the desired outcome – the objective – and what is possible).
Market overview	This provides a brief picture of the market and includes market structure, market trends, and key market segments.
SWOT analyses	These identify your organization's **S**trengths and **W**eaknesses compared with competitors' against key customer success factors, plus your **O**pportunities and **T**hreats. They are normally completed for each key product or segment.
Assumptions	These are the assumptions about such factors as market growth and inflation that are critical to the planned marketing objectives and strategies.
Marketing objectives	These are usually quantitative statements, in terms of profit, volume, value, and market share, of what the organization wishes to achieve. They are usually stated by product, by segment, and overall.
Marketing strategies	These state how the objectives are to be achieved and often involve the 4Ps of marketing: product, price, promotion, and place.
Requirements and budget	This is the full planning period budget, showing in detail, for each year, the revenues and associated costs.

logical sequence: a series of activities leads to the setting of marketing objectives, and the drafting of plans for achieving them.

The formalization of this process is a structured way of:

- identifying a range of options for the organization
- making them explicit in writing
- establishing marketing objectives that are consistent with the company's overall objectives
- scheduling and costing the specific activities most likely to bring about the achievement of the objectives.

The degree to which each marketing planning step needs to be formalized will vary, according to the size and nature of the organization.

DESIGNING THE PLAN

The emphasis of the marketing plan should be on generating information that is genuinely useful, rather than on the procedures and the resulting paperwork. It is also important to pace the work; do not attempt to do too much too quickly. Throughout, make sure that members of staff are trained in the use of procedures.

DEFINITION

Market segment: *a subdivision of a market consisting of a group of customers or consumers with the same or similar needs, which are distinctly different from those of other customers in the market and can be met by tailored offerings.*

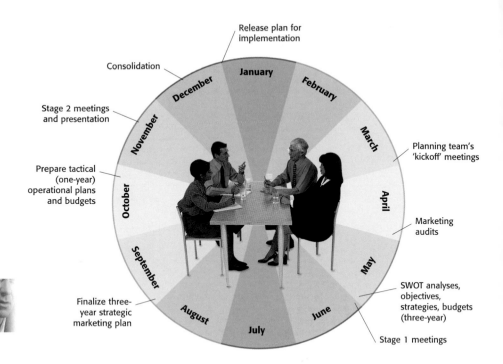

Release plan for implementation

Consolidation

Stage 2 meetings and presentation

Prepare tactical (one-year) operational plans and budgets

Finalize three-year strategic marketing plan

January
February
March
April
May
June
July
August
September
October
November
December

Planning team's 'kickoff' meetings

Marketing audits

SWOT analyses, objectives, strategies, budgets (three-year)

Stage 1 meetings

Creating a timetable for the marketing plan
This sample timetable shows a typical sequence for developing marketing plans. In an ongoing cycle, processes should be scheduled formally, relating the marketing planning process to its output: the strategic/tactical marketing plan.

There are two principal types of marketing plan. These are the strategic and the tactical.

The strategic marketing plan is the written document that outlines:

- how managers perceive their company's market position relative to their competitors' (with competitive advantage accurately defined)
- what objectives they want to achieve
- how they intend to achieve them (strategies)
- what resources are required and with what results (budget).

Until the early 1990s, most organizations planned five years ahead. Today, the typical planning period is three years.

The tactical marketing plan is applied specifically to the first year of the strategic plan. It provides the detailed scheduling and costing of the particular actions necessary for the achievement of that first year's objectives. The tactical plan is thus usually for one year.

The contents of a tactical marketing plan are very similar to those of a strategic plan, except that it often omits the mission statement, the market overview, and SWOT analyses.

The tactical plan goes into much more detailed quantification by product and segment of marketing objectives and the associated strategies. It also has a more detailed scheduling and costing of the tactics necessary to achieve the first year of the plan.

THE ORDER OF PLANNING

Successful organizations always have their strategic plan in place before formulating the tactical plan. In contrast, unsuccessful organizations frequently dispense with a strategic marketing plan, relying largely on sales forecasts and budgets. As a result, many managers end up confining themselves to selling the products and services they find easiest to sell to those customers who offer the least line of resistance. By developing short-term, tactical marketing plans first and then extrapolating them, such managers merely succeed in developing their own shortcomings.

The measure of a good marketing plan is not its 100 percent accuracy in predicting the future. It should capture the essentials of the planning process and distill them into a comprehensive working document. This should not contain so much detail that the major objectives and strategies become buried.

MARKETING OPERATIONS

THE ROLE OF MARKETING OPERATIONS IS TO OPTIMIZE DISTRIBUTION AND PROMOTE THE BUSINESS. THIS ENTAILS STRENGTHENING MARKETING RELATIONSHIPS AND MARKET POSITION. MANAGING THE PLACE, PRICE, AND PROMOTION ELEMENTS OF THE MARKETING MIX IS PARTICULARLY RELEVANT.

DISTRIBUTION CHANNELS

The fundamental role of a company's distribution function is to ensure that the right product is available at the right time. "Place" in the marketing mix determines what channels of distribution are appropriate for the target markets or market segments, and the associated service levels.

The choice of channel(s) must be based on the long-term balance of the benefits and the costs of that choice. This involves key decisions about the use or removal of intermediaries in the distribution chain. It also means that you must carefully consider the implications arising from the physical distribution of all the alternatives.

In recent years, technological advances, most significantly the internet, have transformed the shape of distribution channels. Channel management is now changing and changeable, highlighted by the emergent tactics of disintermediation and reintermediation. It is therefore imperative that you keep your channel strategy under constant review: looking at its levels of efficiency, effectiveness, and sustainability.

DEFINITIONS

Disintermediation: *where the company no longer needs to use intermediaries to create the values sought by customers.*

Reintermediation: *where new types of intermediary (e.g. web-enabled information agents termed "infomediaries") emerge to create more value than was possible in the previous channel structure.*

Service levels: *the extent to which the organization plans to make the product available and to support it in use, e.g. stock availability and after-sales service.*

KEY ROUTES TO MARKET

ROUTE	COMMENTS
Retailers	Stores that sell direct to customers
Wholesalers	Hold stock and distribute it on behalf of supplier
Distributors	Fulfill the same function as wholesalers
Dealers	Often appointed by, or owned by, supplier (e.g. car dealers)
Agents	Do not hold stock, but sell on commission
Value added resellers	Customize specific products for customers, usually in the IT industry
Catalog distributors	Suppliers whose main sales channel is their catalog
Direct mail retailers	Sell direct to consumers via mail to their homes
Franchised outlets	Outlets franchised by famous names
Freight forwarders	Transport specialists who distribute goods in bulk containers
Party sales organizers	Clubs consisting of individuals who sell specific merchandise (e.g. perfume and kitchenware) to other individuals, often from their own homes
Original equipment manufacturers	Manufacture goods for incorporating into other goods (e.g. cars)
Licensed manufacturers/ service operators	Licensed by a principal to produce on its behalf

MAINTAINING CUSTOMER SERVICE

An organization's system of customer service provides a continuing link between the initial contact with the customer, through to the time the order is received, to the time the product is delivered and used. The objective is to continuously satisfy customer needs.

Some marketing and sales managers insist on offering maximum service to all customers, no matter where they are or how profitable they are. Such managers are probably doing their company a disservice. Somewhere between the costs and benefits involved in customer service, a balance has to be found. By reviewing its policy of customer service, perhaps trying out differential service levels for different products or different customers, marketing can enhance its contribution to corporate profitability.

Customer service is an increasingly important factor for both competitive advantage and customer retention. Indeed, the service element is sometimes the only aspect that distinguishes one organization's offers from another's. Also, once a supplier/customer relationship is established, customer service contributes significantly to the augmented product offer, enhancing the value of a purchase and cementing relationships. In some organizations "customer service" is seen as a separate aspect of the marketing mix for which individual plans and strategies are created. The pivotal role of employees as ambassadors of the company, and by processes as the mechanisms of performance, has established "people" and "processes" as other elements of an expanded marketing mix.

THE IMPORTANCE OF PRICE

Price is also a significant component of the offer, since it is one of the determinants of a product's value. A potential customer takes into account not only the cost incurred in making the purchase (transaction cost), but also that incurred in owning or utilizing the product (life-cycle cost). It is this "total cost of ownership" that the customer evaluates against the perceived benefits. Price and associated costs are therefore an important determinant of positioning.

Price is a notoriously difficult dimension of the marketing mix to manage, because it is subject to many pressures that are independent of marketing objectives. These pressures can be internal (from other departments or senior management) and external (from customers, government agencies, competitors, and so on).

The pricing strategy

Maintaining price integrity depends on having a sound pricing strategy. This is a yardstick for making pricing decisions, as well as supporting overall marketing strategy and protecting profitability.

Pricing strategy should reflect the opportunities for value enhancement, based upon building perceived benefits, as well as opportunities for cost reduction to provide cost advantage. Pricing is also

an area of marketing with great potential for increasing short-term profits. But, if managed badly, it can bring a business to its knees. There are many options for using pricing as a flexible "connector," helping to match marketing efforts to customer needs. Pricing variables include:

- price point adopted
- discount structure
- discount amounts
- special offers
- sales (end of season, etc.)
- cost of ownership
- credit terms
- stage payments
- residual value
- leasing arrangements
- financial deals
- psychological elements.

Prices can be seen across a continuum, with low-quality/low-cost/mass-market products at one end, and high-quality/high-cost/select-market products at the other. The most profitable position will be a careful balance that creates the optimal mix. Market leaders rarely share the fear of many managers that unless they offer the lowest possible price they will not win the order. They recognize that a customer buys a "package" of benefits, and the price should therefore reflect the value of the total package.

THE IMPORTANCE OF PROMOTION

Promotion is concerned with the best ways of communicating with the target customers and persuading them to buy the offer. It incorporates selling, direct mail, advertising, and sales promotion.

In practice, promotion falls into two broad categories: the personal and the impersonal. Personal promotion is the role of selling, usually accomplished through a sales force or sales assistants. Impersonal promotion mainly takes the form of advertising and sales promotion. To be managed well, advertising should be regarded as an investment and not a cost. Furthermore, the use of different combinations of message and media provides a flexible advertising repertoire that is tailored to fit most budgets.

The fastest-growing mechanism of promotion is advertising on the internet, which provides a low-cost, high-impact medium for interacting directly with customers across the globe. Virtual showrooms and on-line order processing, information, and support services allow customer-facing operations to be run around-the-clock and be highly responsive to market trends. By tracking and monitoring web shoppers' viewing habits and checking their emailed feedback, businesses can build better customer profiles to support more personalized service strategies and media campaigns.

ORGANIZING FOR MARKETING AND SALES

ORGANIZING FOR MARKETING AND SALES IS A COMPLEX AND CRITICAL TASK THAT UNDERPINS EVERYTHING ELSE. A MAJOR CHALLENGE IS BALANCING RESPONSIBILITY AND ACCOUNTABILITY IN THE MANAGEMENT OF THE MARKETING MIX.

MANAGING THE MIX

Marketing managers obviously want to create an offer that targeted customers find irresistible, and they will manipulate the marketing mix to that end. Many elements of the marketing mix, however, are quite rightly under the control of nonmarketing managers since, to be managed well, they require specialized or technical skills. For example, the development of new products is often the responsibility of research and development specialists – this is the case in the pharmaceutical industry.

Marketing managers are therefore responsible for the profitable sales of the company's products, but without the authority to control all the elements that will promote such sales. This problem leads to the often poor relations that exist between marketing and sales personnel. One attempt to overcome some of these difficulties has been to reorganize a company's activities around its core processes, which either obtain value from suppliers or deliver value to customers.

A PROCESS-ORIENTED BUSINESS

Such a business will change its basis for managing operating units. Instead of, for example, structuring around the functions of operations, finance, human resources, and so on, it will use the processes of new product development, order fulfillment, and cost reduction. Each process will be managed by a team responsible for delivering efficiency in that area, and for meeting the objectives appropriate for competitive advantage. The team may still be product- or market-focused, but its remit becomes multifunctional (encompassing inbound logistics, production, sales and supply, for example), rather than each activity stage being a separate operation. In these circumstances, marketing functions would be accomplished by each of the teams, with ultimate responsibility resting with the top team for each process.

The organization would also include a specialized marketing unit to provide help with specialized topics. Marketing would thus be brought closer to the areas it needs to influence, since much of the marketing mix would be the responsibility of the cross-functional process team.

Under such business process redesign, marketing expertise would be injected into the team either through consulting, training, or contracting out.

CHANGING FOCUS

The issue of organizing marketing and sales effectively has never been so critical. Unprecedented developments throughout the supply chain are seriously challenging the position and structure of marketing. These developments include:

- the decline of traditional brand management as retailers become more powerful and determine their own "shelf strategy"
- advances in "micro marketing" that encourage marketing managers to refine their customer differentiation and targeting practices (such as the use of data mining)
- the reduced effectiveness of mass advertising as media channels proliferate and customers become immune to mass market appeals
- the current popularity of category management as a basis for organizing consumer goods markets.

Another hugely significant development is new technology, especially the internet, which has enabled the growth of "self-service" and the development of the virtual organization. This is an elusive combination of technology, expertise, and networks with little or no physical infrastructure. Marketing is crucial to the establishment, embedding, and excellence of e-commerce and m-commerce.

Resolving the question of exactly how marketing should fit within the structure of the organization involves weighty decisions at board level. The first is whether to have a specific marketing department at all. If this is thought to be the right option, the second decision is what range of activities it should oversee. Once this has been determined, the third decision is how it should be structured and who should do what job. If a separate marketing department is not thought appropriate, it is then more than usually important to establish and maintain strong marketing leadership throughout the organization.

The significance of these decisions is that organizations can provide only the

---

DEFINITIONS

Category management (CM): *the strategic management of a group of products clustered around a specific customer need. This group, or category, is managed as a strategic business unit with clearly defined profitability goals. CM shifts the focus of managers from individual brands to the management of overall categories, as defined by local customer needs.*

M-commerce: *short for "mobile commerce." Business-to-customer transactions are conducted using cellular and internet technologies.*

TYPICAL EVOLUTIONARY PATTERN OF MARKETING

One-man-band
An order taker, probably involved in the technical side

Sales/marketing team
Salespeople use self-generated sales support material

Sales force plus marketing sales support
Marketing provides material and information to support sales activities

Sales force plus ancillary marketing
Marketing expands activities and employs specialists to carry out a range of functions

Separate sales and marketing department
Marketing takes on product or brand management and influences sales strategies

Marketing and sales director
Appointed to coordinate activities

Key
■ *Overall responsibility*
■ *Marketing*
□ *Sales*

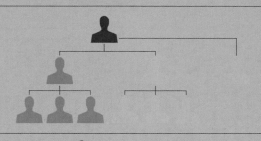
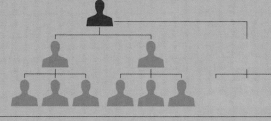
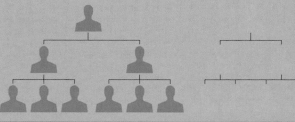
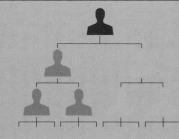

environment within which people carry out their work; they cannot determine how the work is performed. The optimal environment will maintain a productive balance between control and creativity.

An organization's structure and culture have a profound effect on its success. Where marketing and sales are separated at board level, marketing is very much a staff activity, with the real power vested in sales. Since the two jobs are closely connected but fundamentally different, it is important to ensure that marketing's plans are consistent with what sales is actually doing in the field. A strong CEO can ensure that the two areas are sensibly coordinated, but this is often prevented by competing pressures related to issues of production, personnel, distribution, and finance. Where a marketing director oversees both sales and marketing, it is usually easier to achieve coherence between planning and doing.

EVOLVING MARKETING STRUCTURE

In a typical evolutionary pattern of marketing, a company will develop over time from a "one-man band" setup to a multifunctioning super-department that incorporates a whole range of specialized activities. Further growth and increasing marketing sophistication will expand the organization's options.

PLACING THE FOCUS

A key decision for organizations with operations in several regions is whether to centralize or decentralize marketing activities. The ideal arrangement is to organize around a blend of both in order to gain dual benefits. Marketing is put as close to the customer as possible, while some kind of centralized marketing function is maintained. Thus costly and unnecessary duplication is minimized, and economies of scale and effective knowledge transfer are optimized.

AN ORGANIZATONAL METHODOLOGY

Organizations with formal marketing departments need to decide whether to organize around functions, products, markets, key accounts, or geographical area, or to use a combination of approaches to minimize the dangers inherent in any single one. Examples of the latter are businesses that organize around brand managers, but separate the functions of public relations, customer service, and planning; or those that use both product managers and market managers in a matrix-type relationship.

As common sense and market needs are the final arbiters, no one particular form of organization can be considered superior. However, all organizations, of whatever form, must consider:

- marketing "centers of gravity" (i.e. key product/market segments)
- interface areas (e.g. present/future; salespeople/drawing office)
- authority and responsibility
- ease and effectiveness of communication
- flexibility
- human factors (e.g. cultural sensitivities, individual work practices, workplace dynamics).

In the end, however, structure is of only secondary importance in establishing marketing as an effective force within an organization. More significant is the attitude of the managers working within the structures, and the ways in which they influence other managers toward adopting a customer-oriented approach.

the impact
OF THE INTERNET

AFTER EARLY SWINGS OF FORTUNE, IT IS NOW WIDELY ACCEPTED THAT INTERNET TECHNOLOGY WILL CONTINUE TO BE THE BIGGEST AND MOST POWERFUL CATALYST FOR CHANGE IN BUSINESS EVER SEEN. NOBODY CAN PREDICT ITS FULL IMPACT, BUT ALL AGREE THAT IT WILL BE HUGELY SIGNIFICANT AND AFFECT EVERY ASPECT OF DOING BUSINESS EVERYWHERE AND WITH EVERYONE.

In the dot-com world of business and consumer trading, the pace of change is dizzyingly fast – so fast that it can be a threat to survival. As a manager, you must constantly make yourself aware of change in these new business environments. You need to analyze this challenge, deploying smart tools and techniques to identify the moneymaking and money-saving opportunities, and take immediate and nonstop action to address them.

You must understand how internet technology has already transformed traditional business patterns, and be open to further developments, particularly concerning the value chain. You must be able to make the best use of intranets and extranets, and know how to exploit the internet to make valuable short-term, tactical gains.

IN THIS CHAPTER

WIRING THE COMPANY

USING THE INTERNET, A COMPANY CAN COMMUNICATE INSTANTLY BY VOICE, SOUND, VIDEO, IMAGES, AND TEXT WITH ANYONE ELSE IN THE WORLD WHO IS SIMILARLY WIRED. THE TECHNOLOGY'S SPEED AND POTENTIAL GIVE A POWERFUL COMPETITIVE ADVANTAGE TO BUSINESSES THAT ADOPT IT.

THE COMMUNICATION LANDSCAPE

The internet has enabled a growing proportion of businesses, government departments, and individual consumers to communicate with and by anything that can be digitized:

- audio: CDs, DVDs, telephone calls, recorded messages
- images: photos, graphics, diagrams, and computer-aided design
- text: many formats in many fonts; current, archived, and database
- video: archived video, live broadcast television, web cameras
- applications: hosted applications, where users can log on to use software they do not own but just share or rent over the internet, e.g. project management, financial systems, banking, design tools
- trading: business-to-business, business-to-consumer, consumer-to-business, and consumer-to-consumer
- communicating: through forums, discussion groups, emailing, and chat rooms.

Anyone using a phone (landline, mobile, or WAP), a business computer and network, a palmtop device, a laptop, a digital TV, or games console (and many more devices yet to be launched) can contribute to or use the internet.

THE IMPACT OF SPEED

Speed has become a significant force for change. For example, in the travel industry in the late 1990s – at the height of the dot-com boom – the trading values over the internet moved from the equivalent of $3 million per year to $3 billion per year: a step change of 100,000 percent. At that time, less than 50 percent of companies were using internet booking systems for hotel reservations, car rentals, and airline tickets. Now, most people use such systems for business and for personal arrangements.

Traditional processes, traditional slow functions, and traditional attitudes to the way things are done will be relentlessly replaced. Change will be either step change, as seen in the travel industry example and also in the sale of books and CDs, or more gradually incremental. In any case, the drive to cut costs and time by using nontraditional methods will continue aggressively and ruthlessly.

Internet systems enable continual change to be made to business processes at every level. These changes affect how organizations deal with customers, suppliers, and collaborators, and also how the internal processes operate.

One option when faced with such significant change is to read the signs as a kind of "business barroom brawl," with great instability and high risk. This analysis suggests a course of no action, of waiting and seeing, and, when the dust clears, moving in for the kill. But kill what? When and if the dust settles, markets will have changed, customers' expectations and behavior will have changed, and the business landscape will look completely different.

Technology cannot be ignored. Doing nothing is not an option. Being action-oriented is a must.

THREATS AND OPPORTUNITIES TO ESTABLISHED BUSINESSES

The redefinition of business forced by the new opportunities and threats offered by using internet technology presents an urgent need to analyze traditional business models. Media coverage often trails these changes as offering huge cost cuts, and cheap and effective routes to market: a paradise of riches for savvy management and those prepared to take the risk and change their business processes and practices.

New ventures are started that can threaten the established order of existing organizations. As demonstrated in the travel industry, with many new booking systems becoming available on-line, customers find the new purchasing routes attractive, stimulating, and often

significantly cheaper. As the internet has been adopted by new ventures, industries have been changed, forcing established business to adopt these new models or face the threat of failure.

But has the older order been lost in the wake of this technological change? With, according to media estimates, as many as 99 percent of new internet companies failing in their first few years of development, indications are that the traditional companies still have their strengths. They have new business models to use, stabilities to offer, and a real understanding of the markets they have dominated for decades. They are fighting back against the dot coms, deploying their strong market positioning, brand awareness, and financial muscle.

It is becoming increasingly clear that hybrid companies are now winning. These are traditional companies with strong customer service and product line values, adding the dot-com speed and competitiveness to their activities. Companies in the fields of books, travel, banking, airlines, music, and media have adopted, or were forced to adopt, new business models to include the internet component. This is where the new hybrid organizations are seen to emerge.

TRADITION VS DOT COMS

TRADITIONAL COMPANY

Strengths	Weaknesses
■ Brand	■ Weak e-vision
■ Size	■ Lack of e-skills
■ Resources	■ Fear of change
■ Physical presence	■ Old-fashioned
■ Relationships	hierarchy

DOT-COM COMPANY

Strengths	Weaknesses
■ Mind-set/agility	■ Brand
■ Skilled staff	■ Profitable cash-flow
■ Latest IT	■ Business models
■ Internet experience	■ Vulnerability to
■ Speed	market change

RETHINKING THE VALUE CHAIN

Successful businesses always respond to their customers' needs. The value chain exists to serve the customer: the point where the revenue is generated. Smart companies are looking at their value chains as the source of new ideas for implementing internet technologies. Analysis of the value chain must start with the customer and work back through the business functions to the initial development of products and services. The functions should be focused on a clear mission: a business vision. The internet capabilities have brought all this into the spotlight.

A clear plan of where the organization is going and what it is doing can be "turbo-charged" by the smart application of new internet technologies. But a flawed, weak plan, like a poorly serviced car, is more likely to be blown up by the turbo-charger than to perform more effectively.

MAXIMIZE FLEXIBILITY

The key most important change offered by the internet is the ability to enable flexible networks everywhere, so that corporate grandness (that is, "We're so

THE OFFICE OF THE FUTURE

What effects will all these technological changes have on how business is transacted in the traditional office environment? Consider these points:

- why go to the office when you can work from home?
- why have meetings when we can all stay at home and make an internet video call to each other (and multiple calls simultaneously)?
- why have one large office building with our logo on it, when everyone could use remote rented office space by the hour?
- staff often now describe their office environment as a mix of hotel, train, airplane, automobile, home, office, customer site, coffee shop, and so on. Who needs a base office?

Now multiply all these points in your various roles as customer, supplier, head of department, collaborator, and every other means of communication. This will entail significant change to both our private and corporate lives, whether we like it or not.

huge we can do anything") is questioned as a key strength. Each business function can be made to operate better by adding the new capabilities of the internet and applying them to simple, focused projects.

Complexity is the enemy. Better processes are often identified in the early stages of analysis and should be pursued to produce better performance right away. In the fast-moving internet market, tactics may be a better catalyst for change than a grand strategy. Strategy is necessary but, in the internet world, the diversity and potential complexity available make tactics look like the pragmatic route to positive financial results in the short term.

Paralleling incremental improvements, technologies develop and offer new ways to do things. For example:

- digital TVs extend access to networks to a new lower-cost level, without the need for a PC (which requires technical competence and maintenance). Buy a digital TV, plug it in, and get on-line
- the WAP (Wireless Application Protocol) mobile phone enables you to get on-line cheaply from anywhere you can get a signal
- palmtops with internet capability merge the mobile phone function with those of a laptop PC
- bluetooth, the short-range broadcast system, transmits data to your digital devices over a 10–100 yard distance from a transmitter in the shopping mall, the office – anywhere
- networks will expand to receive and transmit an ever-increasing amount of information: anything that can be digitized and anything we can see or hear.

USING INTRANETS AND EXTRANETS EFFECTIVELY

IN A WORLD WHERE ANYTHING THAT CAN BE DIGITIZED CAN BE SENT THROUGH WIRES AND RADIO TRANSMISSION, INTRANETS AND EXTRANETS ARE THE NERVOUS SYSTEM OF AN ORGANIZATION. YOUR ORGANIZATION NEEDS TO GET FIT FOR THE INTERNET-DOMINATED BUSINESS LANDSCAPE, AND STAY THAT WAY.

SPEEDING AND FOCUSING COMMUNICATION

An intranet is a private internet system accessible only by those with the requisite authority within a company, while an extranet includes externally authorized users as well. These external users might be customers, suppliers, or partners. The whole system is usually enveloped in authority levels of access, so that each user sees only what they are authorized to see.

The effective implementation of an intranet and extranet underpins an organization's need to work first on the tactical big internet business wins. Tactical wins produce results in the short term – this year's financial results – rather than a longer-term view of building market share or customer positioning over several years.

As explained earlier, the internal process infrastructures can change with the application of internet technology, especially in the movements from customer to supplier. Analysis of a value chain (that is, how the business is run and makes money) will clarify where the opportunities for maximum savings and revenue generation will be. In the new

internet-enabled world, customers will expect companies to offer new high levels of communication capability: responding promptly to emails, for example, and offering comprehensive information on-line. And, as customer pressure is applied to margins, prices and transaction costs become more transparent.

Staying competitive in these new markets will demand that we reengineer the relationships we have with ourselves, our suppliers, our collaborators, our partners – everyone in the value chain.

SUCCEEDING IN AN INTERNET-BASED BUSINESS

Starting with a clean sheet as they developed in the late 1990s, dot-coms built nontraditional business models. These models did not need to produce profit, market share, or brands, and they did not need to protect channels to market. In this sense, they were disruptive and often not innovative, but they did make traditional businesses rethink how they would protect their current competitive positions. In the longer term, the history of dot coms clearly demonstrates the need for stable and effective business planning based on conventional profit and loss models.

A new term used in the e-business markets is c-commerce (collaborative commerce). This term describes those collaborative efforts and value chains where there is a huge benefit in working together, thus speeding up and reducing the cost of communications requirements.

C-commerce is a new battlefield to enter for traditional businesses. First entrants into the field are building websites that offer a range of services, such as project management, contact lists, managed email directories, discussion groups and forums, and new technologies still searching for new markets.

Adopting new technologies may make you feel as if you are starting out on a journey to an unknown destination: you are aware of the possible risks, you can hear the doubters, but you are moving toward a goal that promises huge rewards for the business winners that make the journey. Like the intrepid explorers of past centuries, corporate management will proceed with care and determination and use corporate muscle to leverage a new winning position.

OPTING FOR QUICK WINS

IN A RAPIDLY DEVELOPING MARKETPLACE, THERE ARE LITERALLY MILLIONS OF OPTIONS FOR UTILIZING INTERNET TECHNOLOGY. ITS SPEED AND RESPONSIVENESS MAKE IT IDEAL FOR SHORT-TERM TACTICAL ACTIONS THAT PRODUCE A POSITIVE RESULT FOR THIS YEAR'S PROFIT AND LOSS BALANCE SHEET.

EMPLOYING WINNING TACTICS

As described earlier, it is important to start from the customer end of your processes and work backward into your organization. Make sure that clients are happy with your response time to their requests for products, services, and information. The internet will save you valuable time and cut administrative costs. Email is a far quicker and more efficient means of communicating than the fax, phone, and postal services.

Your value chain can be a complex business process. You should use the same internet capabilities for both customers and suppliers. Start using e-marketplaces to buy business basics such as furniture and PCs. These open marketplaces are more competitive and faster-reacting than many traditional channels.

ENCOURAGING LOYALTY

Always remember that the internet can commodify products: that is, with little to choose between competing brands, the customer usually opts for the cheapest. This is the other side of the open market coin, and can corrode your customers' loyalty. It is easy for them to access details from your competitors, and the pricing of products becomes more and more competitive. The key is to differentiate your company's offer by adding value and enhancing customer loyalty on your own website. You want to be continually reactive and responsive to those customers and their feedback.

It pays to work as a team with your customers and suppliers. Think about developing extranets to share information with them and simplify the business processes. Start with your key contacts: it is often the top 20 percent of customers who create 80 percent of revenues. The same rule goes for suppliers and costs.

Help customers and suppliers work on internet tactics with you. What stage are they at and how are they changing? What will they need from you in the future? Offer your contacts, provide feedback, or even consider a partnership. Such assistance strengthens relationships and enhances loyalty, as well as offering you the opportunity to ensure your systems are mutually compatible. Web-based forums and discussion groups are an excellent way to get feedback and responses from everybody.

PACING THE CHANGE

Take one step at a time. Do not try and implement everything at once. At any given time, work only on a handful of projects – five at the most. Ensure that the core projects are those that will quickly provide a return on investment. These would include building an effective intranet for all staff use; and also building secure, private extranets where you can exchange information with both your customers and suppliers.

Many of the opportunities offered by technology are very simple, and may be met by the smart use of email (for every communication, internal and external, responding within 24 hours and cutting out the mail, fax, and some phoning), web pages, digital cameras (images can be emailed and often communicate more than text alone), or WAP phones (an internet access method using just a mobile phone, anywhere). Learn from doing the simple things first, then you will be ready for the more complex.

Steps of success for business websites
The internet can be used in a number of interrelated ways to maximize business efficiency. Start with the basics of web access for all employees, building up systems until the whole business is wired.

Set up an eTrading system
This is easy to set up for credit card systems, but will eventually need more sophisticated systems

Set up a system of eProject management
All collaborators with authority to access the project database can manage projects in one system

Use your web facilities to boost eCRM
Customer Relationship Management is greatly improved through your intranet and the shared customer/supplier sites

Enable feedback from customers
An accessible system encourages comments from customers – free market research that keeps you informed

Share a private website with each key supplier
All day-to-day information is shared and accessed by those authorized

Share a private website with each key customer
All day-to-day information is shared and accessed by those authorized

Create an intranet
All staff can access your private intranet and stay in touch with each other. It is the foundation for all following steps

Use email as a communication base
As far as possible, cut out mail, fax, and phone calls, using email for all internal and external processes

Enable web access for all staff
Employees have access to customer and supply sites, and to free business information from a huge array of sources

ADJUSTING TO SIZE

A small company is more likely to be fast and flexible than a larger company, so there are huge opportunities for it to build and grow faster. Larger companies will find the smaller firms pose a significant threat to their profits and ability to compete. A large company should think like a small one: speed in the internet market is often more important than size and financial muscle. Small companies can make decisions faster and implement them more quickly and cost-effectively, while large companies have complex decision-processes. Learn by doing, not by discussing the broader issues and concepts without the action.

BUILDING TO A STRATEGY

Once your tactics have given you excellent delivery of the basics, build beyond these with the more strategic opportunities to revolutionize processes: specifically, communications between suppliers, customers, and anyone else in the value chain. Examine the internal systems for continual improvement, asking those in the field.

CREATING A TACTICAL BUSINESS INTERNET PLAN

TO CREATE YOUR TACTICAL PLAN, YOU SHOULD USE A SIMPLE SEVEN-STEP APPROACH, WHICH ENCOMPASSES THE DISCIPLINES OF MANAGING CHANGE WHILE IMPLEMENTING TECHNOLOGY SYSTEMS. THIS WILL HELP YOU ANALYZE THE OPPORTUNITY AND RISK OF EACH PROJECT AND CREATE A ROADMAP THAT ALL STAFF CAN UNDERSTAND.

FIND A LEADER

As a first step, a leader should be appointed. Internet projects are about change, so processes, functions, and roles will change. Organizational change of this magnitude demands leadership, rather than routine management skills.

Leaders must clear the way, have a vision about where they are going, and inspire enthusiastic teams of followers. Leaders make themselves aware of trends, threats, and opportunities, and developing and breaking technologies.

They are able to see how these can be applied to their organization, and how the technologies can cut costs and speed processes. They communicate this information to their colleagues, and inspire them to take immediate action.

ENGAGE THE BOARD

As the next step, the leader demonstrates to the board of directors the need for urgent change. The focus is on making and saving money. Traditional businesses have had to learn to make real profit from real customers who generate real revenues: the same applies to dot coms.

All business plans, even in the world of the internet, should have a return on investment. In the fast-moving internet environment, a return should come in the early stages of implementation, in less than a year of finding the first, focused, simple e-wins.

ANALYZING BUSINESS INTERNET OPPORTUNITIES

To be successful, a business enterprise utilizing the internet should address each of the six elements in the model below.

Central to the organization is the vision: where the business is going. Vision and the customer function are interrelated, as the vision should be supporting what customers are prepared to buy from the organization, and, conversely, the vision is created or changed by customers' needs.

The internet systems you may want to use with customers will be mirrored by those for suppliers. The issues are very similar: within the same system of internet communication we can be supplier and customer.

The workforce is the talent base needed in the organization that makes everything function. People create and use the processes, which may change with the new technologies that become available. You need to question whether the established processes are still appropriate, or whether they can be replaced or improved by internet systems.

Lastly, the IT infrastructure supports the implementation of the new technologies, and ensures high levels of security and reliability.

Understanding the key issues
Go back to basics and assess how each function of a business works with the others. A clear understanding will enable internet technology to be applied appropriately and profitably.

CUSTOMERS
- Create loyalty
- Deliver acceptable service levels and quality
- Build revenue
- Encourage feedback

TECHNOLOGY
- Ensure cost effectiveness
- Ensure reliability
- Ensure business robustness
- Ensure growth capability

VISION
- Define the mission
- Decide on short- and long-term goals
- Determine what you have to be good at

SUPPLIERS
- Work together closely
- Cut costs
- Ensure quality
- Strengthen relationship with Win–Win contracts

PROCESSES
- Increase speed
- Ensure reliability
- Reduce cost
- Emphasize customer focus

WORKFORCE
- Create a culture where staff buy into the vision
- Ensure the right skills
- Measure performance
- Make customers the focus

INDIVIDUAL COACHING

An individual interview with each board member (or a management team chosen by the leader) gives everyone the chance to speak their mind and share their own department's view of the future (and their personal views on plans to enhance or close activities in their area of concern). With so much press and media coverage surrounding technology issues, managers need to be made aware of the facts and realities rather than the current fashions.

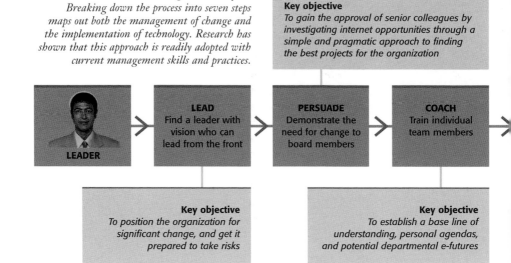

Creating a tactical plan
Breaking down the process into seven steps maps out both the management of change and the implementation of technology. Research has shown that this approach is readily adopted with current management skills and practices.

Key objective
To gain the approval of senior colleagues by investigating internet opportunities through a simple and pragmatic approach to finding the best projects for the organization

LEADER

LEAD
Find a leader with vision who can lead from the front

PERSUADE
Demonstrate the need for change to board members

COACH
Train individual team members

Key objective
To position the organization for significant change, and get it prepared to take risks

Key objective
To establish a base line of understanding, personal agendas, and potential departmental e-futures

At this stage, when meeting in one-to-one interviews, use key questions based on departmental functions to develop an e-business vision of how processes can be done better. Most businesses can be broken down into specific functions; however, each function is interrelated, and no manager truly works in isolation.

WORK OUT THE TOP FIVE ACTIONS
This step includes an appreciation of the organization's value chain, and how the internet may help or replace specific functions. The leader briefs the board on what the internet does for a business – a briefing based on business opportunity and in the language of profit and loss rather than technological terms. An unbiased outside adviser may assist in this process, as an insider may feel too close to the internal politics of the situation if the imperative is big change.

Almost any manager could think of 10 to 20 potential internet uses in his or her own organization. The problem is prioritizing these ideas into a shortlist of five or six that make or save the most money. (You can adjust the actual number to your needs, but there is considerable supporting evidence from research into change management over the last two decades that says five is manageable and maintains focus.)

The key is to find the hidden few ideas that produce the big wins. These will often be deeply hidden to management teams, who may be opting for the most hyped, the most often reported, or their personal favorites rather than those that are the best for the organization.

To set your priorities, assess the ideas in terms of how quickly and easily they could be implemented. Then estimate how much profit they would generate (perhaps considering this as margin, revenue, cost-saving, downsizing, and so on). By prioritizing, you will be able to identify and focus on the top five projects

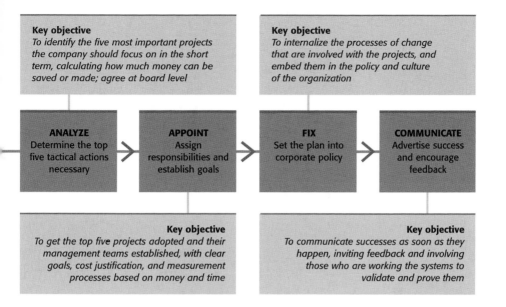

Key objective
To identify the five most important projects the company should focus on in the short term, calculating how much money can be saved or made; agree at board level

Key objective
To internalize the processes of change that are involved with the projects, and embed them in the policy and culture of the organization

ANALYZE
Determine the top five tactical actions necessary

APPOINT
Assign responsibilities and establish goals

FIX
Set the plan into corporate policy

COMMUNICATE
Advertise success and encourage feedback

Key objective
To get the top five projects adopted and their management teams established, with clear goals, cost justification, and measurement processes based on money and time

Key objective
To communicate successes as soon as they happen, inviting feedback and involving those who are working the systems to validate and prove them

rather than the many more that may have been identified by the management team. These five will be the most important, cost-justifiable, profit-making internet activities, as seen over a short timescale.

ASSIGN RESPONSIBILITIES

At this stage the board needs to allocate responsibilities. Who is to do what, by when, and with what resources? Again, outside help can be co-opted. "Nobody knows what they don't know," and in the fast-moving internet market, those who work in it full time are more likely to understand what is going on in it, or the new developing best practices.

A method of measurement is vital. In the US it was reported in the late 1990s that more than 80 percent of internet sites had no return on investment; in other words, they lost money, focus, and market opportunity. Effective cost-justification of each project, and measurement of its success in saving or

making money for the organization, will establish a record of success that the company can build upon in the future. The best practice is then developed in-house with associated learning, skills improvement, and the establishment of an investment foundation.

ENGAGE WITH CORPORATE POLICY

Now the plan needs to be set into corporate policy. Projects need the board's support, which sends a clear message to all that these projects are strategic and have a significant impact on all aspects of corporate activities.

COMMUNICATE SUCCESSES

Finally, communicating what is going on is smart management thinking. It is critical to get valid feedback and involve everyone in checking that the successes are real and valid, and that the new opportunities are workable and of high industrial and commercial quality.

The Role
of the Manager

communication

EFFECTIVE COMMUNICATION IS THE ESSENCE OF
LEADERSHIP AND MANAGEMENT. IT IS NEITHER
TOP-DOWN NOR BOTTOM-UP, BUT TWO-WAY AND
CONTINUOUS. COMBINE DIFFERENT MEDIA AND
TECHNIQUES TO GIVE THE RIGHT MESSAGE TO
THE RIGHT PEOPLE AT THE RIGHT TIME.

There is a huge range of communication channels
available, along with a variety of techniques and means, and
you must learn to master them. At the same time, you need
to remember that all good management depends on
successful personal relationships. These are more likely to
follow if you can develop an informal, relaxed, and friendly
style of interacting with people.

The core skills of reading and writing can always be
enhanced. If you raise your reading speed and improve
your comprehension, while ensuring that your written
words are clear, your overall performance can only be
improved. Two specific areas where you must develop your
communication skills are making presentations and holding
meetings: essential parts of the manager's routine.

There is a specialized area of communication that has
lessons for all forms: negotiation, which aims for a
"Win–Win" result. Good communication of any kind
always aims to meet the needs of all parties.

DEFINING THE MEANS

FOR EFFECTIVE COMMUNICATION, YOU MUST BE AWARE OF THE MEANS AND THE CHANNELS THROUGH WHICH THEY ARE EXPRESSED. A GOOD COMMUNICATOR NEEDS SOME OF THE CHAMELEON-LIKE QUALITIES OF THE GOOD ACTOR; AND, LIKE ACTORS, MANAGERS NEED BOTH TRAINING AND PRACTICE.

THE MEANS OF COMMUNICATION

You must deliver the right message to the right people in the right way and at the right time. Choose whichever of the following five basic methods of communication is best for you, your audience, and your purpose, and master their techniques.

The spoken word

Direct speech, which is the most extensively used approach, is also the most potent because of the unique combination of personality and words. Use the latter with care whether your audience is large or small.

Written communication

In business today, we produce a great range of formal and informal writing, from scribbled notes and emails to long reports and presentations. Whatever the nature and the purpose, always clarify your objectives, thoughts, and facts before putting them down on paper or on screen – and always check the final version carefully before despatch.

Visual images

As all communicators should know (advertisers certainly do), well-chosen and well-designed images convey powerful meanings. Appropriate pictures speak louder than words and help listeners and readers retain the message.

Physical expression

Deliberate use of gestures, vocal variation, and facial expression is relatively uncommon in business contexts. However, unconscious body language is universal and significant. Your own meaning and that of others may be misread and give the wrong signals. Nevertheless, if you understand and use body language effectively, you are likely to increase the chances of a successful encounter.

Mixed methods

The different media affect different areas of the brain, so the more they are used together, the more effective the communication. It is important when combining methods to use each equally well. The credibility of a well-written letter can be destroyed by poor layout, for instance, and a confusing graphic can weaken an important presentation.

THE CHANNELS OF COMMUNICATION

The most common channel of communication is talking informally face to face, but you will undoubtedly have to use some or all of the other main channels (*see* opposite). Note that each of them has its own separate function.

FACE-TO-FACE EXCHANGES

To communicate effectively person to person, you must be articulate and be clear about your objectives. Where and how you communicate, with one person or with many, has a significant effect on the impact of your message, and each form of communication requires different skills.

THE PRIME CHANNELS OF COMMUNICATION

METHOD	COMMENTS
Telephone and teleconferences	The most widely used channel. Choose words carefully to avoid misunderstandings, speak clearly, and be aware of the impact of body language while speaking. Smile to communicate a positive image, and even stand if you feel you need to be more assertive.
Presentations	Can be formal or informal. Good preparation is important. Learn how to deal with impromptu questions and how to speak well "off the cuff."
Q&A sessions	An often underused medium that can provide a valuable, frank exchange of information and views. You need to have good impromptu speaking skills, an excellent understanding of your subject, and a willingness to face criticism and searching questions.
Memos and letters	Indispensable "on-the-record" companions to spoken communications. Make sure all memos and letters are well written and well presented, and do not dilute your impact by sending unnecessary communications.
Reports and briefs	If well organized, they convey important information in an easy-to-follow format and can be referred to again and again. Include only the necessary information and circulate documents only to relevant people.
In-house publications	Written, and therefore permanent. They can disseminate vital company information, or simply give news about colleagues and social events. Can aid morale, but should not be merely a management mouthpiece.
Email	Has overtaken other written forms, being speedy, informal, and functional. Business emails should not be so informal that they become offensive. Keep a back-up of all important communications.
Websites	An "instant" form of communication that must be regularly updated to be effective. Sites must be easy to access and presented in an interesting format. It is always worth employing expert help.
Posters, signs, and noticeboards	Useful for disseminating information and publicizing new developments, though lacking the impact of on-line means.
Broadcasting	Video, film, sound, or multimedia (all can be transmitted over the web). They can have great impact when properly used. As with websites, the more professional the presentation, the better they work.

One-to-one meetings

These are the foundation of human contact, and all managers must master the requisite skills. You need to be a good listener as well as a good talker, and be sensitive to the circumstances. Be flexible. Meetings rarely follow the exact pattern expected by either party.

Small, informal groups

Most work takes place in small gatherings. The interactions of participants play an important role in determining what messages are received. Whether the group is a regular team, or includes outsiders, follow the rules of formal meetings: stick to the point, have

KNOW YOUR AUDIENCE

AUDIENCE	COMMENTS
Superiors	Dealing with superiors requires diplomacy and tact, but do not shy away from such encounters. Be as well prepared as possible, and make sure of your facts.
Colleagues	With colleagues who are equal to you in status, you can be frank and honest. Be positive in your dealings with them, and avoid becoming too competitive.
Subordinates	These are now sometimes called "coworkers" or "associates" to signify that they work "with" their boss, rather than "for" him or her. You should understand their needs and concerns, and communicate to them their role in the wider picture.
Outside suppliers	These need to feel that they are a valued part of the wider team. Both sides need to communicate in a constructive and respectful manner.
Customers	Effective managers spend as much time as possible talking to customers individually. Take great care over all communications with them, especially when handling complaints. Often, diplomacy will take precedence over frankness.
Competitors	Communication with rival businesses is important for cooperation and information, and as a channel to the outside world. Exchanges should be cordial, but beware of divulging any classified information.
Consultants and professional advisers	Effective two-way communication will make the best of this relationship. Both sides should fully understand the brief: ambiguity and confusion can lead to expensive advice being ignored.
Outsiders	Remember that all communication reflects on your organization, either positively or negatively. Take great care with external communication, such as that with the media, national and local politicians, community representatives, and unionists.

a record kept, and circulate a note of decisions and follow-ups.

Larger meetings

These are essential for formal events such as conferences. If you have to speak, good preparation and presentation are essential, and will boost your confidence. You will find it useful to acquire and practice skills in public speaking.

At a distance

The fast-growing new channels, such as email, teleconferencing, websites, and text messaging, are in some ways more efficient at rapid communication. But you must still exploit the unique attributes of mail (including faxing) and telephones, fixed or mobile.

MATCHING THE MESSAGE

Up to a point, you can choose how, where, and what you communicate, but not to whom. You could find yourself with any kind of audience in any setting, using any of the methods and channels. Aim to use the approach that makes your message accessible and effective.

MASTERING INFORMALITY

INFORMAL COMMUNICATION PLAYS A FAR LARGER PART IN MOST MANAGERS' WORKING LIVES THAN FORMAL EXCHANGES. GOOD PERSONAL RELATIONSHIPS ARE THE KEY TO EFFECTIVE MANAGEMENT, AND THESE OFTEN HINGE ON INFORMAL CONTACT.

THE IMPORTANCE OF PLACE

Where you deliver the message communicates strong signals. Going into other people's territories in itself acknowledges their importance in the exchange to follow. Conversely, making people come to your territory projects an image of your superiority. This approach is especially useful if you have to address a disciplinary or performance problem.

In general, you do not want your office to be forbidden or even forbidding territory. People cannot communicate successfully with somebody they cannot see and who never talks to them. As far as possible, operate an "open door" policy.

COMMUNICATING WITHOUT WORDS

Nonverbal communication, including gestures, posture, and facial expression, is vital for getting a clear message across. When communicating informally, body language can help to project a relaxed atmosphere for face-to-face exchanges.

Eye contact and stance are especially significant. Looking directly at the other person, with a smile, if appropriate, delivers a positive message; a shifty glance is negative. Some of the impact is subliminal: we unconsciously notice and appreciate the dilated pupils that show sympathetic attention. Similarly, an upright, attentive posture impresses,

while slouching does not. Getting too close to people may intimidate them, but backing off will lose their sympathy. If a person is lying, their eyes and hands are very likely to give them away. Use your hands to make strong and supportive gestures, or else keep them still. Nervous hand movements betray nervousness.

If you are genuinely relaxed and confident, the right body language is likely to follow. You can, however, develop

NEUROLINGUISTIC PROGRAMMING

Advanced communicators can use neurolinguistic programming (NLP) to strengthen their impact and enhance the comfort of their audience. NLP contends that the way in which people speak shows how they think. Thinking preferences can be categorized by choice of phrase, such as visual: "I see what you mean," and auditory: "This sounds like a problem." Techniques are aimed at creating a rapport, and include using the same imagery as the other person, and mirroring body language.

Manager retains eye contact

Hands rest comfortably in lap

Feet crossed at ankles

Using body language as a technique
Adopting a similar posture to the person you are speaking to, and subtly using the same gestures, will help you establish empathy.

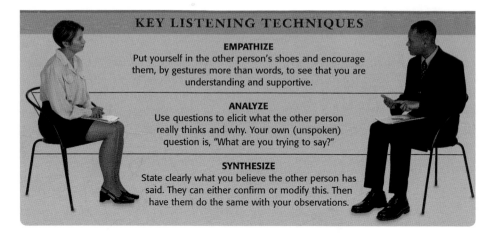

KEY LISTENING TECHNIQUES

EMPATHIZE
Put yourself in the other person's shoes and encourage them, by gestures more than words, to see that you are understanding and supportive.

ANALYZE
Use questions to elicit what the other person really thinks and why. Your own (unspoken) question is, "What are you trying to say?"

SYNTHESIZE
State clearly what you believe the other person has said. They can either confirm or modify this. Then have them do the same with your observations.

a nonverbal vocabulary that becomes second nature, and which can be practiced in front of a mirror, such as:

- smiling, tilting the face, and nodding to indicate approval
- leaning forward to show attentiveness
- holding open hands apart as a request for support.

Always remember that communication is two-way. You not only want to be understood yourself; you want to learn as much as you can from the other person. Watch for their nonverbal signs, too, especially those that show they are not at ease. In this case, the other person:

- will not meet your gaze (wary)
- bites their nails or a pencil (nervous)
- folds their arms (defensive)
- touches their face (avoiding the truth).

LISTENING TECHNIQUES

Good listening techniques are vital, especially in intimate, informal settings. Encourage the speaker by appearing to listen intently, and not interrupting too often. If a person's body language shows that the exchange is not going well, use your listening skills to get the discussion

back on track. Ask open questions ("What do you think we should do about X's career development?"), which will generate discussion and let you deploy the key listening techniques of empathy, analysis, and synthesis. Avoid closed questions ("Should we promote X?") that can be answered with just "Yes" or "No."

All the techniques are subordinate to sincerity. Say what you mean and mean what you say, and show by your nonverbal language that this is the case.

SPEAKING AS A FRIEND

When holding informal, one-to-one discussions, give as much time as necessary. Here, the correct attitude is a model for informal communication in general. You speak as a friend who wants the best for the other person, but who also wishes to ensure that the decision really is in the friend's best interests.

Empathy, analysis, and synthesis thus all come into play. The friendly stance also shows that informal communication is to a significant degree social, a mixing of people at all levels that should lead to good relationships and cement them.

WRITING FOR BUSINESS

GOOD COMMUNICATION OF ANY KIND STARTS WITH A CLEAR OBJECTIVE. THIS IS ESPECIALLY IMPORTANT WITH WRITING, AS IT IS A MORE DELIBERATE PROCESS THAN TALKING. ALL COMMUNICATION IS AN EXCHANGE, SO REMEMBER THAT EVERY DOCUMENT IS ONLY AS GOOD AS ITS RECEPTION.

PLANNING THE PROCESS

Before committing yourself in writing, you should always know the answers to these simple questions:

- Why am I writing this document?
- Who is going to read it?
- What actions and/or reactions do I want from the reader?
- Which format must I use to achieve my aims most effectively?

If an informal, off-the-cuff note, memo, or email will serve your purpose, use it. These formats encourage brevity: never use more words than you need. This saves both the reader's time and your own. Keeping the message terse, yet polite, helps to make the language muscular and clear, as opposed to vague.

But bear in mind that a misconceived note can be just as harmful as an ill-prepared formal report. Always read any document through carefully before sending it, to check that the four questions have been properly answered.

PLANNING THE DOCUMENT

The longer and more formal the document, the more planning it requires. Drafts are often an essential preliminary, though you do not always need to draft a report or proposal in full. A time-saving approach, excellent for organizing thought,

is to jot down the headings and main points to be covered. This will lay down the structure, which always has a major role in the effectiveness and impact. There are three critical structural factors:

- how the document begins
- the sequence that it follows
- how it ends.

Every document has specific aims, which the structure will support. Direct mail specialists know the importance of structure better than anybody. Their

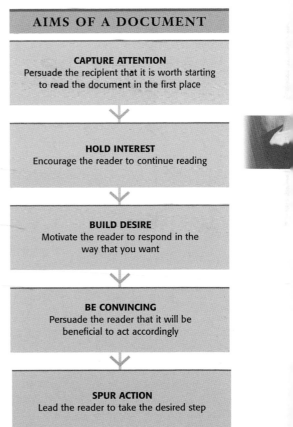

AIMS OF A DOCUMENT

CAPTURE ATTENTION
Persuade the recipient that it is worth starting to read the document in the first place

↓

HOLD INTEREST
Encourage the reader to continue reading

↓

BUILD DESIRE
Motivate the reader to respond in the way that you want

↓

BE CONVINCING
Persuade the reader that it will be beneficial to act accordingly

↓

SPUR ACTION
Lead the reader to take the desired step

letters are "cold calls," written to perfect strangers whose business the letter is intended to win. The writer has to accomplish five tasks, encapsulated into the acronym **AIDCA**: **A**ttention, **I**nterest, **D**esire, **C**onviction, and **A**ction. The five tasks are basic to all business writing, from letters to chairpersons' reports. No piece of writing can succeed unless it engages the reader on all five fronts.

Following AIDCA's logical order will force you to organize your data and thoughts in the most powerful possible sequence. If the technique works with cold calls, where recipients can be initially indifferent or even hostile, it will be even more effective with recipients who start from a position of engaged attention and interest.

TACKLING WRITER'S BLOCK

Even very experienced professional writers are sometimes afflicted with a kind of mental paralysis that prevents them from setting words down. If this happens to you, the worst thing you can do is just sit there looking at a blank page, agonizing. It is possible to break through the block. Start with one simple step:

● Keeping in mind an outline of what you want to say, just start writing, and keep going until you have completed the task. Do not stop, however badly you think the work is going, until you can think of nothing more to say.

Once you have written down all your facts and thoughts, no matter how ineptly, then you can start revising your material. You will find this approach quicker and more productive than constantly going back over your efforts. Usually, you will find that once you have made a start, the writing task becomes progressively easier.

DEVELOPING STYLE

The AIDCA rules are a useful basis, but structure is only half the story. Style is important, and you need to make a conscious effort to develop yours.

Anybody can write well if they adopt a natural, simple style and do not try to be impressive. Avoid unnecessary capital letters, portentous phrases, and archaic words (such as "albeit"). The importance of your document will be in its clarity and concision, not its showiness.

The best writers have a diction unique to them – you can almost hear their voices speaking behind the prose. You could follow their example by writing as you would speak in normal conversation, when most people are capable of being fluent, expressive, and direct. Put words down as naturally and easily as when talking to a friend on a subject you know well. Make sure it really is "a subject you know well" by researching thoroughly. Remember that the hard copy will be a permanent record of any sloppiness.

GOOD PRESENTATION

Presentation matters almost as much as preparation. The document should look clean and inviting.

The blessings of personal computers include spellcheckers and the capability to produce perfect documents with many combinations of typefaces, colors, and formats. But beware of another power of word-processing programs: their ability to reproduce verbatim text that has already been used, so that you can repeat what you have written in another document. The danger is not that the recipient will notice, but that the repetition will stop you from thinking properly about this particular communication.

WRITING TO THE RIGHT LENGTH

Beware of abusing the concentration of your reader. Never add to length without adding to sense – and length, as noted, should be as short as is consistent with achieving your purpose.

Plan what you want to say and then write the whole letter without pause.

Once you have finished, reread the letter, and edit it to a more suitable length, taking care over the structure. Usually, a single page of 8½ x 11 should be enough. You will need to be ruthless with your text – ask someone to help with the editing, if necessary. Remember that the right length applies to words and sentences too: both are usually better shorter.

When writing longer documents, such as reports or proposals, their content may demand a greater length than you would like. It helps the reader if you start with an "executive summary"of your major points, and end with a conclusion that similarly recaps the text. Also, adding headings and subheadings will make the document easier to assimilate.

READING EFFECTIVELY

READING IS AN IMPORTANT PART OF MOST MANAGERS' WORKING DAYS. HOWEVER, MANY READ INEFFICIENTLY, AND NOT NEARLY ENOUGH. READING EFFECTIVELY, QUICKLY, AND WITH GOOD COMPREHENSION LEADS TO GREATER KNOWLEDGE AND BETTER SELF-EXPRESSION. CONCENTRATION IS THE KEY.

READING WIDELY

Many managers largely confine their reading to the correspondence and reports that come with the job. Reading other kinds of material – newspapers, relevant magazines, and serious books – on a regular basis not only trains and broadens the mind, but often transmits valuable information and ideas.

People who read inefficiently claim that they "haven't got time" for anything but their day-to-day business reading. This is usually a mistaken impression. If you plan time, you make time. It is a question of ordering your priorities. You need to make a conscious decision to:

● organize your time efficiently
● increase your reading speed
● improve the efficiency of your memory and comprehension.

SPEED READING

There is a clear link between speed and comprehension. If you have to go back over a passage to understand its meaning, you obviously halve your reading speed. It does not follow, however, that if you double your speed, you halve your comprehension. On the contrary, if you learn to read faster, you actually improve your understanding. You can greatly improve your reading speed by using a few simple steps, as detailed below.

You can also look at how you plan your day. Start by making a reading list (putting the most important items first) and allocate enough time for it. You will use the allocated time still more efficiently by sometimes not "reading" at all. Before you start, glance over the contents, introduction, conclusion, and index (if any) to see what needs reading and what can be omitted. You can also decide whether full reading is necessary, or whether the material can be scanned or skimmed. You may be surprised to find how much you not only notice, but absorb, by turning pages rapidly, running your eye either down the center or in a zigzag down each page.

A great deal of information can also be assimilated from illustrations and other visual material. A caption will often encapsulate a whole point.

You may find a speed-reading course helpful. These courses do not last long, and should not be expensive. They will give you lasting benefit.

Select a passage, count the words, and time your reading. The average is 250–300 words per minute. So a typical book page will take you about two minutes. A speed of 450–500 wpm, covering the page in a minute, is well within your reach. Make that your target.

You may find yourself rereading words, phrases, or even whole passages that you have already read. This "regression" can become an involuntary habit, and a bad, time-wasting one. Keep your eyes moving forward, even if you use your finger or a pointer for the purpose.

Speed up your reading by enlarging the group of words taken in by each small eye movement (what is called a "saccade"), and speeding up the move from one saccade to the next.

Read another passage, following the above rules, and check your time. You should already find a significant and encouraging acceleration.

Increasing your reading speed
Make a conscious effort to read more quickly. First assess your current speed, and then practice the exercises given here. Reading more quickly, but with no less comprehension, means that you will have time to expand the range of your reading matter.

IMPROVING THE MEMORY
Absorbing what you read is, of course, vital, and that involves another mental power: memory. Most people complain about weakening memory as they grow older. This is almost always an unchecked impression, which may not be factually true. The performance of memory, like that of reading, can be consciously improved. Again, you may find courses or instructional books useful.

Memory fades over time: even a day after reading and understanding a passage, 80 percent of what you have read will be lost. This is a good reason for not using memory superfluously. For instance, there is no point in memorizing telephone numbers and addresses that are listed either on hard copy or on disk.

Even if you have an excellent memory, though, the most reliable and convenient way of recalling what you need to remember is properly taken notes.

LEARNING FROM BOOKS

An effective way of learning from books is to follow this method:

- Study for a certain period (say, one hour).

- Wait for a tenth of the time spent studying (in this example, six minutes), and review what you have learned.

- Then wait for 10 times the study period (in this example, 10 hours), and review once again.

With application, and repetition, you should find that your recall of what you have learned improves significantly.

TEST YOURSELF

Reread the sections on increasing your reading speed and improving your memory, and then tackle this exercise:

- When you have read to the end of this paragraph, you will have covered 700 words on "Reading Effectively."

- Write down what you have comprehended and can recall from this whole section.

- The 700 words should have taken you about two and a half minutes. If they took longer, or if your recall was inadequate, read the instructions again.

- Wait 24 hours and try again, using what you have learned. You will be pleasantly surprised by the improvement.

Self-instruction is an important principle. Every time you read a passage, or take notes, you have an excellent opportunity to improve your mental performance. Pay close attention to what you are doing, and how, and with what results, and you will find yourself raising comprehension and speed without further effort. You can always do better, and the methodical approach provides the most emphatic benefits.

TAKING NOTES

Note-taking is an essential part of recording and recalling material, whether written or spoken. Being able to make your notes quickly is important, and again, classes and manuals can help you master techniques such as shorthand and speedwriting.

Working from written material, the faster you write, the less your note-taking will slow your reading. If you do not mind defacing the pages, you can underline or highlight key points as you read, and write them down later. This is a particularly efficient method.

Fast-writing techniques are even more important when taking notes from speech. People speak much faster than they can write: a fast writer sets down 1,000 words an hour; a speaker will manage over nine times as many in the same time. Unless you are an expert in shorthand, that leaves no option: you have to edit what you hear, concentrating on key points. Exactly the same approach is required with written material.

A number of people use Mind Maps®. These were devised by Tony Buzan as a

means of making visual notes, and include quickly sketched pictures to summarize points as well as words. They can be used for taking notes during presentations, interviews, and so on, and for abridging written work. In a Mind Map®, the facts and ideas heard or read are grouped together as branches and subbranches off central keywords, phrases, or thoughts. This follows the key organizing principle of the brain, which works in patterns and memorizes by association.

Use association deliberately (for instance, linking a person's name to a physical feature, or to the place where you met), and memory will improve.

MAKING PRESENTATIONS

AS A MANAGER, YOU SHOULD EXPECT TO
MAKE PRESENTATIONS OFTEN, AND SOMETIMES
ON MATTERS OF CRUCIAL IMPORTANCE FOR
THE ORGANIZATION AND YOUR OWN CAREER.
THOROUGH PREPARATION IS A VITAL PART OF
EXCELLENT PRESENTATION.

THE IMPORTANCE OF PREPARATION

Always allow enough time. You will need
at least twice as long to prepare than for
delivery, sometimes far longer. If the
preparation means writing out a speech
in full, a 25-minute talk will need 4,000
words, or about five hours' writing time.

The time factor is one compelling
reason for speaking from notes.
Composing presentations in this
condensed way saves a great deal of
writing time and makes you speak rather
than read from a script. Reading is
generally less effective, hampering the
eye contact you must have with the
audience. Even if the address must be
prepared in full, it is more effective to
condense the document into notes and
give the talk from these.

STRUCTURING THE ADDRESS

Build your case in a logical order, with a
series of connected points or headlines.
Allow two minutes for each major point.
If you are not using visual aids, a dozen
headings will cover that 25-minute talk.
If you are using slides or overheads, allow
three minutes per point. Always try to:

- Begin your notes by writing down
  your objective.
- Ask: "What will make this presentation
  a success for me and the audience?"
- Be very clear and sure about that
  purpose before deciding the structure.
- Reflect your aim in the first few
  minutes of the speech.
- Tell the audience clearly and strongly
  what you are going to say.
- Emphasise what you have said with a
  concise recap in your conclusion.

Timing your presentation
*Getting the balance of a presentation right is
important. The example here breaks up a short,
15-minute speech. Allow about three minutes for
each main topic, leading and following them with
an introduction and conclusion of similar length.*

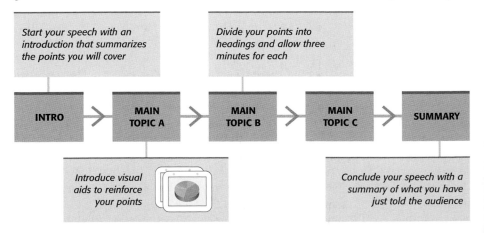

Start your speech with an
introduction that summarizes
the points you will cover

Divide your points into
headings and allow three
minutes for each

INTRO → MAIN TOPIC A → MAIN TOPIC B → MAIN TOPIC C → SUMMARY

Introduce visual
aids to reinforce
your points

Conclude your speech with a
summary of what you have
just told the audience

PERSONAL PRESENTATION

How you look and sound is important. Your delivery should be confident, your speech clear and unhurried, your movements natural. You should look the part in dress and appearance. All these essentials can be improved by training. Less important but effective techniques, like the injection of humor or using audience participation, require practice as well as instruction.

MAKING A VISUAL IMPACT

Images have a greater impact than words on the human brain: audiences retain images much better than unaided speech. Retention is most effective if speech and images are combined. Excellent graphics are possible with modern technology. Any form of projection works well, but slides relayed through a PC are the most effective. With a presentation program (enlist help if necessary), it is possible to compose, adapt, or replace the material to suit your audience. Beware, though, of the common trap of placing too much information on a single slide. Remember **KISS**: **K**eep **I**t **S**imple, **S**tupid!

MAKING IT MEMORABLE

To ensure you make a lasting impact, give the people present tangible reminders to take away: high-quality hard copy and copies of slides. For the same reason, always keep your last point for the conclusion. You told them what you were going to say, you said it, and now you are reminding them of what you said. Never be afraid of repetition.

The length of the presentation is also critical. The longer you have spoken, the more information the audience has to remember, and the less they will recall. The average human attention span varies from 20 to 40 minutes. Any speech longer than this risks losing the audience. If your material is so substantial that it requires a very long presentation, you should break it up into chunks lasting no longer than 40 minutes. Use the breaks for stretching the limbs, changing the subject, or for questions.

DEALING WITH QUESTIONS

Allow time for questioning. It establishes a lively relationship with the audience and by definition deals with points that are of interest. You can also exhibit your command of the subject in a natural, unrehearsed way. To ensure an adequate flow of questions:

- Ask: "Can I have the first (or next) question, please." rather than "Are there any (or any more) questions?"
- Alternatively, ask for written questions to be handed in during breaks.
- Plant questions with members of the audience, to be used as a last resort.
- Do not insist on questioners giving their names: that increases shyness.
- Repeat the question, in case it has not been properly heard (and to give yourself more time to think).

ACHIEVING THE PURPOSE

Questionnaires circulated to the audience can be useful for gaining feedback on the effectiveness of a presentation. However, simply asking for ratings on a scale of 1 to 10 is not useful. If you want to use a questionnaire, revisit your objectives and relate the feedback questions to those aims. If the respondent indicates that the target was missed, find out why, and ensure that you do better next time.

MAKING MEETINGS WORK

MEETINGS ARE THE PRIME MEANS OF MANAGEMENT ACTION AND COMMUNICATION. WHATEVER THE TYPE OF MEETING, THERE IS ONE UNVARYING FACTOR: PURPOSE. THERE MUST BE AN OBJECTIVE, WHICH CAN BE ACHIEVED ONLY BY BRINGING CERTAIN PEOPLE TOGETHER AT A CERTAIN TIME.

DEFINING THE MEETING

Whether the meeting is ad hoc, called for a specific reason, or formally scheduled as part of the operational structure, ask these essential questions:
- What is the aim of the meeting?
- Does each proposed participant really have to be there to achieve the aim?
- If so, what contribution are they expected to make?

The purpose of the meeting should determine how it is conducted.

NUMBERS AND TIMING

Remember: the fewer the people, the more effective the meeting will be. The optimum number of active participants peaks at about seven, so whoever convenes the meeting must be ruthless about invitations. So must the invitees: if you are invited and do not think your presence is essential, say so, and stay away. Whatever the type of meeting, only people specifically relevant to the objective should attend.

The chairperson must ensure that all present make the required contribution. That points to a strong reason for keeping down numbers. Suppose that each person needs to speak for 15 minutes; then four contributions take an hour, which is an acceptable length for a meeting. A dozen speakers, however, need three hours, or double the desirable maximum time for a meeting (after about one and a quarter hours, people start to repeat themselves).

The chairperson, ideally after an hour or so, should sum up the consensus. This is possible, however, only if the agenda is timed to provide a useful framework. Items on the agenda should be realistically paced, allowing enough time for each of them. If there are too many potential attendees to allow reasonable timing, then revise the invitation list. You can also delegate decision-making to sub-committees of manageable size.

ORGANIZING THE MEETING

You need to have good organization, both before and during a meeting. Before the meeting, make sure all paperwork is distributed well ahead, and that the participants are fully briefed. Whoever is

---

CHECKLIST

✔ *Except in an emergency, distribute the agenda and all relevant papers to attendees well in advance.*

✔ *Insist that people attend with full knowledge of what has to be discussed, so that time will not be wasted on updating.*

✔ *Do not let meetings deteriorate into point-scoring, adversarial debates.*

✔ *Have every participant state his or her viewpoint clearly and forcefully. Allow questions after any contribution.*

✔ *See the chairperson's job as steering the discussion toward consensus, not refereeing a verbal boxing match.*

actually leading the meeting must remain in control throughout, ensuring fruitful discussion and positive results.

Even brainstorming sessions, and other unstructured meetings, are more effective for being disciplined. Set time limits, and insist that everyone comes with two or three ideas, to be taken in rotation. Make sure that each contribution is treated with respect, never derision.

STRUCTURED MEETINGS

With structured meetings, including boards and other committees, there should be no divergence from the agenda and its timing unless there is good reason and the meeting agrees. Do not allow the minutes of previous meetings to take up too much time: raise any discrepancies before the meeting begins, and ensure they are corrected. "Matters arising" from the minutes should not start dealing with major issues. Such matters can be covered by written reports or by scheduled items.

Always start at the appointed time or before (if everybody is present). The chairperson especially must be punctual.

MEETINGS AT A DISTANCE

All the rules of good meetings apply equally to video-conferencing and telephone conferences. The role of the chairperson becomes even more decisive when people are not in the same room, because eye contact is impossible.

Such considerations mean that electronic meetings will probably never take the place of face-to-face encounters. However, they are far preferable to delaying discussions until everybody can be in the same place at the same time.

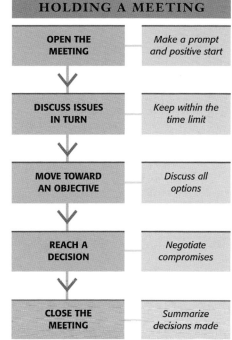

HOLDING A MEETING

| OPEN THE MEETING | Make a prompt and positive start |

| DISCUSS ISSUES IN TURN | Keep within the time limit |

| MOVE TOWARD AN OBJECTIVE | Discuss all options |

| REACH A DECISION | Negotiate compromises |

| CLOSE THE MEETING | Summarize decisions made |

ENDING AND REVIEWING THE MEETING

Whatever the nature of the meeting, the ending is very important:
- The chairperson sums up the main points settled.
- Follow-up actions are agreed and allocated, complete with deadlines and personal responsibilities, and listed in the minutes.

The minutes should be written clearly and accurately from notes, approved by the chairperson, and distributed to all parties within 24 hours of the meeting.

The chairperson, alone or with a close associate, also needs to conduct a personal post-mortem. Did the meeting achieve its objective? If not, why not? Identifying the reason for any failure will help future meetings to be more positive.

HOLDING NEGOTIATIONS

WITH BOTH PARTIES SEEKING THE BEST RESULT, NEGOTIATIONS ARE INHERENTLY ADVERSARIAL. THIS MAKES IT DIFFICULT TO FOLLOW THE USUAL RULES OF GOOD COMMUNICATION. YOUR GOAL IS A "WIN–WIN" SITUATION THAT SATISFIES BOTH PARTIES.

PLANNING TACTICS

Negotiation theory hinges on the concept of needs. Before setting out your proposals, consider what the other side needs from the negotiations. Do not think of a winning proposal as a Mafia-style "offer they cannot refuse." Rather, make an offer that is too good to refuse, that creates a "Win–Win" situation.

How can you work toward satisfying their needs (while never, of course, relinquishing your own)? This initial approach requires much subtlety, since the other side will demand more than it hopes to receive, and will expect you to do the same. That is why it is vital, early in the proceedings, to determine your ultimate acceptable position. This is not a target, but a limit. You must believe, basing your belief on the thorough research that is an essential preliminary, that the other side will also find this ultimate settlement to be a "win."

You have two key tactical weapons at your disposal: timing (when you make, modify, or refuse proposals) and change (how you shift the ground to a position more favorable to success). That means deciding such issues as how to:
- improve an offer
- revise your own proposal
- reject the other side's proposal
- introduce new elements.

Preparing for negotiations
Before going into negotiations, you need a sound plan: an ultimate goal, and a strategy for achieving it. You must be absolutely clear in your own mind about both your own role and tactics and those of individual team members.

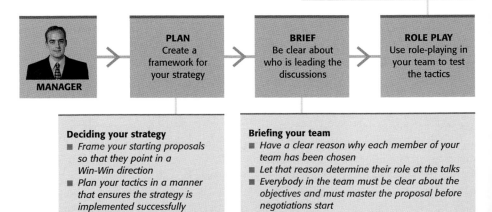

Reviewing your plan
Always hold team meetings before and after each session to evaluate the situation and confirm tactic

MANAGER

PLAN
Create a framework for your strategy

BRIEF
Be clear about who is leading the discussions

ROLE PLAY
Use role-playing in your team to test the tactics

Deciding your strategy
- *Frame your starting proposals so that they point in a Win-Win direction*
- *Plan your tactics in a manner that ensures the strategy is implemented successfully*

Briefing your team
- *Have a clear reason why each member of your team has been chosen*
- *Let that reason determine their role at the talks*
- *Everybody in the team must be clear about the objectives and must master the proposal before negotiations start*

DEFINING THE ROLES

If more than one negotiator is required, using your team in role-play exercises will demonstrate whether you have the right members in the right roles. The best-known role division is "good cop/bad cop," in which one member of a two-person team plays the tough, no-compromise role, and the other is the conciliatory, "I'm on your side" friend.

SIMPLIFY THE ISSUES

Keep all documents as lean and brief as possible. Concentrate on the main points, and avoid getting bogged down in detail. If the other side produces complex, lengthy documents, take time out to reduce their arguments to succinct, clear summaries on which you can base your response.

NEGOTIATING TECHNIQUES

A basic technique is repeating the other side's arguments, which first clarifies the issues. Then, by seeming to speak for them, you move toward the position of working for their needs rather than your own. In a fruitful negotiation, the other side will adopt the same approach, which greatly increases the chances of a speedy and secure compromise.

"Compromise" is not a popular word, since it is thought to imply weakness. But compromise is the essence of Win–Win. An outright victory may seem desirable, but the consequences may not be so pleasing. For example, if you want to negotiate the lowest price possible for a supply contract, this may mean financial loss for the supplier. This apparent "win" will actually result in losses for you, if the consequences are poor quality and unreliable delivery. Modern purchasing

USING ARBITRATION

Occasionally, communication breaks down altogether, and performance and good faith are in dispute. If this is the case, arbitration may help to keep the lines of communication open. Each side sets out its case for independent scrutiny, and then studies the other side's version. This process in itself may remove misunderstanding and achieve agreement of disputed facts.

If external negotiations reach an impasse, a court of law might give you more than an arbitrator would. However, the time and expense, as well as the risk of losing, argue strongly against litigation. Also, the fact that both sides agree to arbitrate provides a valuable assurance that the result will be accepted as fair, even if the negotiations themselves fail to achieve a satisfactory outcome.

concentrates on performance before price, negotiating long-term relationships in which the two sides combine to generate and share operating economies.

Negotiations over supply, however, may well be internal rather than external. Companies are often organized into separate businesses, with units bargaining between themselves. Here the case for Win–Win is overwhelming, since the best interests of the organization as a whole take precedence. But it is hard to keep politics and personalities out of internal negotiation, and it may be wise to agree on a neutral arbitrator.

AVOID IMPASSE

It may well be that the other party simply refuses to agree. In this case, all you can do is keep talking, trying to find a way through; or bring the negotiations to an end, either temporarily or permanently. A deadlock is in nobody's interest.

managing
PEOPLE

MANAGING PEOPLE IS ABOUT ORGANIZING AND MOTIVATING INDIVIDUALS TO WORK TOGETHER TO ACHIEVE CERTAIN GOALS. MANAGERS MUST UNDERSTAND PEOPLE'S NEEDS AND BEHAVIOR TO BECOME EFFECTIVE LEADERS WHO CAN INSPIRE AND DEVELOP TEAM MEMBERS.

There is no inherently right or wrong way to manage people – different situations will require different approaches – but there are some general techniques that may be applied to build a management framework that suits your team and your objectives.

To be a good manager, you must build on your technical skills by developing leadership qualities. You need to understand what really motivates people, the dynamics of teamwork, and recognize when and how to delegate. Managing people involves constructive reviews of their work, and a program of training and development, supported by coaching and mentoring, to maximize employees' skills and unlock their potential. You must also develop sensitive interpersonal skills and learn to use them to resolve individual difficulties and deal with conflict.

MOTIVATING PEOPLE

BEING MOTIVATED IS MORE THAN JUST BEING HAPPY OR SATISFIED IN A JOB. MOTIVATED PEOPLE WANT TO DO THE VERY BEST THEY CAN – NOT FOR YOU, BUT FOR THEMSELVES. MOTIVATION IS A FEELING WITHIN A PERSON, NOT SOMETHING YOU CAN IMPOSE.

UNDERSTANDING MOTIVATION

Motivation lies at the heart of managing people, and goes far beyond praise for a job well done. As a manager, you need the skills to understand and create the conditions in which all team members can become motivated. This is a huge challenge: different people will respond to different conditions, and these conditions can change over time.

As a starting point, it is worth examining two models of motivation that are commonly referred to in management theory: Abraham Maslow's "hierarchy of needs," and what Frederick Herzberg called "motivators and hygiene factors." Maslow suggested that the needs of an individual grow progressively: when a lower-level need is satisfied, the individual seeks fulfillment at the next level up. He or she would not seek to fulfill "self-actualizing" needs, those at the highest level, until all the needs below have been met. In practical terms, this means that employees will not truly do their very best unless they feel safe, respected, and valued. So if your team's lower-level needs are under threat, from fear of layoffs, for example, they may not respond positively when you encourage them to do their best.

IDENTIFYING FACTORS

Herzberg carried out extensive research into people's attitudes to their jobs. He found that some factors previously believed to be motivational did little more than contribute to job satisfaction: these are what he termed "hygiene factors." Their absence or poor quality caused dissatisfaction, but their presence did not increase motivation. People were actively motivated by a range of other factors: motivators. The absence of these would

Maslow's Hierarchy of Needs

SELF-ACTUALIZATION
Development of own potential, finding self-fulfillment

SELF-ESTEEM
Approval from others, recognition, achievement

SOCIAL
Acceptance from others, affiliation, belonging

SAFETY
Feeling of security, not fearing danger

PHYSIOLOGICAL
Basic requirements of life, such as food and drink

This simplified model of psychologist Abraham Maslow's theory illustrates the sequence of satisfying needs. Not until those at the lower level have been satisfied can the higher needs be tackled. As an individual draws near to satisfying a particular need, the one above becomes more of a priority. A satisfied need is no longer a stimulus.

HERZBERG'S HYGIENE FACTORS AND MOTIVATORS

HYGIENE FACTORS	MOTIVATORS
■ **Company policy** The rules and regulations that govern how the organization goes about its business.	■ **Achievement** Doing a good job: meeting and exceeding goals.
■ **Supervision** The way employees are managed when carrying out day-to-day tasks.	■ **Recognition** Managers and colleagues acknowledging an individual's achievements.
■ **Interpersonal relationships** Relationships with colleagues in the workplace.	■ **Work itself** Employees believing that the role they fulfill is important.
■ **Working conditions** Working hours, workplace layout, facilities, and technical equipment.	■ **Responsibility** Giving employees ownership of their work by giving them freedom in how they carry out their tasks.
■ **Salary and benefits** Fair compensation in the form of basic income, plus fringe benefits, bonuses, vacations, and company car.	■ **Advancement** Employees making progress not just through promotion but also through opportunities for development.

not necessarily cause dissatisfaction, but their presence was generally motivational.

In his analysis, Herzberg separates satisfaction from motivation. In your role as manager, you can influence many hygiene (satisfaction) factors and all of the motivating factors.

MOTIVATED OR NOT?

A motivated team member is usually energetic and enthusiastic, performing consistently well and actively seeking greater responsibility. Such an individual is not intimidated by the prospect of change, and has a positive approach to challenges. A highly motivated team member can help lift the spirit of the rest of the team, and draw them toward greater achievement.

In contrast, demotivated team members will often appear not to care about their tasks and goals. As a result, their performance can be poor, and they will shirk responsibility. They may frequently arrive late, or be absent altogether. They may exaggerate the slightest problem, and consequently find change difficult to cope with. Demotivation is infectious. If a single demotivated member is failing to deliver on obligations to customers and to the rest of the team, then without remedial action other members of the team may eventually follow suit.

GETTING TO KNOW YOUR TEAM

The first step in creating motivating conditions for your team is to get to know each one of them as an individual. Their self-confidence, abilities, values, and expectations play an important part in their ability to become motivated.

Do not assume that what motivates you will automatically work for other people. Some people work simply for money and may be demotivated by, say, having additional responsibility. Try to figure out what personal goals the individual is trying to achieve through work – to gain recognition, for example, or improve lifestyle. The most difficult people to manage are those who cannot articulate their needs. In this case, some form of psychometric testing may indicate their preferred ways of behaving and relating to other people. More importantly, it may reveal main sources of motivation.

CREATING THE CONDITIONS

While getting to know people, bear in mind that some principles of motivation are almost universally applicable.

Match the people to the skills

People who are confident in their job will be more satisfied than those who feel overloaded, or whose current skills do not match requirements. Reassess the team's workload where necessary, and use training to improve ability.

Work to clearly defined goals

Make sure goals are manageable and achievable, and people know exactly what is expected of them. If they have a part in defining their goals, they will be all the more satisfied when they achieve them.

Reward achievements

Reward is not just about money: by itself, money does not motivate people to perform better – it merely prevents dissatisfaction. Throwing money at a motivation problem will yield only short-term results. Think about nonmonetary reward: positive feedback, taking an active interest in the individual's career, increasing responsibility in recognition of ability. Find out what drives the individual, and use that knowledge to develop suitable rewards.

MANAGEMENT AND LEADERSHIP

TO MANAGE PEOPLE EFFECTIVELY, YOU WILL NEED TO USE BOTH MANAGEMENT SKILLS AND LEADERSHIP ABILITY. THE CHALLENGE LIES IN APPLYING BOTH TYPES OF SKILLS APPROPRIATELY IN A GIVEN SITUATION TO DELIVER A SUCCESSFUL OUTCOME.

DISTINGUISHING BETWEEN MANAGEMENT AND LEADERSHIP

Management is essentially about steady-state processes. In broad terms, it deals rationally with such complexities of organizational life as problem-solving, planning, budgeting, and controling.

Leadership is fundamentally about personal behaviors and styles. It appeals to the emotions, seeking to align people behind a vision and inspire them to make that vision a reality. This is especially important in times of significant change.

Amid the practicalities of working life, this distinction is not so cut and dried. Leadership and management may demand different skills, but they are not mutually exclusive. They may be closely interlinked, depending on the situation. Most so-called "management" roles will be neither entirely steady-state, nor entirely about change. They will be partly about organizing people to achieve and partly about motivating and inspiring them. So any effective "manager" will need to be able to display a combination of both management and leadership skills.

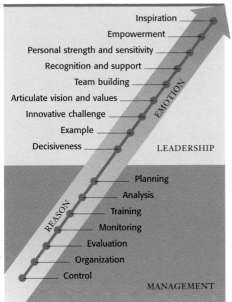

Based on a diagram produced by the UK Ministry of Defence

Inspiration
Empowerment
Personal strength and sensitivity
Recognition and support
Team building
Articulate vision and values
Innovative challenge
Example
Decisiveness
LEADERSHIP

EMOTION

Planning
Analysis
Training
Monitoring
Evaluation
Organization
Control
MANAGEMENT

REASON

Distinguishing management and leadership
The two roles, of management and leadership, may be viewed as existing on the same continuum. At one end, management controls systems and processes on a rational basis, while at the other end, leadership appeals to emotion through style and behavior.

of people behind radical change, or to encourage them to participate in suggesting change. There are a number of theories about management style, but at its simplest level, it can be viewed as a continuum hinging on the level of involvement in decision-making.

The directional style
At one end of the continuum is the directional style, where the manager simply tells people what to do. This style is most appropriate in exceptional circumstances: some kind of crisis, or when dealing with difficult employees.

The democratic style
At the other end of the continuum is the democratic style, where the manager actively engages the team in decision-making and seeks consensus. This style is particularly effective if it is important for the team to fully accept the decision and to take action as a result. It is frequently employed to ensure that organizational change is more effective.

Adapting the style
In most situations, managers will adopt a style between these two extremes: from "selling" their decision to the team, to encouraging the team to make its own decision but reserving the right to change it if necessary.

As a general rule, a management style that encourages involvement will produce a more positive reaction from employees, but can be too time-consuming a process for most routine decisions.

CHOOSING AND APPLYING MANAGEMENT STYLES

Your management style must be carefully matched to the management task. For example, the approach you would take to manage a group of administrators processing forms would be significantly different from the approach needed to manage a group of research scientists. So there are two initial elements to consider: what kind of people you are managing, and what kind of tasks they are fulfilling. You can then consider which management styles may be appropriate.

The use of the plural is deliberate; effective managers are aware that there is a whole range of management styles, and know that they must choose the right one to suit a particular situation. For example, the steady-state style required to deal with the group of administrators mentioned above would be very different from the style required to align a group

KNOWING YOURSELF

To apply the appropriate management styles successfully, it is very useful to have a thorough knowledge of yourself. You need to recognize your own behavior, and how you interact with other people. This may sound an obvious course to many people, but some individuals are wholly unaware of the impact they make on others, and their life and work may suffer as a result. So it is worth making the effort to find out what you are really like.

There are many ways of doing this, but one useful method of gaining insight is by taking psychometric tests. There is a wide range of such tests, to assess elements of personal style and behavior, capacities, and attributes. It is worth researching which one will be of most benefit to you. You could probably get advice from your human resources department. The output from these tests will be invaluable to you not only as a manager, but also as a team member and a subordinate.

A less formal method of understanding your own behavior is to solicit direct feedback from the people you work with: your team, your peers, and your own manager. Use real-life examples, and ask your colleagues how you could have done better in managing a particular situation. You should encourage them to focus on your behavior rather than the specific actions you took.

At first, your colleagues – especially those who report to you – may find this awkward, but over time their candor will increase. It may be useful to encourage subordinates by relating feedback you have received from other colleagues and asking them to comment on it.

Choosing the right style

While some managers will naturally use more than one style, others will have a single dominant style. Many have a tendency to overuse the style they feel comfortable with, often applying it in situations where it is clearly unsuitable. A good example of this is a manager using a directional style when it is vital for the team to commit to doing something differently or better. Such an approach here is rarely successful. A democratic style is more likely to have the desired result, because members of the team will feel they have been involved in the decision-making. They will feel that they "own" the decision.

TAKING ACTION

Some managers choose not to work on their management style, believing it to be part and parcel of their personality. But, with commitment to improvement, and a willingness to learn and adapt, they can begin to introduce additional styles into their repertoire, and possibly change their dominant approach.

The success of adopting a suitable management style can be measured in a number of ways, including:
- the team's success in achieving goals
- staff turnover among team members
- absenteeism among team members.

However, relying on these measures alone means that you may be unaware of problems until it is too late. A more constructive approach is to emulate or seek coaching from other managers who are demonstrably respected by their teams and who achieve results.

No manager is perfect; everybody needs to work on their weak points and build on their strong points. Consider this as a challenge to you in determining your own development. Positive feedback will reassure you that the effort you make to understand and influence your management style is worthwhile.

BUILDING A TEAM

TO BUILD AN EFFECTIVE TEAM, YOU NEED TO COMBINE THE SKILLS AND PERSONALITIES OF THE INDIVIDUALS INVOLVED TO ACHIEVE SHARED GOALS AND OBJECTIVES. YOU MUST UNDERSTAND THE CONDITIONS REQUIRED FOR GOOD TEAMWORK AND PROVIDE THEM.

THE BENEFITS OF TEAMWORKING

People can often accomplish much more by working together than they can by working separately. Even just making people feel like part of a team, instead of isolated individuals, helps them achieve more and feel more committed. An effective team can share and exploit its full range of talent and expertise, and compensate for individual weaknesses.

WHAT MAKES A TEAM?

Simply bringing together a group of people does not necessarily mean that they will function effectively as a team. A successful team needs:
● diversity of membership
● common and challenging goals
● involvement of team members
● good communications.
Underlying all these elements is the basic necessity of strong leadership. Strong does not mean dictatorial. Rather, it means that you take an overview of the team situation and create an environment in which the members can combine their skills to achieve objectives.

A WELL-BALANCED TEAM

Team membership is not just about bringing together functional expertise: it is also about personality and attitude. The psychologist Meredith Belbin has

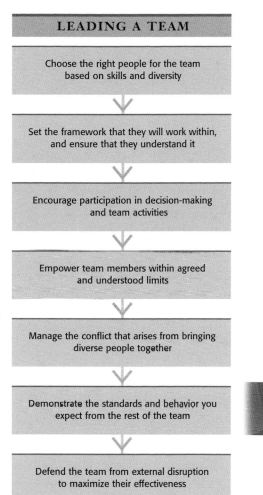

LEADING A TEAM

Choose the right people for the team based on skills and diversity

Set the framework that they will work within, and ensure that they understand it

Encourage participation in decision-making and team activities

Empower team members within agreed and understood limits

Manage the conflict that arises from bringing diverse people together

Demonstrate the standards and behavior you expect from the rest of the team

Defend the team from external disruption to maximize their effectiveness

distinguished nine team roles that need to be covered to deliver optimum team performance (*see* page 174). This does not mean you need to slot one team member into each separate role. Most individuals have certain styles and attributes that enable them to fulfill more than one role. Work with the team to ensure that the

BELBIN'S NINE TEAM ROLES

ROLE	ATTRIBUTES
Plant	■ Creative, imaginative, unorthodox ■ Solves difficult problems
Resource investigator	■ Extroverted, enthusiastic, communicative ■ Explores opportunities ■ Develops contacts
Coordinator	■ Mature, confident, a good chairperson ■ Clarifies goals, promotes decision-making, delegates well
Shaper	■ Challenging, dynamic, thrives on pressure ■ Has the drive and courage to overcome obstacles
Monitor evaluator	■ Sober, strategic, discerning ■ Sees all options. Judges accurately
Teamworker	■ Cooperative, mild, perceptive, diplomatic ■ Listens, builds, averts friction, calms the waters
Implementer	■ Disciplined, reliable, conservative, efficient ■ Turns ideas into practical actions
Completer	■ Painstaking, conscientious, anxious ■ Searches out errors and omissions ■ Delivers on time
Specialist	■ Single-minded, self-starting, dedicated ■ Provides knowledge and skills in rare supply

whole range of roles is covered, and to establish your own roles. You will be the "coordinator," and may also need to take on those team roles that remain unfilled, even if they are a poor fit with your usual ways of working.

SETTING TEAM GOALS

All team members must know exactly what they are expected to achieve at a number of levels. You will need to:
● develop a team vision and goals
● ensure that every team member knows what to do to contribute to team goals
● review how team goals relate to wider organizational goals.

Without this clarity, there is the danger that team members will duplicate some roles and miss others completely, or that they will lose sight of the overall objectives. The team should carefully map each member's responsibilities and roles, and ensure that everybody is clear about who does what. This is the basis for team identity and commitment.

INVOLVING TEAM MEMBERS

To get the team fully aligned behind goals, you need to involve them in the setting of those goals and then carry through that involvement into all aspects of the team's work. Everybody should be equally involved in the team's activities and decisions. You will need to actively manage the process: push shy members forward and tactfully rein in the more vociferous. To ensure that everyone is working within the same framework, explain how the team will approach problem-solving and decision-making.

STRENGTHENING THE TEAM

Build team identity by bringing the members together to work, to train, or to play. Encourage open communications by giving people the confidence and freedom to express their views.

Some managers use substitute team tasks such as outdoor adventure courses to build up a team. These do bring people together, but there is a danger that the team may see them as just a game. In any case, they should be seen as no more than a supplement to the management tasks

required to build an effective team: they will not compensate for deficiencies in setting goals or roles, or in flawed decision-making processes. The most useful team-building events mirror in some way the team's real-life activities.

DEALING WITH TEAM PROBLEMS

Most team problems are caused by a breakdown in trust: a commitment has not been met, or confidence has been betrayed. You can help prevent this by setting clear standards and managing performance consistently. Leadership and consultation can develop common team values that are acceptable to all members.

Never put all your faith in team management to the exclusion of people management. A team functions well only with skilled and motivated individuals, so take time to meet each of those individuals to discuss their concerns.

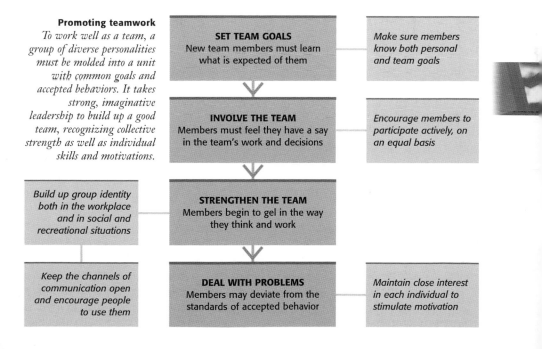

Promoting teamwork
To work well as a team, a group of diverse personalities must be molded into a unit with common goals and accepted behaviors. It takes strong, imaginative leadership to build up a good team, recognizing collective strength as well as individual skills and motivations.

SET TEAM GOALS
New team members must learn what is expected of them

Make sure members know both personal and team goals

INVOLVE THE TEAM
Members must feel they have a say in the team's work and decisions

Encourage members to participate actively, on an equal basis

Build up group identity both in the workplace and in social and recreational situations

STRENGTHEN THE TEAM
Members begin to gel in the way they think and work

Keep the channels of communication open and encourage people to use them

DEAL WITH PROBLEMS
Members may deviate from the standards of accepted behavior

Maintain close interest in each individual to stimulate motivation

DELEGATING WORK

DELEGATING CERTAIN TASKS OR PROCESSES TO OTHER MEMBERS OF THE TEAM ALLOWS YOU TO USE YOUR MANAGEMENT TIME MORE CONSTRUCTIVELY. DELEGATION HAS THE ADDITIONAL BENEFIT OF HELPING THOSE MEMBERS TO DEVELOP NEW SKILLS.

WHAT IS DELEGATION?

Delegation is deciding which tasks to do yourself and which to pass on, and to whom. Honest delegation may mean giving up tasks you enjoy. Sometimes, if there is no competent team member to delegate to, it may mean doing relatively junior tasks yourself, at least temporarily.

Delegation is more than just handing down a task: you are also asking a team member to take on the responsibility for carrying out that task and the authority to act on your behalf. But you retain accountability: the buck stops with you.

WHAT TO DELEGATE

List the tasks that constitute your role. Reflect on your own career plans and consider which skills you need to keep fresh. Decide which tasks you must do yourself, and which could be done by someone else, even if this would mean an initial dip in quality or speed.

You are delegating authority for the task as well as its execution, so choose tasks that are reasonably self-contained. For example, it would be easy to delegate preparation of the weekly sales report, but almost impossible to delegate your relationship with an important customer. Delegating a whole task, though, will aid the individual's personal development and foster a sense of achievement.

Some managers see delegation as a license to get rid of all the tasks that they find too boring or too difficult. Do not fall into this trap – it is all too transparent to your team. Delegating tedious tasks will demotivate, and delegating tasks that are too hard is dangerous, because it will undermine your authority with the team.

ALLOCATING TASKS

Deciding who should be responsible for the task is about more than just assessing competence, though competence is a vital ingredient. You should try to select a team member who already has the required knowledge and skills for the job, or could easily attain them through training or coaching.

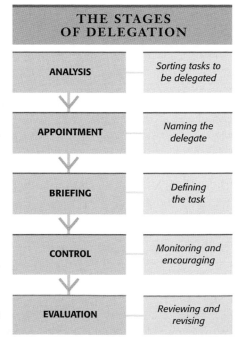

THE STAGES OF DELEGATION

ANALYSIS	Sorting tasks to be delegated
APPOINTMENT	Naming the delegate
BRIEFING	Defining the task
CONTROL	Monitoring and encouraging
EVALUATION	Reviewing and revising

COMMON PROBLEMS

ISSUE	CAUSE
You refuse to delegate	■ You fear that subordinates will fail. ■ You believe you can carry out the task more quickly and/or better than any other individual. ■ You fear that delegating the task will be seen as "unloading" it, and therefore resented.
You delegate the wrong tasks	■ The task is too difficult for you. ■ You want to absolve yourself of responsibility. ■ You have not fully considered the competencies required and their fit with the individual.
You interfere/A subordinate exceeds authority	■ A two-way problem with a common cause: you have not established a firm structure with clear limits of delegation.

There are other factors to consider, not least how comfortable the individual will be with this added responsibility. Some employees relish it and see it as part of their personal development. Others find it stressful and resist extra work; they should do their fair share on the team, but they may not be your first choice when you are delegating parts of your own role.

Another factor is whether the member you intend to delegate to can in turn delegate part of his or her own role. As a general rule, delegation should be encouraged as far down the organization as skills and comfort will permit. If you can find the optimum level, you yourself will not only work more efficiently but will also motivate and develop the team.

STRUCTURED DELEGATION

The team member needs to understand what is being delegated and why. You must be very precise about the limits of authority so the individual can build up a picture of the task, its context, and their place in it. Clarify how you will supervise the task and assess performance.

Be prepared to adjust your style: an increasingly confident individual may resent your "interference." Be clear right from the start about the controls, but also stress that you are there to offer any support and advice. This should help to prevent the unhappy situation where you feel that the individual is overstepping their limits, but he or she feels that you are interfering unnecessarily.

Finally, ensure that anybody else who will be affected by the newly assigned responsibility is informed, partly to avoid confusion but also to motivate the individual through public recognition.

EVALUATION

When the delegated task is completed, it is important to review it. Concentrate on what went well. This will give you useful guidelines for future decisions about delegation, and also help the individual concerned in his or her personal development. At this stage, you may also want to consider whether there appears to be any need for a permanent change to the individual's role.

CONDUCTING REVIEWS

IN A FORMAL REVIEW, A MANAGER MEETS A TEAM MEMBER TO DISCUSS HIS OR HER PERFORMANCE OVER A GIVEN PERIOD, AND TO SET FUTURE OBJECTIVES. THERE MAY ALSO BE SOME DISCUSSION OF FUTURE POTENTIAL, AND HOW IT MAY BE FULFILLED.

DOING REVIEWS WITHIN PERFORMANCE MANAGEMENT

Some organizations regard performance reviews as little more than a regular form-filling chore. But a review can provide an invaluable opportunity for the manager and the team member to exchange views. In many organizations, reviews link back into a performance management system and forward into a schedule of training and development.

A performance management system
Here, individual performance is linked to organizational goals. The individual's goals are set within this context. Performance is supported, and regularly monitored through the review system.

A performance management system links an individual's performance to overall organizational goals. The system supports the manager in:
- determining what is expected of the individual
- providing support to achieve objectives
- regularly reviewing what has been achieved
- managing performance when appropriate
- revisiting goals that have been set.

THE ROLE OF REVIEWS
A formal review enables the manager and the team member to review his or her work as a whole. They can discuss what was good and not so good, and identify training and development needs. It can fulfill other purposes as well: to provide input to the annual pay review, or to look forward to the individual's future potential and aspirations.

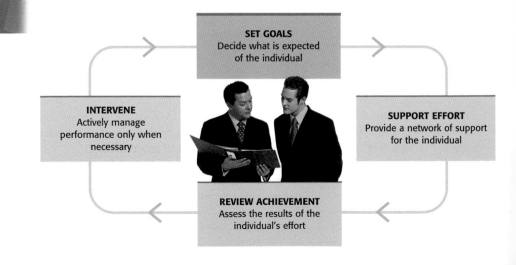

SET GOALS
Decide what is expected of the individual

INTERVENE
Actively manage performance only when necessary

SUPPORT EFFORT
Provide a network of support for the individual

REVIEW ACHIEVEMENT
Assess the results of the individual's effort

PREPARING FOR A REVIEW MEETING

CONSIDERATIONS	KEY POINTS
Performance during period since last review	What went well? What went less well? Were objectives met? Do you have evidence to support these views? What factors might have contributed to performance?
Performance in previous periods	How does performance compare? If there is a noticeable difference, what may have contributed to that difference? (For example, development activities may have had an impact.)
Development needs	Are there obvious needs that you can identify and are willing to suggest? You will also need to consider the individual's potential career path in answering the question.
Accuracy of your view	Do other people (colleagues, internal customers, subordinates) hold the same views? Gather their opinions even if no formal 360-degree feedback process is in place.
The right tone	What tone will be appropriate for the meeting? Although the appraisal process will probably have been imposed, you can set whichever tone will work best for getting the most useful response from the particular personality.
Specific questions	Do you have some specific questions ready? Drafting some open questions before the meeting will avoid the need to ad-lib (when you may be on the spot).

It is important for both parties to be clear what the discussion is primarily about: is it about performance, pay, or potential? If employees see a review as **an** opportunity for pay negotiation, they will be unwilling to admit to shortcomings. The same applies to potential: if the individual feels that the need for, say, a time-management course diminishes his or her chance of promotion, then this additional element is likely to hinder the appraisal process.

Remember that you should not wait until a review meeting to discuss performance. Make it part of your routine supervision. What you have to say in an appraisal meeting should reaffirm points you have discussed previously, not be out of the blue.

PREPARING FOR THE REVIEW

First, schedule the meeting to allow both parties adequate opportunity to prepare. You will probably be working to a set format requiring systematic preparation. If 360-degree feedback is used (*see* page 180), you will need to set aside time to consult the relevant parties. You should plan the meeting thoroughly. Your careful preparation will become apparent during the meeting, and will be seen as a mark of respect by the subject. It will also enable you to feel more relaxed.

Choose a location conducive to an open and frank discussion: possibly off-site or away from your usual office, to separate the discussion from routine supervisory activity. Be sure to set aside a reasonable amount of time. It will be

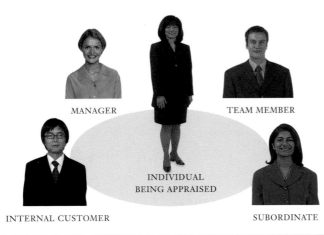

MANAGER

TEAM MEMBER

INTERNAL CUSTOMER

INDIVIDUAL
BEING APPRAISED

SUBORDINATE

Using 360-degree review
This system of review takes an all-around view. In assessing an individual's performance, feedback will be needed from a number of work contacts, including other team members, internal customers, and subordinates, as well as the manager. This is a very useful process, but time-consuming: allow enough time to collect all the data.

frustrating for both parties if the discussion is rushed or interrupted. The time required will depend on the nature and extent of regular one-to-one discussions: if this is known territory for both of you, less time will be required.

REVIEWING PERFORMANCE

Take care how you handle this discussion. You may have done most of the preparation, but you should not do most of the talking.

Most managers find it easy to praise, but difficult to talk about problem areas. Do not shrink from these: the meeting is an opportunity for constructive criticism. If poor performance is not confronted, the individual's longer-term development is put at risk. In giving negative feedback, be sensitive and listen to the employee's point of view. He or she may feel that factors outside their control have prevented them from achieving objectives: a change in company policy, for example.

Any shortcomings can be identified as issues to solve rather than statements of blame. Analyze causes and seek possible remedies. If the individual recommends the solution, it is more likely to work.

SETTING OBJECTIVES

All reviews should include setting objectives. A simple acronym reminds you that they should be SMART: **S**pecific, **M**easurable, **A**greed, **R**ealistic, **T**imed.

A SMART objective specifies the required result, with a suitable measure attached so both parties know when the objective has been achieved. Objectives should be achievable, but not too easy: "stretch" targets give a real sense of accomplishment when they are achieved. Always set a target date for completion.

CAREER PLANNING

A discussion about performance will often highlight training or development needs. You may also identify longer-term career objectives and what help is required in achieving them.

ENDING THE MEETING

You should carefully document what has been discussed and agreed, and thank the individual for their time and effort. Assure them that you will act promptly on identifying any potential development opportunities, and will provide regular feedback on progress.

TRAINING AND DEVELOPMENT

TRAINING IS VITAL TO ENSURE THAT EMPLOYEES FUNCTION COMPETENTLY AND SAFELY AT WORK, WHILE DEVELOPMENT INCREASES THEIR SKILLS AND ENCOURAGES PROGRESS. THESE PROCESSES ARE SUPPORTED BY COACHING AND MENTORING.

DIFFERENT KINDS OF TRAINING
Training is not always concerned with the skills required for the individual's current role. It can also cover refresher training to keep skills up to date, additional tools to cover other people's jobs, and organizational knowledge.

ASSESSING TRAINING NEEDS
Your starting point in assessing an employee's training needs should be his or her current job, and the competencies required to do it effectively and safely. Does the individual have all the necessary skills, or is there room for improvement? If you identify areas that need help, what form should this help take? It may be anything from some on-the-job coaching to a formal, full-scale training

course. If you do decide on a plan of action, would this be useful for other team members too? Try to look beyond the individual and assess the needs of the entire team. It is possible that no formal training for an individual is required at all, and that the desired result could be achieved by a combination of job redesign and on-the-job coaching.

Also, bear in mind that people tend to forget new skills very quickly if they do not use them. The acid test for a formal training decision is: will the employee "use it or lose it"? If they are likely to lose it, postpone training.

CHOOSING THE TRAINING METHODS
Having assessed the training need and established that specific action is indeed required, you must now decide how the

Hierarchy of training needs
After basics such as health and safety have been covered, training is skill-specific, updated when necessary. Personal needs vary, and should also be addressed. When fully competent, an employee may have further training to cover colleagues' jobs.

FURTHER TRAINING
To cover other people's jobs

TOP-UP TRAINING
Specific to the individual's job

PERSONAL TRAINING
To improve such skills as time-management

TASK-RELATED TRAINING
Specific to the individual's job

ORGANIZATIONAL TRAINING
Such as company orientation

CHOOSING A TRAINING METHOD

METHOD	ADVANTAGES	DISADVANTAGES
On-the-job training For specific task(s)	■ Comparatively inexpensive ■ No outside trainers required ■ Relevant to individual's tasks ■ Does not require time away from workplace ■ Individual puts theory into practice right away	■ Colleagues may not have effective teaching skills
In-house training course For specific area of expertise	■ Highly relevant to organization ■ Good opportunities for networking within organization ■ Facilitates lateral communications within organization	■ May not be relevant to specific task/role
External training course Tailored for the organization or available to all	■ Carried out by trained professionals ■ Custom course highly relevant ■ General course gives chance to network with, and learn from, individuals with similar roles in other companies	■ Both types very expensive ■ General course may not be entirely relevant

training should be carried out. This depends on a number of factors:

● how many people need training (an entire team or a single new member?)
● the skills required and the level to be attained
● how urgent the training need is.

There are three main methods of training usually available:

On-the-job training

In a typical situation, a new recruit will be "shown the ropes" by experienced members of the team.

In-house training courses

These are usually run by professionals within the organization, and commonly apply to a broad cross-section of workers (as in training in computer processes).

External training courses

There are two types. One is specifically developed for the organization or the team by an external supplier. The other is available to all interested organizations, and the individual attends as a delegate.

EVALUATION AND FOLLOW-UP

After the training, always carry out some kind of evaluation, together with the employee. You need to know whether the desired improvement has been achieved. This will guide your future decisions about investment in training.

Help the trainee to make the best use of the new skill, both in the current role and in passing on knowledge to the rest of the team where appropriate. At this stage you may need to start thinking about further development opportunities for the employee.

THE IMPORTANCE OF DEVELOPMENT

While training improves an individual's ability to carry out tasks within a specific job, development adds to people's overall skills, and is not necessarily related to current tasks. If done well, development supports employee motivation, sending a message that they are valued.

Development may be seen as a low priority when balanced against other demands on a manager's time. But if skilled team members are not supported in developing their careers, they will move on. From the organization's point of view, it is much more cost-effective to develop existing staff than it is to recruit and train new staff. Taking a proactive approach is more likely to keep your team members efficient and committed.

HELPING PEOPLE DEVELOP

Take time, possibly during a review, to ask about career aspirations, and what kinds of experience or training might help the individual. Beware of raising expectations or making any promises. If employees' aspirations are unrealistic, advise them to think again: chasing unattainable goals is a certain route to dissatisfaction. Conversely, people may underestimate their own abilities, and need your positive encouragement to achieve their potential.

Based on this discussion, you may seek development opportunities within your own team, elsewhere in the organization, or even outside it.

Opportunities in your own team

First look for approaches that will develop the individual and will help attain team goals. The aim is to increase an individual's experience and skills. Consider the following options:

- introducing cross-training to develop team members' breadth of skills and flexibility
- setting up separate projects and delegating responsibility for them
- promoting team members, either temporarily to cover a post or permanently.

Promotion is the ultimate way of keeping development within the team – it also demonstrates your willingness to recognize and reward good performance.

Opportunities within the organization

Depending on the development need, the most appropriate opportunities may be elsewhere in the organization. For example, if you are currently managing a clerical processing function and you have a capable team member who aspires to a career in brand management, you could consider a project in marketing.

On some occasions you may lose a team member permanently, but do not be deterred by this possibility. You should always do your utmost to ensure that your team is aware of opportunities elsewhere in the organization.

Opportunities outside the organization

Some companies sponsor nonvocational courses (such as internet use for manual workers), or temporarily send employees into other organizations. For example, a commercial organization may allow an employee to take a temporary aid assignment in a developing country.

Opportunities beyond the organization

Sadly, on some occasions you and the employee may conclude that the best development action for him or her is to leave the organization. If this happens, be supportive. You will have a short-term problem in recruiting and training a new team member, but an employee who feels trapped in a job can be highly destructive to team morale and performance.

There is a further incentive for a helpful approach. An employee who has been properly supported in such a time of transition will retain a positive attitude to the organization, which will add to its reputation as a committed employer.

COACHING AND MENTORING

Training and development are supported by coaching and mentoring. Coaching is linked to training, in that it is about improving performance, usually in the short to medium term. It is an intrinsic part of a manager's role – giving extra help to team members who need it – even if it is not listed in the job description. Mentoring is a longer-term activity, more closely linked to personal development. It may be part of your job, though not with a member of your own team.

Coaching

Coaching is applicable at all levels of the organization to develop and enhance the required skills for the job. It assumes that the employee already has a degree of competence, but needs help in one or more of the following areas:
● skills enhancement
● on-the-job capability
● solving specific problems
● acclimatizing to organizational change
● personal attitude/outlook.

The coaching and mentoring roles
A coach and a mentor have skills in common, but apply them differently. A coach focuses on specifics, in the shorter term, while a mentor views the whole picture, in the longer term.

There are some similarities between on-the-job training and coaching, but coaching is a much more dynamic, motivational process, demonstrating a high level of interest in the individual employee. The coach must move with the learner along a continuum of improvement. If the coach gets stuck, the learner may lose self-confidence and cease to improve.

Coaching needs to be approached in different ways, depending on the phase of learning of the individual. In coaching a complete beginner, you may have to carry out a task and then have them mirror the activity: this is akin to instruction. As they acquire a basic skill-set, the coaching approach will change: you now ask them to identify where they need help to enable them to achieve their goals. You can then work with them to improve in these specific areas.

When coaching an individual with a high degree of technical competence, your role may change again to assist him or her by placing the emphasis on self-reflection and analysis. Throughout any coaching process, however, you need to apply the core communication skills of empathy and active listening.

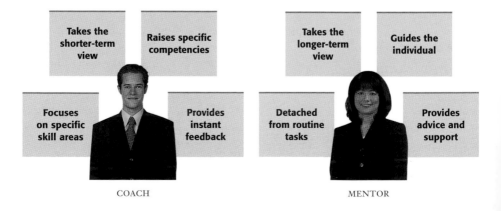

| Takes the shorter-term view | Raises specific competencies | | Takes the longer-term view | Guides the individual |

| Focuses on specific skill areas | Provides instant feedback | | Detached from routine tasks | Provides advice and support |

COACH   MENTOR

Mentoring

A mentor is essentially a trusted adviser and confidant(e). The role requires a detached, overall view, which means that an individual's immediate manager, or indeed anyone else in that individual's management chain, would not be a suitable mentor. The "big picture" would always be clouded with routine concerns.

While you cannot mentor any member of your own team, as a manager you can still have a part to play in organizational mentoring. You may mentor an employee who is studying for professional qualifications that you have already attained. Or you may mentor a new recruit to the organization to ensure that he or she makes the most of the opportunities available.

A mentor may remain with the individual throughout his or her career in a specific organization, but this will very much depend on their "fit" over time. With the increasing confidence that comes with experience, an employee may decide that the appointed mentor is no longer a suitable role model, at a personal level. An experienced mentor will realize this first, and will normally seek to end the mentoring relationship.

DEALING WITH PROBLEMS

A MANAGER INEVITABLY HAS TO DEAL WITH DIFFICULT PEOPLE AND SITUATIONS IN THE WORKPLACE. MANY OF THE ISSUES WILL ARISE FROM NEGATIVE ATTITUDE AND POOR PERFORMANCE, AND YOU NEED A GENERAL FRAMEWORK TO TACKLE THEM.

THE GOLDEN RULES

Whatever the specifics of a particular problem, whatever the claims and counterclaims of a contentious issue, there are certain standards of behavior that you as a manager should maintain:
- be firm, but scrupulously fair
- be clear and honest
- be constructive in your comments and suggestions
- always look for a positive outcome and encourage others to do so
- take action early: do not put things off and let the problem grow
- document discussions and actions
- remain calm.

WHERE TO START

Sometimes you will have no choice but to discipline an individual, for example in the case of gross misconduct such as being drunk at work. But in less serious cases, such as poor timekeeping, the first step is to try to get to the bottom of the issue by opening up a dialogue.

Schedule a meeting as soon as possible with the individual concerned to explain what is worrying you. Illustrate the problem areas using measures and examples wherever possible. Explain what you expect from the individual, and seek his or her views on how things could be improved. The session should end with the drawing up of a simple action plan, which will probably detail the required action from both parties.

Sometimes even defining the problem may not be as easy as it sounds, and you may need to decide whether some kind of counseling is needed.

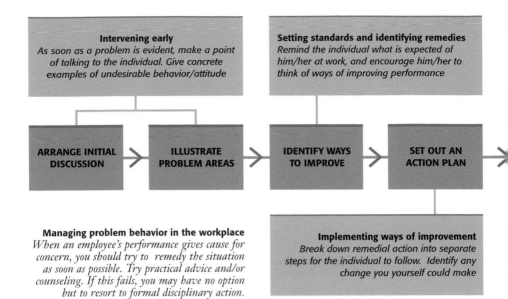

Intervening early
As soon as a problem is evident, make a point of talking to the individual. Give concrete examples of undesirable behavior/attitude

Setting standards and identifying remedies
Remind the individual what is expected of him/her at work, and encourage him/her to think of ways of improving performance

ARRANGE INITIAL DISCUSSION → **ILLUSTRATE PROBLEM AREAS** → **IDENTIFY WAYS TO IMPROVE** → **SET OUT AN ACTION PLAN** →

Managing problem behavior in the workplace
When an employee's performance gives cause for concern, you should try to remedy the situation as soon as possible. Try practical advice and/or counseling. If this fails, you may have no option but to resort to formal disciplinary action.

Implementing ways of improvement
Break down remedial action into separate steps for the individual to follow. Identify any change you yourself could make

COUNSELING

Your discussions may suggest that the team member has problems, personal or work-related, that they are struggling to resolve. Counseling may help.

Counseling is about helping people to help themselves by looking at the problem from a different perspective, and finding the self-confidence to work out a way forward. It is not just about giving advice, nor about being some kind of corporate psychiatrist. As a manager, you aim to use counseling skills rather than to be a counselor.

These counseling skills are vitally important in managing people, and are similar to coaching skills. Whatever the context, you will benefit from these skills every day of your career as a manager:
- "active" listening: using careful listening combined with questions with the intention of gaining a better understanding
- empathy: understanding how things seem to the other person
- respect: treating the individual and his or her views with consideration.

You should always aspire to being approachable, so team members feel they can raise any problematical issue with you. In some instances you will be able to help the individual through work-related and personal issues.

GETTING OUTSIDE HELP

Where serious personal issues such as substance abuse or bereavement are concerned, few managers are qualified to provide counseling support. Even if you have the requisite skills and experience, you may feel uncomfortable about the prospect of counseling a team member in such sensitive areas.

In these circumstances, you should avoid counseling yourself and find some other form of support for your colleague.

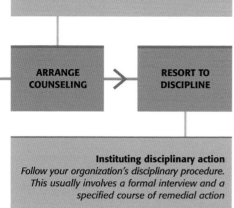

Providing support
Give counseling to the employee yourself, if appropriate, or bring in other people to help, from inside or outside the organization

ARRANGE COUNSELING

RESORT TO DISCIPLINE

Instituting disciplinary action
Follow your organization's disciplinary procedure. This usually involves a formal interview and a specified course of remedial action

Many organizations have an employee assistance program, which offers confidential counseling. If not, you could assist the employee by finding a suitable external counselor. Your human resources department may be able to help you. In any case, you should take great care not to seem dismissive, and should at least listen to the problem and express interest and sympathy.

In the case of serious workplace issues, it may be that the individual's line manager is part of the problem, so counseling from that person would be inappropriate and unhelpful. Here, you can only seek mediation by a third party, such as an uninvolved manager or an independent mediator.

But counseling, of whatever kind, may fail to help the individual change behavior. If this proves to be the case, you may as a last resort need to consider disciplinary action.

DISCIPLINARY ACTION

Before resorting to disciplinary action, you should have carried out the processes outlined earlier. If it comes to such action, you should view it as a way to help people get back on the right course, not to punish them for wrongdoing. If disciplinary action starts to be perceived as vengeance, it will undermine trust and may invoke trade union intervention. It is not the manager's role to dispense punishment or dismiss someone because of a personality clash.

You should also familiarize yourself thoroughly with your organization's disciplinary procedure. If professional advice is available from human resources, make full use of it. You must be sure of your ground, so get your facts right and, if possible, ask a trusted colleague to confirm your objectivity.

CONDUCTING THE DISCIPLINARY INTERVIEW

A disciplinary interview should be carried out in private, but both parties should invite witnesses. The individual should be informed formally of the grievance against him or her, and given the opportunity to respond fully to it.

The appropriate course of action then needs to be finalized. In the interests of fairness, this should be based on the facts and the context, and in line with similar action in the past.

You should make a careful record of the decisions made, and any actions required by either party. It is to be hoped that by invoking the disciplinary process, you will signal your determination to resolve the matter and this, supported by the documented actions, will be sufficient to achieve a satisfactory outcome.

problem-solving AND DECISION-MAKING

AS A MANAGER, YOU WILL SPEND MUCH OF YOUR TIME DEALING WITH PROBLEMS AND MAKING DECISIONS. FOR EFFECTIVE MANAGEMENT, IT IS ESSENTIAL TO DISTINGUISH BETWEEN THESE TWO PROCESSES, WHICH ARE SEPARATE AND DISTINCT, AND REQUIRE DIFFERENT APPROACHES.

Problems and decisions are such a large part of working life that many managers take them for granted. Indeed, there is confusion over just what constitutes a problem and what constitutes a decision. Often, issues are clumped together as the familiar catch-all "problem." But for the most effective solutions, you should use different skills.

You need first to understand the crucial differences between a problem and a decision. To solve a problem, you must find the root cause by gathering information. Similarly, the decision-making process needs information from everybody concerned. Once the cause has been identified, or a decision made, then you need to know the best way of implementing the solution.

IDENTIFYING PROBLEMS AND DECISIONS

IN TYPICAL SITUATIONS, A PROBLEM ARISES FROM A MALFUNCTION OF SOME KIND, WHILE A DECISION IS NEEDED WHEN ONE COURSE OF ACTION AMONG OTHERS MUST BE CHOSEN. IT IS IMPORTANT TO DISTINGUISH BETWEEN THESE TWO PROCESSES, TO DETERMINE THE APPROPRIATE RESPONSE.

IDENTIFY THE ISSUES

Managers have to deal with vast amounts of information, which seems to increase as technology improves. To stay in control, you should make a habit of regularly reviewing the issues you have to deal with, and be aware of changing priorities as situations evolve. Take a few minutes each morning or each week to write down all the matters that concern you. Make sure you understand them fully and have an approach to deal with them. In this way, you can make a complex picture much more manageable.

Defining complex issues
When a situation demands your attention and is not immediately identifiable as a problem or a decision, you need to follow a logical sequence of analysis to define the kind of issue it is.

When any issue is brought to your attention, you should first assess it and identify it. Your first question is whether it is truly relevant to your work. If it is clearly outside your area, have nothing more to do with it. Limit yourself to situations that require your action.

Having decided that an issue is relevant to you, ask yourself if it is clearly defined. If it is, then your course of action will follow accordingly. You may identify a certain issue as an undoubted problem: a vital piece of machinery is down and it must be fixed to restore the production process to working order. Or you may identify another issue as an undoubted need for a decision: you have a choice of three good candidates for one position, and you must do the choosing.

If things are not so clear-cut, you need to break down the issue to its component parts. Ask other people for their opinions (encouraging them to think broadly). List all the answers, then review the list and ensure that each item is clear and understood. Sometimes asking more

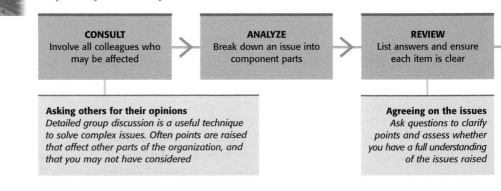

CONSULT
Involve all colleagues who may be affected

ANALYZE
Break down an issue into component parts

REVIEW
List answers and ensure each item is clear

Asking others for their opinions
Detailed group discussion is a useful technique to solve complex issues. Often points are raised that affect other parts of the organization, and that you may not have considered

Agreeing on the issues
Ask questions to clarify points and assess whether you have a full understanding of the issues raised

questions to explain a point further will bring a new insight. You will not just fall into the trap of focusing on one element and missing others that may be equally or even more important.

When you define a given situation as either a problem to be solved or a specific decision to be made, you are simplifying the whole picture, and beginning the process that will lead to a solution.

CLARIFY THE PROBLEM

Some "problems" are so simple that the solution is immediate. Paper jam in the printer? Let someone ease out the mangled paper and reset the machine. More challenging problems are those that not only disrupt the usual working procedure but also threaten serious repercussions; often they are not readily explicable. One such situation would be if the quality of your product appeared to be failing. The first indications would probably be customers complaining, with the product being rejected and returned at an accelerating rate.

An urgent problem indeed: but how to tackle it? It may seem so huge as to be too diffuse, making it difficult to pinpoint cause and effect. All managers have their own approach to dealing with

issues, and no doubt have some success some of the time. Yet in many cases people are probably not aware of the actual process they are going through, and are therefore unable to understand why sometimes things go badly wrong.

You have to trace causes of problems back to their roots. The only way that the problem can be eliminated is by finding and removing that cause: the "finding causes" process, addressed in the next section (*see* page 193), should be used here. A rigorous system of logical and analytical thought is essential to clarify the issues. This rational approach can enhance the chances of a successful outcome, and is particularly helpful when working in a group. Problems can be solved more effectively when people are working together and not trying to place blame on others. In the example of product failure, collaboration may help to illuminate the problem. People may separately identify:

- new system errors
- high staff turnover leading to under-par work
- inferior raw materials
- price perceived as too high by the market
- higher-quality product provided by competitors.

Thus wide-ranging underlying causes can involve both working processes and materials, and outside circumstances. Once you can identify each element contributing to the overall situation, the way ahead becomes clearer.

You should not only be aware of problems once they occur. Sometimes you can look ahead and forecast potential problems, and prevent them from causing trouble in the future: foresee and forestall.

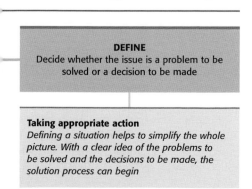

DEFINE
Decide whether the issue is a problem to be solved or a decision to be made

Taking appropriate action
Defining a situation helps to simplify the whole picture. With a clear idea of the problems to be solved and the decisions to be made, the solution process can begin

IDENTIFY THE DECISION

While problems by their very nature can be frustratingly diffuse, decisions – again by their very nature – can be much more focused. You want a particular outcome. You have a finite number of choices. So establish the criteria, the parameters, and choose. Again, a rigorous and logical analysis is vital. And it is especially important to realize early on when a decision needs to be made, as this can build in that valuable commodity: time.

Decisions may follow from the identification of an earlier problem. If raw materials were a contributing factor to the poor performance of your product, you may need to change your supplier. The selection of a new supplier is actually a choice between several possible suppliers: a decision. Once this has been understood, you can start the decision-making process.

Of course, a decision may be demanded by many factors operating in the working environment, and not only prompted by a specific problem. To refer to an earlier example: you have three good candidates for one position. This, again, is not a problem. The situation has not arisen from an unwanted deviation in the accepted norm. You have more than one solution to a given situation, and this requires a decision.

TACKLING THE ISSUES

If you have many issues to work on, you may have to concentrate on the most important. Identify which areas will give you the highest payback in terms of the best outcome in the quickest time. Early successes are important, as they show progress and are motivational.

Before starting to work on an issue, define and agree on the outcome. Ask what will constitute success. Sometimes it will be very clear: a "new system errors" problem, for example, would be solved by elimination of the errors. But sorting out the "high staff turnover" may require some research into what the acceptable level of turnover would be.

Find out who needs to be involved in order to resolve this issue. Who is likely to have information, who will be affected by the outcome, who has strong opinions about this, and who is an expert in this area? As well as internal colleagues, think about external contributors such as customers, suppliers, industry experts, academics, and consultants.

Finally, set some deadlines to ensure that the work will get done. Structure a reasonable timetable. Set aside time in your calendar and get agreement from others involved to do the same.

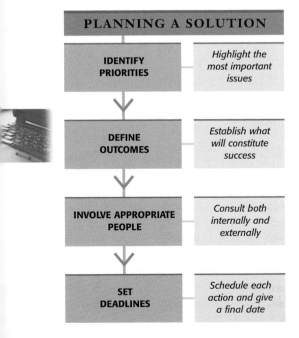

PLANNING A SOLUTION

IDENTIFY PRIORITIES	Highlight the most important issues
DEFINE OUTCOMES	Establish what will constitute success
INVOLVE APPROPRIATE PEOPLE	Consult both internally and externally
SET DEADLINES	Schedule each action and give a final date

FINDING THE CAUSE OF A PROBLEM

ONCE AN ISSUE HAS BEEN DEFINED AS A PROBLEM, THE ROOT CAUSE OF IT MUST BE IDENTIFIED. ONLY WHEN THIS HAS BEEN ESTABLISHED CAN THE APPROPRIATE ACTION BE TAKEN TO ELIMINATE THE PROBLEM. CERTAIN TECHNIQUES WILL HELP YOU HERE.

THE RELEVANCE OF EXPERIENCE

Once a problem has been clearly defined, there is often a tendency to "trial fix" it. Someone has an idea of cause, based on previous experience, and tries a corrective action. If that does not make the problem go away, another fix is tried. This approach can go on for some time until eventually the right fix may be found, but it is hardly effective in terms of cost or time.

A more productive approach based on experience is that employed by troubleshooters. Some people seem to be natural troubleshooters, able to home in on cause quickly. Their initial focus is typically not on causes but on the effects of the problem. These effects are often all too visible, and they hold the clues that lead back to the cause. These people are still using experience, but are typically gathering more data before attempting to reach a conclusion.

AGREE ON THE PROBLEM

As the clues to discovering cause lie in the effects of the problem, the first step is to ask questions to gather relevant information about the problem, such as what exactly is affected and what is wrong with it. There may be some misunderstanding about what the actual problem is, especially if different people are seeing only a part of the problem as it relates to them.

For example, if a product is being bottled but slightly underfilled, this could have domino effects for quality control and distribution. Lack of good product could mean that there are delays in getting stocks to the customer, and if any of this bad product has reached the customer, this could lead to further complaints. The various managers in this

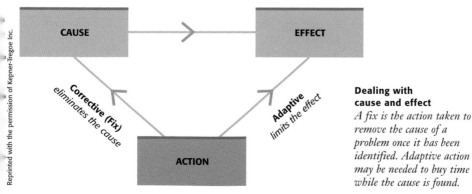

Dealing with cause and effect
A fix is the action taken to remove the cause of a problem once it has been identified. Adaptive action may be needed to buy time while the cause is found.

scenario will all be seeing different problems. The production manager has a "bottles underfilling" problem, while the quality assurance manager has a "high rejects" problem, the distribution manager has "lack of product," and the customer service manager is dealing with "customer complaints."

The underlying problem is that the bottles are not being filled properly, and the cause of this must be found. But other actions are needed to deal with the other effects. Only when the various parts of the situation are recognized is it possible to resolve it effectively.

GATHER INFORMATION

Once the essential problem has been agreed on, there is more information to be obtained, such as its location, timing, and size. Where and when does the problem occur, and how big a problem is it?

If this information is collected and organized, it can provide many ideas about the cause of the problem. It also serves as a blueprint against which these possible causes can be checked. Any cause must be able to explain how the effects are happening, and the cause that best explains all the information is most likely to be the right one.

When information is being gathered, remember that other people may have key pieces of data. For example, the user, the customer, the machine operator, and the supplier may all know something useful. Unfortunately, even experienced troubleshooters may ignore this valuable source of detail. Car mechanics and computer engineers often try to tackle problems with very scant information from the driver or computer user.

ROOT OUT THE CAUSE

When the effects are understood, then it is appropriate to start looking for cause. Experience is important here, too. Study the information you have gathered and ask yourself, and others, what could have caused this. If experience does not lead to any possible causes, there are techniques, such as formulating fishbone diagrams, that can prompt creative thinking.

Combining ideas is an important method to find cause, as many problems will occur only when there have been several contributing elements happening at the same time. Individually they may

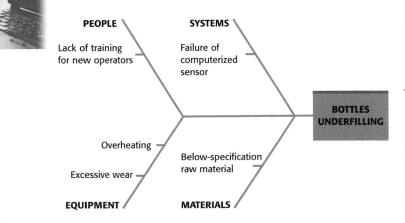

PEOPLE

Lack of training
for new operators

SYSTEMS

Failure of
computerized
sensor

**BOTTLES
UNDERFILLING**

Overheating

Below-specification
raw material

Excessive wear

EQUIPMENT

MATERIALS

**Using fishbone
diagrams for analysis**
*Fishbone diagrams
encourage a more
focused discussion by
concentrating the
thinking around specific
areas. In this example,
the problem is written
at the end of the
"spine." The four
"bones" are the relevant
sectors, with specific
causes listed on them.*

not cause a problem but, if they occur at the same time, they will do so.

Most problems are caused by a change. Everything was functioning well but now it is not, so something must have changed. Identifying exactly what it is that has changed can be another good way of getting ideas for cause.

JUSTIFYING THE CAUSE

When you have identified a list of causes, review them to see which one best explains the information you have about the problem. If you did a good job earlier of gathering data, you will have a better chance of finding the best fix.

You should then check if this cause is the right one before putting the fix into place. This may require a visual check: if the most likely cause is a worn part, go and look at it. Sometimes a test or experiment may provide the proof, or you may need to ask some questions to confirm your ideas. The goal should be to ensure that the root cause has been identified and that any fix will therefore eliminate the problem.

It may also be necessary to step back and consider other factors contributing to the cause. Systems and processes may need to be changed to ensure that future problems do not occur.

THE DECISION-MAKING PROCESS

WHENEVER YOU ARE FACED WITH A NUMBER OF DIFFERENT COURSES OF ACTION TO RESOLVE A SITUATION, YOU WILL HAVE TO MAKE A DECISION. OFTEN A DECISION WILL HAVE SIGNIFICANT REPERCUSSIONS, SO IT IS VITAL TO MAKE AN INFORMED CHOICE.

IDENTIFYING THE RIGHT APPROACH TO DECISION-MAKING

As mentioned earlier, sometimes a decision is needed to get the best fix for a problem. But other decisions are often related to finding ways to do work better, or to make it easier for others to do their jobs. Irrespective of the reason for the decision, a logical approach will improve the chance of making a good one.

When making decisions, you need to understand the impact of your choices. In some decisions, the results may be the same whatever course of action you adopt. If, for example, you have to allocate a project to one member of your team, and they are all equally capable of doing the work, it will not matter which one you choose. If all the alternatives open to you will achieve your objectives equally well, and have the same amount of risk (*see* page 197), you may just as well pick one out of a hat and not waste too much time thinking about it.

Similarly, small decisions are quickly guided by asking some simple questions:
- What criteria am I trying to meet?
- What are the choices?
- Which one best fits my criteria?
- What is the downside of this choice?

If the downside outweighs the benefit, look at the next best fit until you find one with which you are comfortable. For

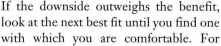

decisions that are going to have a great impact, where the final choice is likely to mean the difference between significant success and failure, it is worth investing time to get it right.

GATHERING INFORMATION

As with the previous section on finding causes, gathering data is very important in decision-making. However, one difference is in the timeframe. When gathering information about a problem, you are looking at something that has already happened, and you can therefore get factual information. In the case of decision-making, you are gathering data that will affect behavior now and in the future, so you will probably have to make a number of assumptions.

For example, when choosing a supplier you may want a local company, so you select one that manufactures in the next city. However, six months later that supplier decides to move operations to another country. You had assumed that the company would remain local; you should have checked your assumption before making the decision.

USE A LOGICAL APPROACH

A rational approach to decision-making would start by gaining agreement on the criteria of the decision. Once these have been agreed upon, it is a relatively simple task to assess the alternative choices against the criteria. Figure out what you need in order to make this decision a success. When compiling your

AVOIDING THE PITFALLS OF DECISION-MAKING

There are many pitfalls awaiting the decision-maker, who may well be unaware of any of them. The most common ones include:
- having a favorite alternative
- ignoring risks
- not searching for alternatives
- focusing on only one aspect of the decision.

Many managers approach a decision with a preferred alternative already in mind. This can create difficulties when a group of managers are making a decision together and they each have a different favorite alternative. In this case the discussion will typically focus on the alternatives or choices, with each person focusing on what is good about their personal favorite and not taking into account the others' alternatives. This kind of meeting will usually be unproductive. It may result in the most senior person, or the most persuasive speaker, getting the alternative of their choice. This will not necessarily be the right choice for the group or organization.

Getting too caught up in the benefits of a choice and not considering the risks can be very dangerous. For example, offering a sales job to an industry expert who knows all the aspects of your market may seem like a good idea, but if it turns out that the person lacks interpersonal skills and upsets all your customers, your choice will not achieve the results for which you had hoped.

Sometimes poor decisions are made because not enough alternatives have been explored. For example, when looking for a new supplier of a product, it may be tempting to consider only the two suppliers you are already using for other products. After all, you know them and you are satisfied with their service so far. However, unless you look for other possible suppliers you will not really know if your current ones are the best.

Finally, putting too much weight on one aspect of the decision can lead you down the wrong path. Among the most common examples is always going for the cheapest option available, or always considering only the short-term benefits. Both these approaches can lead to inappropriate choices.

information, think about other people who may be able to contribute, including:

- colleagues
- senior managers
- customers
- suppliers
- industry experts
- shareholders
- subordinates
- stakeholders in the decision.

Different people may have relevant input to different parts of the process. For example, when a new computer system is being selected, senior managers and colleagues may want to contribute to the criteria with ideas around cost or functionality. Meanwhile, suppliers and industry experts are certain to have information about alternative systems that are available.

If you actively seek out the range of possible choices, you will increase your chances of success. When you have a list of the choices, eliminate those that you know will not meet your standards. Consider how well the remaining choices match your set of criteria.

WEIGHING UP THE RISK

You must always consider the risks inherent in a decision as well as the benefits. When you have narrowed down your top alternatives, you should review them for any downside. If you identify any risk, this can be weighed against the benefits, giving a balanced decision.

For example, a start-up company may offer a software package that seems to meet all your requirements for tracking your sales and marketing efforts. You would have to weigh that benefit against the fact that the supplier and product do not have a track record of success. This could be a big risk.

The level of acceptable risk will vary between organizations and individuals. Some people may be willing to take a big risk if the proposed action offers the chance of significant gain. Other people may be much more comfortable with a low-risk alternative, even if they have to compromise on benefits.

Once the decision has been made and the risk accepted, then it is possible to minimize that risk (*see* page 198).

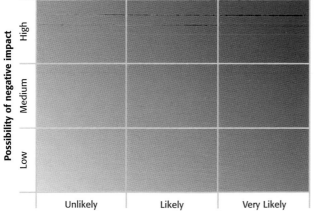

Possibility of negative impact — High / Medium / Low

Likelihood of risk occurring — Unlikely / Likely / Very Likely

Assessing risk in decision-making
All but the most simple, straightforward decisions will involve an element of risk. The rational approach is to balance it against the possible benefit. Try to assess the likelihood of the risk occurring, and how bad an effect it would have if it came about. Then you will know how risky your decision may be.

Key
■ *Significant risk*
□ *Smaller risk*

IMPLEMENTING SOLUTIONS TO PROBLEMS AND DECISIONS

ONCE THE ROOT CAUSE OF A PROBLEM HAS BEEN DISCOVERED, OR A DECISION HAS BEEN MADE, YOU SHOULD THEN FOCUS ON THE IMPLEMENTATION OF THE FIX OR THE DECISION. YOUR PREVIOUS EFFORTS WILL BE WASTED IF THE EXECUTION IS POOR.

UNDERSTANDING RISK AS PART OF THE SOLUTION

Risk, as has been seen, is an important consideration in the decision-making process. Now, in the implementation phase, you need to do something about those risks. There are several options to consider:

- accept the risk
- stop it from happening
- be ready to deal with it when it occurs.

The first option is viable if the risk is small with a low impact. Some known risks could be avoided by adopting a different course of action. If, say, you were concerned about possible late delivery of a part because the supplier had a poor delivery record, you could arrange to pick up the part and eliminate that area of concern.

Sometimes you cannot stop problems from happening, but you can be ready for them. For example, every time you conduct a fire drill in the workplace, or get a supplier to sign a confidentiality agreement, you are preparing for a future problem. You hope that the problem will never happen but, if it does, you will be better prepared.

It is worthwhile spending some time identifying these kinds of problems, so that preventive and contingent actions can be put into place. This can save valuable time and money.

LOOKING FOR OPPORTUNITIES IN THE SOLUTION

As well as understanding and managing the procedures related to implementing solutions, it is useful to look for extra opportunities. Additional benefits can often be identified and capitalized on.

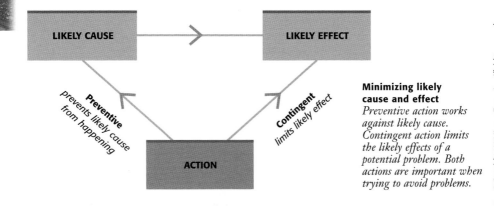

Minimizing likely cause and effect
Preventive action works against likely cause. Contingent action limits the likely effects of a potential problem. Both actions are important when trying to avoid problems.

When you are implementing something new, there is sometimes a chance to achieve more than you originally set out to do. For example, if you are stopping production to replace a part of the machinery, consider whether there are other jobs that can be done at the same time while the machine is down. Or, if you are training members of staff in one part of the business, perhaps you could include people from another area, who would benefit from the same training without increasing costs.

THINKING IT THROUGH

After you have carefully worked out and implemented your solution, asking some pertinent questions can ensure things continue to run smoothly. For example:
- Who should know about this implementation?
- Have we dealt with any related issues?
- When do we need to review this?
- Has our fix worked?
- Are our assumptions holding true?

Effective communication is always very important, in any area of management. In this case, the chances are that you have made changes that will impact on other areas of the business or customers and suppliers. If they are not informed of these changes, you could be storing up more problems for the future.

If you have dealt with a problem, or made and implemented a decision, remember that there could be related issues that still require some action. For example, a faulty product in the factory may have been corrected, and this is fine. But what if some of the product got out to customers? They may face problems with it. You may also want to look at limiting any other damage caused.

MANAGING THE WORK

Where implementation of a solution is complex, it is worth treating it as a project, a subject in itself. However, a checklist for implementation is useful; here are some questions to consider:
- Is the result agreed upon and understood?
- What work needs to be done?
- Who will do it?
- How much will it cost?
- What resources will you need?
- how long will it take?
- When do you need to start?
- What should be done first?
- How do the tasks relate to each other?
- What could go wrong?
- What opportunities do you have?
- How will you track the activity?

Reviewing the situation regularly to check that your solution is working could be important. Some solutions may be only temporary, or may develop further problems that were unforeseeable.

If you have done a thorough job of finding the right cause of a problem and selecting an appropriate fix, then that fix should work, but sometimes it is only possible to know that you have got it right after you have implemented the process. It is important to monitor the results of your implementation.

Similarly, check any assumptions you made when making a decision. Do they hold steady when you take action? If you find inconsistencies, you may need to act to get things back on track.

Finally, review the outcome and identify the lessons learned. Incorporate your learning into future plans, and so ensure continuous improvement.

change
AND INNOVATION

IN A CONSTANTLY CHANGING WORLD, IT IS
ESSENTIAL THAT ORGANIZATIONS ARE ALSO ABLE
TO CHANGE. TO BE SUCCESSFUL, THEY MUST
CONSTANTLY STRIVE TO ADAPT TO NEW
CHALLENGES. THE CHANGES MAY BE INNOVATIVE,
STRATEGIC, PHYSICAL, OR BEHAVIORAL.

As a manager, you need first to understand why
organizations have to be prepared for change, and that
change may be either innovative or strategic. Innovative
change is continuous improvement within the framework
of existing resources, while strategic change involves doing
something new. Each process requires a different approach.

Most managers can plan and execute physical changes
successfully. It is in the area of behavioral change that they
have the most difficulty, and you need to understand the
influences here. To implement change successfully, you
have to create the right conditions for motivating and
involving people; one of these is the commitment to
effective leadership. Crucially, you can maximize your
chances of success with a careful evaluation of your plan.

RECOGNIZING THE NEED FOR ORGANIZATIONAL CHANGE

IN A FAST-MOVING, HIGHLY COMPETITIVE WORLD MARKETPLACE, ORGANIZATIONS NEED TO CHANGE TO STAY ALIVE. FOR COMMERCIAL ORGANIZATIONS; THIS MEANS THEY MUST REMAIN PROFITABLE. FOR PUBLIC SECTOR ORGANIZATIONS, IT MEANS THEY MUST DELIVER "BEST VALUE" SERVICES.

SUPPLY AND DEMAND

Modern technology and the accompanying advances in both physical and electronic communications have made it possible for an individual working anywhere in the world to develop something that can, in a few short years, challenge giants. The reasons are simple.

First, supply has outstripped demand. The familiar world of finite supply and infinite demand, where all suppliers could earn a living whatever they produced, has been replaced by a world of infinite supply and finite demand. The customer, not the supplier, is now "king." This has increased competition, with market share being the key goal: companies that want to grow in a finite market must target someone else's customers.

Second, there is the development of the international company with its global business strategies. Such companies target markets throughout the world, and are prepared to spend vast sums of money promoting themselves. Their manufacturing strategies ensure that they have highly productive specialized plants in strategic places around the world to service these markets, thus minimizing production costs. They develop pricing policies to ensure competitiveness in local markets, and can afford to weed out local competition if it becomes a problem.

Third, the emergence of physical and electronic communication networks has provided a reliable means of transporting goods and information quickly from one place to another. It has enabled "new age" organizations to provide instant access to their products and services around the world through the internet.

GETTING READY FOR ORGANIZATIONAL CHANGE

All of these developments mean that organizations must adopt strategies for integrating continuing change into their operating procedures. These change procedures take two forms:

- Innovative change procedures: those that enable organizations to improve the effectiveness with which they use their existing resources.
- Strategic change procedures: those that enable organizations to change what they do and the way they do it.

CHECKLIST

✔ *Dedicated to customer satisfaction*
✔ *Continually seeking new and better ways of doing things*
✔ *Committed to reducing costs*
✔ *Value employees/encourage development*
✔ *Determined to remain competitive*
✔ *Committed to shareholder value.*

IDENTIFYING THE NEED FOR INNOVATIVE CHANGE

INNOVATIVE CHANGE IMPROVES WHAT WE ALREADY DO. THESE IMPROVEMENTS MAY INVOLVE CHANGES IN WORKING PRACTICES AND PROCESSES; CHANGES IN DESIGN, ASSEMBLY, OR DELIVERY OF PRODUCTS; OR CHANGES IN MATERIALS MANAGEMENT.

CHANGES IN WORKING PRACTICES

Changes in the way people actually do their jobs involve a number of factors, including the introduction of team-working, flatter structures, performance management, and self-management. The biggest changes in working practices in recent years have been:

- the change from single skill to multiskilling, which has enabled organizations to create small multi-purpose teams, thus optimizing the use of people
- the move from traditional hierarchical organization structures to flatter organizations focused on results rather than status
- the introduction of "empowerment" to solve organizational problems through permanent work teams and cross-functional teams.

CHANGES IN WORKING PROCESSES

Changing the way that work is processed through organizations and the way it is done takes two forms:

- new organizational processes, aimed at shortening order-cycle times
- new work processes, aimed at reducing the time taken to do a specific job.

Reducing the order-cycle time – the time taken from receipt of an order or work instruction to the delivery of the product or service – involves mapping the order-cycle processes and then analyzing them to reduce wastage. Making reductions in order-cycle time can yield very significant improvements in productivity: a reduction of 10 days, say, in a 30-day order cycle increases productivity capacity by a third.

Work process innovation, involving employees in seeking ways of doing work more effectively, has been enormously beneficial in terms of both improving productivity and enhancing worker motivation. Various methods have been developed to enable this improvement, the best known being the Japanese JIT ("Just In Time") and Kaizen (which is about continuous, gradual change).

The key point here is to have a tangible methodology which can be promoted throughout the organization, and through which results can be monitored and controlled.

CHANGES IN DESIGN

Original designs for both products and services reflect the conditions prevailing at the time they are developed. As time goes by, technology and materials change – as do people's needs for services and the way these are delivered.

To remain competitive, producer organizations need to constantly review how they make things: the process, materials, equipment, and so on – indeed, whether they should be making some components at all. Equally, service providers need to constantly review their services and make continuing changes to ensure their survival.

CHANGES IN
MATERIALS MANAGEMENT

Materials management, often referred to as the management of the "logistics" chain, has led to very significant savings for organizations. Improvements are focused on the control of the flow of components into organizations and out again as products on a Just-In-Time basis.

Many organizations use specialized suppliers for this service. These suppliers take responsibility for both the materials management process and, more recently, for the purchasing of parts, components, and services. Economies of scale can be very considerable.

IMPLEMENTING
INNOVATIVE CHANGE

Whether change takes place in the private or public sector, the same policies and procedures of implementation apply.

Innovative change starts with senior management deciding on the introduction of a policy of continuous improvement, and determining the methods they will use. They may choose, for example, the JIT tool mentioned earlier, or TQM (Total Quality Management), or TPM (Total Productive Maintenance).

Once the tools have been chosen and deployed, and people trained, the results become the responsibility of the workers and the first-line managers. Continuous improvement involves all employees in a process of investigation that results in hundreds of small changes, most of them

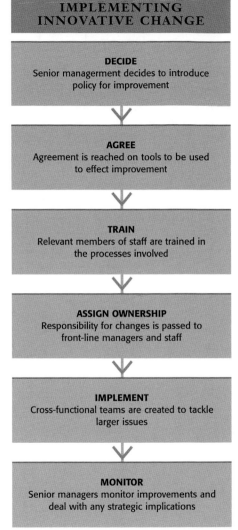

IMPLEMENTING INNOVATIVE CHANGE

DECIDE
Senior managerment decides to introduce policy for improvement

AGREE
Agreement is reached on tools to be used to effect improvement

TRAIN
Relevant members of staff are trained in the processes involved

ASSIGN OWNERSHIP
Responsibility for changes is passed to front-line managers and staff

IMPLEMENT
Cross-functional teams are created to tackle larger issues

MONITOR
Senior managers monitor improvements and deal with any strategic implications

actioned by supervisors and their teams in the workplace. Larger changes that overlap departmental boundaries are carried out by cross-functional teams. Senior management's chief involvement is in authorizing any strategic changes that arise, and monitoring the benefits of ongoing improvements.

IDENTIFYING THE NEED FOR STRATEGIC CHANGE

STRATEGIC CHANGE INVOLVES A CHANGE OF DIRECTION: DOING SOMETHING NEW OR IN A DIFFERENT WAY TO MAINTAIN OR ENHANCE THE ORGANIZATION'S SUCCESS. SUCH CHANGES MAY AFFECT THE PRODUCT, ITS DESIGN, PRODUCTION, PRICE, MARKET, PROMOTION, DISTRIBUTION, OR FIELD SUPPORT.

MAINTAINING SHAREHOLDER VALUE

The primary force driving strategic change in both the private and public sectors is economic. In the private sector, shareholders set the desired level of income, while customers (the market) determine the actual income through their buying choices and the amount they are willing to pay. Performance standards are set by the competition.

The task of management is to stimulate the required level of demand by satisfying customers' needs, and to control operating costs to ensure that shareholders' expectations are met.

This inevitably means change. Products, no matter how efficiently they are produced, will at some point become outdated. Technological advances have led, for example, to the replacement of typewriters by computers, resulting in the closure of "old technology" plants and of the investment in new ones.

Markets, no matter how secure they seem, change with the changing tastes of customers. For example, water was once regarded as an unmarketable commodity; today a huge variety can be found in stores across the globe. No matter how well controlled, production costs in developed economies inevitably become too high, and lower-cost opportunities need to be explored. This is exemplified in the decision of many major western companies not to invest in their home country, but to move production to other countries where labor and operating costs are significantly lower – those in central Europe, for example.

The main factors impacting the profitability of firms in the private sector, and thus the strategic decision-making process, are:

- changes in the desirability of the product or service being offered
- changes in the price
- changes in the size of the market – the volumes it will absorb
- changes in the way the product or service is promoted
- changes in the way the product or service is distributed
- changes in the way the product or service is supported in the field
- changes in the costs of labor and operations.

CHANGES IN PRODUCT DESIRABILITY

Products – and services – need to change to reflect changing market conditions. People want products that they feel will enhance their lifestyles. Cell phones are popular, for example, because they enable people to contact each other when they want to, wherever they are. Prepacked food is popular because it requires no preparation and emphasizes convenience. Advances in technology enable suppliers to meet old needs in new ways, and so steal others' market share.

CHANGES IN PRODUCT PRICE

Price changes are usually reductions, driven by competitive pressures. They have become a powerful factor of modern industrial life – organizations must have a low cost base to survive.

Alcatel, one of the largest French communications companies, is a case in point. It forecast in 1999 that to remain competitive, it would have to achieve a 5 percent year-on-year reduction in production costs over the five years up to 2004. It made a strategic decision to do so.

CHANGES IN MARKET SIZE

The volume of products that can be sold in any given market is finite, and always changing. It is a big task to change the production capacity of an organization, either up or down. Managers need to be fully aware of the implications of change in market size and production capacity to manage these changes effectively. The problems in the steel industry since World War II are a good example of what happens when change is not managed well. Steel is a market that is characterized by over-supply due to new (cheap) capacity and reducing demand, and many suppliers are suffering.

CHANGES IN PROMOTION

People buy what they see. Effective promotion is basic to commercial success. It takes two forms:
- awareness: creating an awareness of the product or brand, usually through some form of advertising
- availability: having the product or service where the buyers are.

Changes in the way products are promoted and their availability have a significant impact on sales. Personal computers are an interesting example. Most of the industry sells either through its own sales forces or through retailers, including mail-order houses and value-added resellers. The highly successful US computer maker Dell uses a different model, linking its promotion to supply through direct distribution, including the internet. Similarly, if your child's favorite breakfast cereal, as promoted on early morning TV, is not on the supermarket shelf, you buy a product that is.

CHANGES IN DISTRIBUTION

Overnight delivery of goods and services is now commonplace in the developed world. The internet and e-commerce are in the process of changing for ever how things are bought. The ease with which they can reach consumers is shown by the Napster case, and the demand by the

CREATING CHANGE IN THE PUBLIC SECTOR

Strategic change in the public sector differs from the private sector in that government sets the service levels and the investment it is willing to make to achieve these. Public sector managers have the task of delivering the level and quality of services required within the cost parameters. Performance standards are set by comparison with best-in-class performance.

Thus for the public sector, strategic change is focused mainly on the need to balance service requirements, that is, what is desired by consumers, and the aspirations of their elected representatives and legislation, against the funds available.

industry to have it closed down and replaced by "industry-approved" retailers only. The Napster site was created to allow people to swap music free of charge (enabling an individual to buy a new CD and share it). The music industry took Napster to court for breach of copyright; as a result, Napster was ordered by a US judge to stop the practice.

CHANGES IN FIELD SUPPORT

People buying expensive products or services expect a backup service, which historically meant suppliers establishing support networks in areas where they wished to trade. With new ways of distribution, suppliers can now reach many more customers, often where they have no established support facilities. In this case, suppliers must find new ways of supporting them. They may, for example, replace direct employees with agency agreements, or offer replacement products rather than repair.

CHANGES IN LABOR AND OPERATING COSTS

Materials and production technology costs are fairly standard, no matter where in the world goods are produced. The real differentiation is the cost of labor and operations. Senior managers must continually seek the lowest cost base in order to remain competitive, and be prepared to move plant, design, and expertise to optimize economies.

IMPLEMENTING STRATEGIC CHANGE

Strategic change is a onetime activity, directly linked to the organization's business goals. It is the responsibility of senior management, who plan resources, communicate about, and directly manage

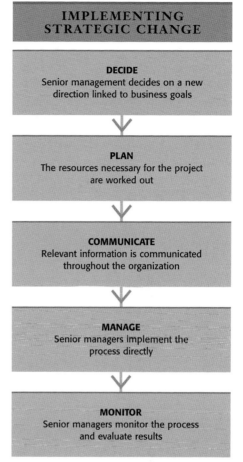

IMPLEMENTING STRATEGIC CHANGE

DECIDE
Senior management decides on a new direction linked to business goals

PLAN
The resources necessary for the project are worked out

COMMUNICATE
Relevant information is communicated throughout the organization

MANAGE
Senior managers implement the process directly

MONITOR
Senior managers monitor the process and evaluate results

the process. A good example of strategic change would be the competition between the Betamax and VHS home video systems. The Sony corporation introduced Betamax in the mid-1970s, while a rival electronics manufacturer was developing a similar system known as VHS. Despite its reported audio and visual inferiority, the VHS system met with huge commercial success, whereas Betamax was left behind. Sony subsequently scaled-down its Betamax program and today produces VHS recorders.

CHANGING BEHAVIOR

WHILE MOST CHANGES MAY APPEAR TO BE TECHNICAL, THEY ARE ALL ESSENTIALLY ABOUT PEOPLE AND THEIR BEHAVIOR. AT ITS SIMPLEST, CHANGE INVOLVES INCREASING KNOWLEDGE AND DEVELOPING NEW SKILLS; ON A LARGE SCALE, IT DEMANDS THAT ALL EMPLOYEES MODIFY THEIR BEHAVIOR.

WHO CHANGES AND WHY?

All change affects people to a greater or lesser extent, depending on what kind of change it is. If it is a new product or service, or an improvement such as reducing tool changeover times on production machines, the main changes will be felt at the operating level. If, however, the change has to do with behavior – improving staff motivation, for example, or teamworking – then the onus is on management change.

To ensure the success of a change program, everyone in the organization must change to some degree. In practice, this means understanding two forces:
● what influences behavior
● what motivates people to change.

BEHAVIORAL INFLUENCES

There are five factors that influence the way people behave at work: knowledge, skills, beliefs, environment, and purpose.

The influence of knowledge

This is what people must know to be able to do what is required, and it is the easiest element to change. Introducing staff to an upgraded software package, for example, may require users to be taught new commands, but most people can cope. There is no need to let go of existing knowledge, only to acquire more.

The influence of skills

Skills are the abilities people need to carry out new tasks, and they may be physical or behavioral. Physical skills are needed for physical tasks: becoming computer literate means acquiring keyboard skills, and so on. Behavioral skills are needed to "get things done." Learning how to conduct meetings, or manage customer relations effectively, means learning a range of process and interpersonal skills.

Skills are more difficult to change or develop than knowledge, as they often involve changes in instinctive behavior patterns. It takes time to change an employee's instinctive response to a customer query from "What do you want?" to "How can I help you?"

The influence of beliefs

Beliefs determine attitudes, which in turn determine whether knowledge and skills are applied in practice. People can be given the knowledge and skills they need to work in a different way, but they may not apply them because the proposed new way of working cuts across their belief systems. Thus training supervisors to carry out team meetings will not, of itself, ensure that such meetings are run well. This can be ensured only through monitoring and control. Beliefs are very difficult to change as they require people to let go of established behavior.

The influence of environment

An organization's environment affects people's behavior by rewarding desired behavior and correcting undesired behavior. It is "subconscious" in that one cannot touch it, yet it is the key determinant of people's behavior at work. With people, "What you stroke [reward] is what you get." Successful organizations are successful because they encourage people to behave effectively; ineffective organizations fail because they accept ineffective behaviors.

The influence of purpose

Purpose is determined by the collective beliefs of the organization's leaders, and creates the environment. Purpose is enshrined in the organization's vision of the future, and its values. Leaders with a clear vision of the future and a common purpose create an environment that encourages productive behavior, while leaders with no common sense of purpose create only confusion.

THE BEHAVIORAL EQUATION

It is the combination of these five factors that determines effectiveness. Purpose creates the environment. Environment provides the "reward and punishment culture" that determines the motivation of employees. Simple changes, such as the introduction of new technology, can be achieved through appropriate training

to provide the knowledge and skills to do the job, and the introduction of controls to ensure effectiveness. On the other hand, the introduction of a 360-degree performance review procedure requires both training and facilitation to change "beliefs." Adopting any management philosophy requires the development of a comprehensive implementation strategy involving all parts of the equation.

THE MOTIVATORS OF CHANGE

Human beings are naturally resistant to change. To accept it, they need to be motivated. People will accept change if they perceive it to offer:

- the opportunity for significant gain
- the avoidance of significant pain.

Successful change initiatives combine the twin motivators of gain and pain, offering gain but with a clear downside if things go wrong (pain). For example, a supervisor introducing teamworking can balance the additional work involved against the benefits for team members (sharing the savings achieved through increased productivity).

IDENTIFYING BEHAVIOURAL INFLUENCES

INFLUENCE	DESCRIPTION
Knowledge	What people need to know to do the job, building on existing knowledge.
Skills	The abilities, physical or behavioral, that people need to carry out new tasks.
Beliefs	Determine whether people will apply their new skills and techniques in practice.
Environment	The key determinant, created by the organization's purpose, that sets standards of what is acceptable.
Purpose	Determined by the organization's vision, and creates the environment.

CREATING THE CONDITIONS FOR SUCCESSFUL CHANGE

SUCCESSFUL CHANGE INITIATIVES ARE MADE, NOT BORN. YOU NEED A STRUCTURED APPROACH FOR PLANNING THE BEHAVIORAL ASPECTS OF CHANGE INITIATIVES, WHETHER THE CHANGE IS INNOVATIVE OR STRATEGIC.

CREATE A FRAMEWORK FOR CHANGE

The behavioral aspects inherent in any change must be properly considered. The following sequence of actions can be used for any "size" of change, whether this is individual change, changing the way of working in a department, or total organizational change.

To develop the framework for your change program, consider each of the sections in turn.

DEFINE THE DESIRED CHANGE

Whether the change involves a dilemma to be resolved or an opportunity to be taken, you should start by producing a statement setting out what is to be changed and why. If others are involved, the proposal should be discussed with all stakeholders to gain understanding and agreement that this is the real problem to be solved. Remember Peter Drucker's dictum: "You can always put right the wrong solution on the right problem; what you can never put right is the right solution on the wrong problem."

STATE THE REQUIRED OUTCOMES

What results should the changes produce? A 20 percent increase in profitability, for example? A higher level of customer satisfaction, a more highly motivated work force, to be seen as a "best-in-class supplier"? Make sure that you use simple language to "visualize" the change – words that can easily be communicated to employees.

The best way to "visualize" change is to identify an organization that you would like to resemble, and use it as a benchmark. You can then arrange for employees to "see" what things will look like after the change.

RELATE CHANGE TO A VALUED GOAL

Things that are measured get done. The reason for the change must be linked to a valued business goal, otherwise it will not survive. Managements whose personal reward is linked to shareholder value are motivated to maximize the share price. To ensure the sustainability of change, there must be an underlying reason for the project, which is important to those who have the power to make it happen. This needs to be clearly defined and understood by all involved.

COMMIT TO LEADERSHIP

For change initiatives to be successful, whatever their scope, senior management must both agree to the change and be committed to its implications. Leading change means being involved and also being willing to change yourself. There is no value in introducing teamworking to increase productivity if management refuses to let go of the decision-making process. Clarify what commitment you need from whom and develop a strategy for getting it.

UNDERSTAND THE BEHAVIORAL IMPLICATIONS

What changes in knowledge, skills, beliefs, environment, and purpose – the behavioral equation – need to take place to support the proposed change? What changes are required in the current reward systems to promote the desired new behaviors?

Both the direct and the indirect implications need to be reviewed, listed, and understood before the change process is started. Introducing a pay scale by results, for example, means linking the reward to the ability to pay; it means change for managers (monitoring and control) and for the accounts department. It also creates expectations for individuals, who will be led to think: "If I play my part to the best of my ability, I will be rewarded accordingly."

For example, it is not possible to introduce a program of Total Quality Management (which is about constantly improving processes and products) with any chance of success if senior management do not believe in quality (although many organizations have tried!). Improving product quality inevitably involves design, purchasing, sales and finance, and, most importantly, a change in management attitudes.

CHOOSE THE RIGHT TOOLS

All change programs are really projects, thus the basic tool of change management is project management. However, different changes will be based on different operational tools. The two broad areas of change, innovation, and strategy, each use different approaches.

Tools for innovative change

While the delivery of innovative change is the responsibility of employees, it is the responsibility of senior management to introduce the procedural tools that integrate continuous improvement into the day-to-day management practices of organizations, and to monitor their long-term effectiveness. Successful innovative change is based on simple repeatable processes that can be easily monitored and controlled. These set out the structure of the activity and how it will be managed and controlled.

Today there are many tried, tested, and valuable processes that can be used. For example, in addition to the Japanese Kaizen method mentioned earlier, used to deliver continuous improvement, the Malcolm Baldrige/EFQM (European Foundation for Quality Management) Excellence models can be used for re-engineering business processes. This measures the health of a business using nonfinancial methods. There are many ways in which TQM can help to improve performance, while keeping total customer satisfaction as an approach to focus customer service, Six Sigma to improve quality, and Team Briefing, or 360-degree Appraisals, to improve internal understanding (*see* pages 244–5).

Once the right tool has been selected, the next step is to develop an outline plan for implementing it, along with procedures for monitoring and control. Note that it is important at this stage to determine the conditions for rewarding the desired behaviors, and correcting those members of staff who do not conform.

Tools for strategic change

Strategic change is by its very nature a "onetime" activity: once the change has been made, the project is complete. Strategic changes fall into three main categories, as follows:

- technical – for example changing technology, targeting new markets, moving production from a high-cost to a low-cost area of the world
- procedural – changing the way things are done, for example, outsourcing logistics, integrating information systems, achieving accreditation to some recognized standard
- managerial – changing the way that the organization is managed: for example, flattening the structure, introducing self-managed work teams or performance management.

All the methods described earlier that deliver innovative change can have a strategic application, too. The Balance Scorecard approach, in addition, is an increasingly used methodology for combining strategic and tactical considerations. However, it is more likely that each organization will introduce those changes that best suit its particular circumstances, and will therefore tend to develop its own model.

INVOLVE ALL THE STAKEHOLDERS

For any change to be successful, all stakeholders in the organization must be involved in the process.

While most of these individuals cannot influence the "what" of the change, they can certainly influence the "how." You should identify all those people who will be affected by the proposed changes, and make a point of talking with them. Discuss the details of the plan and ask for their views. If these stakeholders are involved before the die is cast, they are much more likely to feel that they "own" the change and are committed to it. This will make implementation of the plan easier.

USE A STRATEGY TO CREATE BEHAVIORAL CHANGE

The implementation of most changes is relatively easy from a technical perspective. The problem is to gain the commitment of all those employees who will have to work with the change.

The only way to gain commitment is through genuine involvement, and one very effective way of doing this is through using "in-plant action learning." This method uses cross-functional teams of specialists and people from the areas affected by the proposed project, as the primary implementers of change.

Once senior management has decided what it wants to do, mixed teams are set up to implement the processes. These teams, which are supported by a facilitator, receive some initial training in problem-solving and teamworking. They then work directly for a sponsoring manager, thus involving all employees in the change process and encouraging commitment to it.

MONITOR AND CONTROL THE PROCESSES

Both the process of implementation and the result being achieved must be measured. Targets should be agreed upon and performance indicators identified, while performance must be regularly reviewed. This allows management to monitor and control the progress of the change.

LEADING CHANGE INITIATIVES

LEADERSHIP IS THE ABILITY TO INSPIRE OTHER PEOPLE TO DO WHAT IS REQUIRED TO ACHIEVE THE ORGANIZATION'S DESIRED GOALS. IN THE FIELD OF CHANGE AND INNOVATION, LEADERS PROVIDE WHAT IS NEEDED TO ENSURE CHANGE INITIATIVES ARE DELIVERED SUCCESSFULLY.

IDENTIFYING THE LEADERSHIP FUNCTION

Effective leadership is crucial for successful change at every level in the organization. When introducing major change, it is the task of the management team to provide this leadership and to ensure that it is reflected down the organization. For local change, it is the responsibility of the supervisor or team leader to provide the leadership.

It is important to remember that people facing change are being asked to enter the unknown. The leader is the one who provides the vision of the future, who inspires people's confidence that the future, after the change, will be better than today, and that he or she knows how to get to the destination.

There are the many definitions of leadership, but a good working guide is to consider it as motivating people to accomplish defined objectives willingly. This definition highlights two key features of leadership:
- it is concerned with harnessing people's drives, needs, and wants
- it is goal-orientated.

These features relate in different ways at the process level and the behavioral level.

At the process level, leaders must:
- have a vision of the future
- identify clear goals about what to change and why
- communicate clearly and be willing to debate issues
- agree how to implement the change, and involve people in the process
- clarify roles and controls
- agree how open, two-way communication will be maintained throughout the implementation of the change
- manage the process to ensure that the project is successfully delivered.

At the behavioral level, leaders must:
- develop trust through open two-way communication
- respect people and treat them with dignity
- be involved at every stage in the process to maximize ownership
- recognize employees' knowledge and skills
- be available to help
- be seen as a leader by others.

In practice, leading successful change projects means:
- agreeing on the objectives
- deciding on the tasks
- planning how they will be done
- organizing the resources
- communicating tasks
- making people responsible
- monitoring and controlling.

Good leaders understand this and behave accordingly. Leadership is an essential skill, which all managers need to learn.

EVALUATING CHANGE INITIATIVES

MOST CHANGE INITIATIVES THAT FAIL DO SO BECAUSE THEY DO NOT REFLECT THE NEEDS OF THOSE INVOLVED. THE RISK OF FAILURE CAN BE MINIMIZED BY ASSESSING WHETHER CHANGE INITIATIVES HAVE BEEN DESIGNED WITH BEHAVIORAL IMPLICATIONS IN MIND.

USING THE CHECKLIST

The assessment of change is best done by a small team, as this creates the opportunity for debate. Choose a change you are planning. Give each member of the team a copy of the checklist. They should study all the questions, section by section, and answer yes or no to each. Any undecided response should be counted as a negative. Then collate the copies of the checklist.

For an exercise in retrospective evaluation, use the checklist to assess a recent change initiative.

Any questions with a "no" answer will identify a weakness, which demands swift and appropriate action.

Definition of the dilemma to be resolved or opportunity to be taken	
1 *Is there a clear statement setting out what is to be changed and why?*	YES / NO
2 *Has this been discussed with all involved to gain understanding and agreement?*	YES / NO
3 *Is the focus on problems, not symptoms?*	YES / NO

Statement of the desired outcomes	
4 *Is there a clear statement setting out what will be different at the end of the change process?*	YES / NO
5 *Has this been discussed with all involved to gain understanding and agreement?*	YES / NO
6 *Has a benchmark organization been identified?*	YES / NO

Commitment of the senior management team to the leadership of the initiative	
7 *Is the senior management team really committed to change?*	YES / NO
8 *Do all members understand the implications for them?*	YES / NO
9 *Will they all survive the process?*	YES / NO
10 *Does the desired outcome have a direct relationship to a valued business goal?*	YES / NO

Stakeholder involvement through creating the motivation and commitment to change	
11 *Have the key stakeholders been identified?*	YES / NO
12 *Have they been involved in designing the change?*	YES / NO
13 *Is there evidence of this?*	YES / NO
14 *Is it likely they will cooperate?*	YES / NO
15 *Is there evidence that their views have been taken into account?*	YES / NO
16 *Have both plus and minus motivators been identified and built into the plan?*	YES / NO

Choice of the "tool"	
17 *Has the change been categorized as innovative or strategic?*	YES / NO
18 *Has a suitable tool been selected to implement the change?*	YES / NO
19 *Does everybody know what it is?*	YES / NO
20 *Does everybody know how it will work?*	YES / NO
21 *Is it known who has used it before?*	YES / NO
22 *Is it known what their experience was like?*	YES / NO
23 *Would you recommend it?*	YES / NO

Use of a disciplined, action learning-based implementation strategy	
24 *Is there a composite program covering the change?*	YES / NO
25 *Does it have milestones, timescales, costs?*	YES / NO
26 *Has it been communicated to all concerned?*	YES / NO
27 *Is someone at senior level taking responsibility for managing the implementation?*	YES / NO
28 *Does it embrace learning opportunities and have the capability for change?*	YES / NO
29 *Is it based on "action learning"?*	YES / NO

Focus on measuring success	
30 *Have performance indicators been identified and targets agreed?*	YES / NO
31 *Is there an effective monitoring and control structure in place?*	YES / NO
32 *Is the information being used to control the implementation?*	YES / NO
33 *Are the necessary changes being made?*	YES / NO

International Management

operating
A GLOBAL BUSINESS

THERE IS A GLOBAL MARKETPLACE FOR GOODS AND SERVICES, WHICH IS ENERGIZED BY AN INCREASING MONEY MOBILITY AND ACCESS TO NEW COMPUTING AND COMMUNICATIONS TECHNOLOGIES. TO BE EFFECTIVE AS A GLOBAL MANAGER, YOU NEED TO UNDERSTAND HOW A SUCCESSFUL TRANSNATIONAL BUSINESS WORKS, AND DEVELOP THE APPROPRIATE SKILLS.

You should first understand the essential structure of a global business. It is not the same as a multinational or pan-regional organization; it balances the global and the local in particular ways. It also demands special skills from a manager. You need to have a creative mix of professional and personal qualities that allow positive, culturally aware relationships, and you must be a true cosmopolitan.

To appreciate the demands of global strategy, you also need to recognize the vital "push–pull" factors that drive risk and opportunity in the global marketplace. Here the internet is particularly important, providing as it does a global "community" of interrelated parties. Whatever the strategy, it should be carefully mapped out, focusing on specific areas and utilizing all available operational tools.

THE ESSENTIALS OF GLOBAL BUSINESS

BEING "GLOBAL" IS NOT SO MUCH ABOUT WHERE YOU DO BUSINESS AS HOW YOU DO BUSINESS. A GLOBAL COMPANY ACTS IN AN INTERNALLY COORDINATED WAY TO BALANCE THE BENEFITS OF RESPONSIVENESS TO LOCAL MARKETS WITH THE BENEFITS OF GLOBAL ECONOMICS.

GLOBAL BUSINESS IN CONTEXT

A tight global structure may not suit every international business. A global manager must know organizational options to make good structural choices. The best way to understand being "global" is to make comparisons with two other types of organizational structure: the multinational and the pan-regional.

The multinational structure

A multinational structure involves working within several countries. Corporate headquarters, in this case, is located in France, but each country business has a relatively high degree of autonomy to satisfy the specific demands of its local marketplace. The multinational is in essence a collection of domestic businesses.

There are drawbacks to this structure, including:

- potentially high levels of fragmentation in the overall business
- entrapment of resources in country units
- duplication, for example, in R & D, marketing, human resources, IT functions in each country
- suboptimization, as each country battles with others to maximize their results and gain and protect resources.

The primary advantage of the multinational organization is its high degree of understanding and ability to respond to each country's local conditions and customers.

Compare the multinational model with a pan-regional structure.

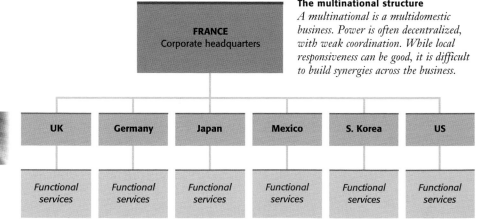

The multinational structure
A multinational is a multidomestic business. Power is often decentralized, with weak coordination. While local responsiveness can be good, it is difficult to build synergies across the business.

FRANCE
Corporate headquarters

UK	Germany	Japan	Mexico	S. Korea	US
Functional services	*Functional services*	*Functional services*	*Functional services*	*Functional services*	*Functional services*

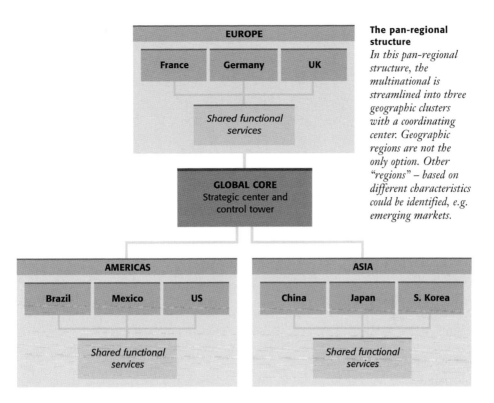

The pan-regional structure

In this pan-regional structure, the multinational is streamlined into three geographic clusters with a coordinating center. Geographic regions are not the only option. Other "regions" – based on different characteristics could be identified, e.g. emerging markets.

The pan-regional structure

In this case, local geography is secondary to regional geography. Markets within a similar geographic region – Asia, the Americas, and Europe – are "bundled" together. In the example given, the regions are connected to a global core that is responsible for overall global strategy and coordination. Each region is responsible for business results in its area. The regions may create shared function services among their businesses, for example, in regional marketing and advertising, and IT.

The pan-regional structure reduces fragmentation and encourages increased efficiency and the development of synergies. Compare these two models with a possible global structure, in which geography plays a secondary role to business units with global responsibility.

The global structure

In this scenario, a balance is attempted between:

- a global executive core
- global strategic business units
- shared services
- local activities.

The global executive core is responsible for overall global strategy and leadership. The global strategic business units are responsible for the performance management of products and services on a global basis. They may also be responsible for key processes. High level teams may work across the strategic business units to manage common brands. Shared services are those

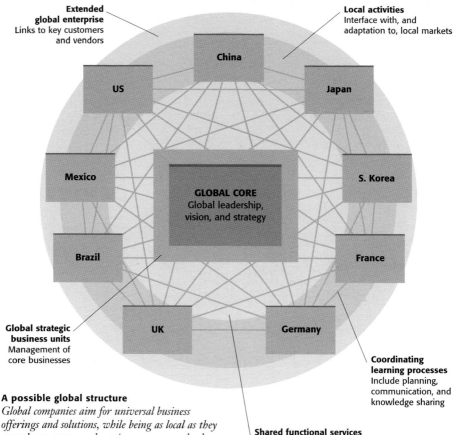

Extended global enterprise
Links to key customers and vendors

Local activities
Interface with, and adaptation to, local markets

China

US

Japan

Mexico

GLOBAL CORE
Global leadership, vision, and strategy

S. Korea

Brazil

France

Global strategic business units
Management of core businesses

UK

Germany

Coordinating learning processes
Include planning, communication, and knowledge sharing

A possible global structure
Global companies aim for universal business offerings and solutions, while being as local as they must be to attract and retain customers and talent. All leaders need to ask: "What are the global and local consequences of the decision I am making?"

Shared functional services
Include purchasing, research and development, and global marketing

functional areas that cut across the business as a whole, for example global marketing, global research and development, global IT, and global human resources. Local operations are those activities conducted in each specific market, for example promotions.

In reality, a business may have different structures in various parts of the company. Some parts of the business may be more conducive to globalization than others: for example, prescribed

drugs as opposed to over-the-counter drugs that tend to have deeper ties to the local marketplace.

OPERATING GLOBALLY

To derive the greatest benefits of globalization, managers need to use the following operating principles to guide their decision-making:

Integration

Integrating the international network so that they operate as one company worldwide, presenting a consistent face to customers.

Flow

Allowing resources (for example, capital, people, information) to circulate to those areas of the global business where they can add most value at a particular point in time.

Leverage

Utilizing resources, such as knowledge, facilities, systems, and people, across the global network to create world-class efficiency and effectiveness throughout the operation.

Optimization

Generating the best possible results for the total organization, rather than just the narrow pursuit of local success.

It is important to keep in mind that optimize does not mean compromise. To optimize is to make the whole system as effective as possible, in order to create the most favorable conditions for the growth and success of the total organization. For example, the country manager wants to maximize sales and so offers local customers a full range of products with as many options as possible. Meanwhile, the global strategic business unit manager will want to minimize costs. The optimal solution is likely to be an offering consisting of a subset of products with the most popular features. The goal of neither manager is maximized, but the overall result will be best for the company.

THE SKILLS OF A GLOBAL MANAGER

SUCCESSFUL GLOBAL MANAGERS UNDERSTAND THE KEY OPERATING PRINCIPLES OF SUCCESSFUL TRANSNATIONAL BUSINESSES. THEY SEE BEYOND "TRIBAL" BOUNDARIES, WHETHER PSYCHOLOGICAL OR CULTURAL, AND PURSUE THE APPROACHES THAT ADD OPTIMAL VALUE FOR THE COMPANY.

THE COSMOPOLITAN WAY OF BUSINESS

A global manager must be cosmopolitan. Every "tribe," whether national, local, organizational, professional, or functional, has different understandings of how the world works and what is to be valued. The accounting culture, for example, has a worldview very different from that of the marketing or engineering culture. At a national level, the bullet-point presentations of the Americans may not be welcomed by the French, who often want a demonstration of complex and logical thinking. The cosmopolitan sees the value in both and can generate business value from the diversity of worldviews. This way of thinking often requires the ability to blend seeming opposites – for example, local autonomy and central control, competition and cooperation.

A cosmopolitan mindset involves sensitivity and openness to learning. We must invest time in becoming sensitive to how others across the globe think and work so that we can avoid cultural surprises, make appropriate adaptations, and do business together without destructive misunderstandings. We must learn that the feeling, thinking, and behavioral habits with which we are culturally familiar, while still being applicable in some situations, might have limitations in others.

Suppose, for example, that two pharmaceutical companies are being merged – one German and the other French. Typically, the German approach to developing and producing a new drug will be very linear and predetermined: step 1, step 2, and so on. It may take 10 months from input to output, but the quality of the final output is guaranteed 100 percent. The French company's approach is likely to be more nonlinear, in which the processes unfold over time: the output from one phase determines what the next phase will look like, and so on. After six months the French might well be producing the new drug at the following quality levels: 80 percent is equivalent to the German standard and 20 percent is below. To the German mindset, such an approach can appear inefficient and unmethodical. However, the French might well get to market-testing first.

In this scenario, the French approach might be most applicable to new product development, while the German approach might be more applicable to manufacturing the final product. The cosmopolitan challenge is to act out of rational choice and derive value from differences rather than flow along the channels of cultural habit.

EMBRACING PARADOX

Many of the issues faced in global businesses do not lend themselves to easy "Yes" or "No" answers. The complexity of the global environment is such that, as indicated in this section, the response needs to be "Both/And." A global business is by nature a living contradiction. It needs all the benefits of size (for example, market presence, economies of scale, purchasing power) as well as the benefits of small organizations (for example, focus, speed, flexibility, responsiveness).

One key tension in any global business is centralization/decentralization. A rational mix of the two approaches ("glocalization") is likely to be the best approach. Your customer base, for example, is likely to make global, regional, and local demands and will need to be managed accordingly. Research and development may well be suited to global integration, while sales may need to be localized.

A key challenge for the global manager is to use contradictory forces in the business to generate creative ideas and competitive advantage. Often a busy manager opts for one side of a paradox over the other. But this does not produce radical breakthroughs or create new competitive space for the company.

GLOBAL MANAGEMENT CAPABILITIES

The complexity of the global business environment demands that we develop new capabilities for managing ourselves, managing cross-border relationships, and managing the transnational business. Working across borders often challenges traditional management assumptions. What is perceived to be good individual feedback in the United States may be viewed as personally demeaning in Asia. The global manager is challenged by multiple economic, financial, regulatory, technological, and cultural environments. This global mix can only be managed through collaboration with others inside and outside the business.

GLOBAL MANAGEMENT CAPABILITIES

MANAGING OURSELVES	MANAGING RELATIONSHIPS	MANAGING THE BUSINESS

MANAGING OURSELVES

■ Curiosity: Actively seek out international experiences and other resources for increasing global knowledge.

■ Flexibility: Adapt to changing circumstances and be resourceful in devising ways and means for being effective in new situations.

■ Objectivity: Challenge existing mental models and biases, and be open to learning from perspectives that may often be counterintuitive.

■ Patience: Set realistic expectations for yourself and others when dealing with the unfamiliar.

■ Resilience: Keep working through conditions of high uncertainty and ambiguity.

■ Self-reflection: Spend time drawing lessons from past experiences.

MANAGING RELATIONSHIPS

■ Collaboration: Seek to create or integrate ways of working that enable everyone to generate business value.

■ Crosscultural communication: Develop shared understandings despite language and style differences.

■ Empathy: See the world from another's cultural perspective and do not rush to judgment.

■ Influencing: Connect with the underlying logic of different cultural groups to maximize persuasiveness in making presentations, supervising, etc.

■ Negotiating: Recognize and adapt to differences in the style of bargaining and managing conflict.

■ Networking: Develop an extensive web of relationships inside and outside the organization that extend the reach and richness of personal and local resources.

MANAGING THE BUSINESS

■ Conceptualizing: Identify patterns within the complex global environment to increase managerial understanding and effectiveness.

■ Culture-building: Act as a role model for those values and norms of behavior that both leverage diversity and promote inclusion, for example, respect, fairness, and sharing.

■ Environmental scanning: Gather and analyze information from local and global sources to identify business risks and opportunities and support ongoing strategic thinking.

■ Integrating: Think beyond either/or answers to generate both/and solutions to complex problems.

■ Optimizing: Balance global and local needs to generate the best possible results for the whole organization.

■ Partnering: Manage relationships with global alliance partners, suppliers, distributors, etc. to generate new value for the business.

IDENTIFYING GLOBAL RISKS AND OPPORTUNITIES

MANAGING IN A GLOBAL BUSINESS NEEDS A THOROUGH UNDERSTANDING OF THE DYNAMICS OF RISK AND OPPORTUNITY. THE RISK OF NOT PURSUING A GLOBAL STRATEGY PUSHES YOU INTO THE GLOBAL MARKETPLACE, WHILE THE OPPORTUNITIES AVAILABLE THERE PULL YOU INTO IT.

global risk, may find itself out of business – sooner rather than later. A company that does not pay attention to pull factors, which relate to global opportunity, may find its scope for growth eroding rapidly. The global risk-opportunity profile provides insights into the global business

THE GLOBAL RISK-OPPORTUNITY PROFILE

A company that does not pay attention to push factors, which relate to managing

Using a global risk-opportunity profile
You need to determine the mix of push and pull factors on the company and how they affect its success. This profile for a US-based insurance company shows which choices should be prioritized.

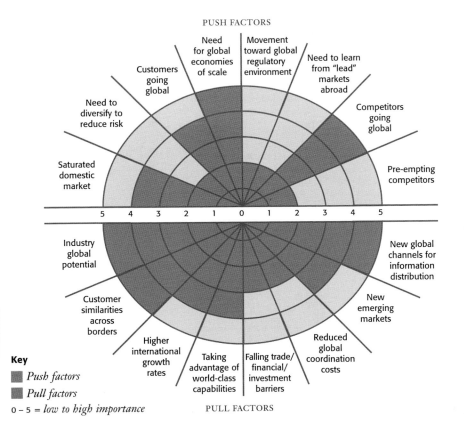

PUSH FACTORS

Need for global economies of scale

Movement toward global regulatory environment

Customers going global

Need to learn from "lead" markets abroad

Need to diversify to reduce risk

Competitors going global

Saturated domestic market

Pre-empting competitors

5 4 3 2 1 0 1 2 3 4 5

Industry global potential

New global channels for information distribution

Customer similarities across borders

New emerging markets

Higher international growth rates

Reduced global coordination costs

Taking advantage of world-class capabilities

Falling trade/ financial/ investment barriers

Key

▓ *Push factors*

▓ *Pull factors*

0 – 5 = *low to high importance*

PULL FACTORS

landscape upon which the company is trying to compete. At left is a global risk-opportunity profile for a US-based insurance company.

On the push side, the company is experiencing pressure from competitors who are going global and reducing costs. This creates a need for the company to achieve greater economies of scale and be price competitive. This pressure is intensified by customers who are going global, and by an increasingly saturated domestic marketplace for insurance.

On the pull side, strong opportunities are seen because of global potential in the insurance industry as a whole (increasing middle-class populations around the world are more aware than ever before of the benefits of insurance and can afford it). The higher international growth rates in many emerging markets, coupled with new distribution systems such as the internet, make the global marketplace attractive. The company also feels it has world-class capabilities in its organization which are currently underutilized.

THE INTERNET AND GLOBAL BUSINESS

One of the greatest global risks and/or opportunities in today's environment is the internet, and it deserves special attention. It provides a global electronic community in which sellers and buyers, suppliers and distributors, employers and employees can make fast decisions together based on real-time information.

A global internet presence is relatively easy to establish, so small, flexible companies can compete successfully with the corporate goliaths. The internet provides a powerful new channel to

> **CHECKLIST**
>
> *To increase your company's competitiveness using the internet, ask:*
>
> ✔ *Is your website "global friendly"?*
> ✔ *What are you doing to build e-loyalty among your customers?*
> ✔ *Have you built an extranet?*
> ✔ *Do you have a corporate intranet to connect your global employees?*
> ✔ *Have you explored how the internet can help you cut out the information middleman?*
> ✔ *Are you mining the nuggets of global data gathered on your customers and products?*
> ✔ *Are you training your people – including executives – to pursue the internet advantage?*

customers, to different customer segments, and new opportunities for increased brand recognition and development.

Imagine the likely scenario of 700 million people on-line worldwide, with nearly half in Europe and the fastest growth in the Asia–Pacific region. *What are the implications for your business?* Imagine an increasing number of users interacting on the web in languages other than English – Chinese and Japanese, for example. *What are the implications for your business?* In future the worldwide use of wireless devices to access the internet will be greater than the use of PCs. *How will your company adapt?*

Business-to-business e-commerce on a global scale is now a key component of many global strategies. Global business-to-consumer e-commerce is smaller, but it will increase as consumers enjoy on-line shopping and their security fears diminish.

MAPPING A GLOBAL STRATEGY

MAPPING AND EXECUTING A GLOBAL STRATEGY ARE PART OF THE SAME DYNAMIC AND INTERRELATED PROCESS OF CREATING VALUE FOR STAKEHOLDERS IN THE BUSINESS. THINK OF THEM AS BEING NECESSARILY INTERDEPENDENT.

THE ELEMENTS OF MAPPING

When mapping a global strategy, we need to focus attention on the following: terrain, targets, tools, and tests.

TERRAIN: SCENARIO PROFILES

The global risk-opportunity profile given before provides a quick assessment of why a business may need to be thinking and operating globally. But be warned: this profile can change quickly. The global market never sleeps, and obsolescence is only an idea away. It is important to scan continually for the most significant trends – economic, legal, political, technological, sociocultural, industrial, and those of competitors.

A global analysis needs to result in scenarios of possible future conditions. Generating scenarios enables decision-makers to identify the mix of strategies that are most likely to produce the best results (given the range of uncertainties in the environment).

TARGETS: INVESTMENT PRIORITIES

Strategic targets need to be identified in three critical areas: customers, products and services, and markets. Which customers – at global, regional, and local levels – present you with the best potential for generating revenue at the lowest possible cost? Given your target customers, what are your strategic products and services? Do you have

Profiling targets
Global strategic goals and objectives can only be determined after a careful analysis of the likely revenue-cost profiles of potential targets over a period of time. Matrices such as these can help identify these profiles.

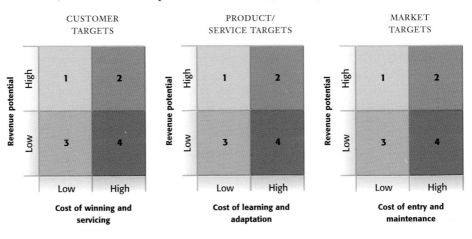

CUSTOMER TARGETS

PRODUCT/ SERVICE TARGETS

MARKET TARGETS

Cost of winning and servicing

Cost of learning and adaptation

Cost of entry and maintenance

existing products and services that require little learning and adaptation for the global marketplace? Which markets offer the best opportunities for revenue generation at the lowest costs of entry and maintenance?

Targets for customers, products or services, and markets can be visualized in a set of matrices, as shown at left. Quadrant 1 offers the best choice of targets (high revenue potential and low costs). We should not, however, fail to consider opportunities to target in Quadrants 2 and 3. Targets in Quadrant 2 have high revenue potential, but they also have high costs. Are these costs likely to decline over time? Would strategic partnerships help reduce the cost burden while maintaining the revenue attractiveness? Potential targets in Quadrant 3 have low revenue potential but also low costs. Is the revenue potential likely to change over time as the market develops?

TOOLS: CAPABILITY ASSESSMENT

You need world-class capabilities to execute strategy successfully – otherwise you do not have the tools to do the job. You must develop, acquire, or outsource the requisite tools, which are of four types: identity, infrastructure, performance, and relationship, as documented in the next section. Alternatively, partnering with others who already have these tools is a widely used option.

TESTS: PERFORMANCE INDICATORS

The profitability of the company is an indicator of its performance, but another is the company's ability to perform well across many other key areas. The chart on the right lists those factors to measure.

USING PERFORMANCE INDICATORS

The task here is to identify performance indicators that show how well you are leveraging tangible and intangible assets globally. Financial results comprise one indicator, but are not sufficient for assessing performance sustainability into the future. The following is a list of some performance indicators relevant to the global context:

- level of global representation on the board
- customer satisfaction with quality and consistency of global support and service
- employee satisfaction with, and commitment to, common corporate culture
- utilization of common systems and processes worldwide
- ability to implement common global standards
- global brand recognition
- speed of best practice exchange between global operations
- speed of information exchange to support the formulation and implementation of strategies
- speed of creating, absorbing, and utilizing new knowledge throughout the network
- ability to put the right individuals and teams in the right place at the right time
- speed of translating local ideas into global products
- speed to open new markets
- extent of and satisfaction with global shared services
- ability to identify and partner with resources inside and outside the global network, for example, customers, suppliers
- ability to recognize and exploit opportunities for streamlining the global network and creating synergies.

EXECUTING A GLOBAL STRATEGY

TO TRANSLATE ITS GLOBAL STRATEGY INTO ACTUAL RESULTS, A BUSINESS NEEDS TO UTILIZE ALL OF THE VALUE-GENERATING CAPABILITIES IT ALREADY HAS, CAN DEVELOP, BUY, OUTSOURCE, OR OBTAIN BY PARTNERING WITH OTHERS. THESE CAPABILITIES CAN BE THOUGHT OF AS OPERATIONAL TOOLS.

OPERATIONAL TOOLS

A successful global business is built upon having a meaningful identity, a strong infrastructure, high performance, and skilled management of relationships – all at world-class levels.

IDENTITY TOOLS

These are the capabilities needed to provide those inside and outside the business with a clear sense of what the business does and what it stands for in the world – for example, qualities such as global vision and values, development and communication, worldwide brand management, and advertising. Brand names such as Johnson & Johnson, Disney, and Volvo carry meaning as well as information.

INFRASTRUCTURE TOOLS

To create a winning global infrastructure, the business must develop its capabilities for organizing. The configuration of its value chain activities around the world must satisfy the demands of the top and bottom lines (revenues and costs), while allowing the flexibility to adapt to the needs of strategic customers. It must also put robust coordinating processes and systems in place – for example, planning, decision-making and communication pipelines – to enable efficient global collaboration. Technology will play an increasingly important part in the global infrastructure as businesses seek to exploit the benefits of being virtual.

PERFORMANCE TOOLS

These tools relate to expertise in the company. There are two types: first, the specialized performance tools – the traditional functional areas such as research and development, manufacturing, marketing, and human resources. They are reservoirs of skills and know-how. A great deal of emphasis in recent years has been placed on the importance of processes, but we should not neglect the importance of functional depth. For example, car and motorcycle manufacturer Honda is a highly successful global company that maintains very high levels of functional expertise.

The second type of performance tool to be developed is generic, for example, customer-focus, constant innovation, and knowledge sharing. We should expect everyone in the business to contribute to building these capabilities.

RELATIONSHIP TOOLS

Global companies rely heavily on collaboration across the organization – as in new product development teams, who also be highly proficient in working with "external" parties, such as customers, vendors, and alliance partners. Too many

DEVELOPING GLOBAL CAPABILITIES

OPTION	PROS	CONS
Developing capabilities in-house	■ Hands-on control over the development process ■ Close linkage to the specific capability needs of the company	■ Possibility of limited mindsets and skills in the existing company ■ Large potential investments in recruitment and training programs
Acquiring capabilities through mergers and acquisitions	■ No need to develop capabilities from scratch ■ High degree of control	■ Large up-front investment ■ Lengthy integration process ■ May need to purchase redundant or unwanted capabilities ■ May inherit hidden problems
Outsourcing	■ Eliminate or minimize development costs ■ Significantly reduce administration costs ■ Can shop around for the best capability fit without purchasing "extras"	■ Reduced control ■ Ongoing investment ■ Increased dependence on external sources
Partnering	■ Little or no up-front investment ■ Access to broader range of mindsets and expertise	■ Issues of organizational and cultural fit ■ Partnership problems, for example, control, roles, and responsibilities, varied levels of commitment, effort, and investment ■ Dependence on the success of the partner

transnational mergers and acquisitions, for example, fail to add value because of cultural difficulties.

Global collaboration requires people who are well trained and proficient in cross-cultural communication, teamwork, and negotiation skills. It also requires the development and nurturing of an organizational culture that encourages collaborative leadership across borders and an openness to learning.

THE GLOBAL/LOCAL MIX

In the very near future, being a global manager may not be an option but an absolute requirement. Even the most

local of jobs are likely to have a global dimension. You might have to make sure, for example, that decisions on promoting products locally are in alignment with global brand strategies. Or you might have to make sure that criteria for local suppliers fit with global standards.

In essence, the successful operation of a global business depends on managers being able to:

- see the global implications of the local requirements
- see the local implications of the global requirements
- create the best mix for the customer and the company.

managing
ACROSS CULTURES

WHEN YOU ARE DOING BUSINESS OUTSIDE YOUR HOME COUNTRY, IT IS A CONSIDERABLE CHALLENGE TO COPE WITH A CULTURE THAT IS DIFFERENT FROM YOUR OWN. THESE DIFFERENCES MAY BE SUPERFICIAL OR PROFOUND, BUT IN ANY CASE YOU MUST BE AWARE OF THEM, RESPECT THEM, AND INDEED CELEBRATE THEM.

To work and live fruitfully in these different cultures, you need to develop an underlying intercultural competence. The crucial element is reconciliation: acknowledging the legitimacy of cultural differences, and integrating them in a mutually beneficial partnership. Working in different cultures can be a source of personal growth: back home, you should be even more effective in your own culture.

You must first be aware of the range of variables that make up cultural diversity. These can be defined in a number of dimensions, or categories, and they provide a framework to respond to the practicalities of life. With an awareness of specific norms and values in individual societies, you can then consider how such knowledge can be applied to business procedures, and how you yourself can adapt accordingly in your management role.

IN THIS CHAPTER

DEFINING CULTURES

WHEN WE ARE LIVING AND WORKING IN ANOTHER CULTURE, WE ARE USUALLY AWARE OF CULTURAL DIFFERENCES SUCH AS DRESS, FOOD, AND BASIC BEHAVIORS. MUCH MORE IMPORTANT FOR EFFECTIVE INTEGRATION ARE DIFFERENCES AT A DEEPER, IMPLICIT LEVEL, OF WHICH WE ARE OFTEN UNAWARE.

ANALYZING THE
STRUCTURE OF CULTURE

The culture of any society around the world can be compared to an onion. It has layers, which can be peeled off. Three distinct layers can be distinguished:
● the outer layer
● the middle layer
● the inner layer.

The outer layer contains those elements that people primarily associate with culture: the visual reality of behavior, such as clothes, food, language, and architecture. Wherever they are, they will readily recognize the differences compared to those they are familiar with at home. This is the level of explicit culture.

The middle layer refers to the norms and values that a community holds: what is considered right and wrong (norms), or good and bad (values). Norms are often external; each society superimposes them on its members, reinforced by measures of social control. Values tend to be more internal than norms, and most societies do not have many means of controlling their enforcement. Values and norms structure the way people in a particular culture behave. But they are not visible, despite their influence on what happens at the observable surface, in the outer layer of culture.

The inner layer is the deepest: the level of implicit culture. Understanding the core of the culture onion is the key to working successfully with other cultures. The core consists of basic assumptions, series of rules, and methods that a society has developed to deal with the regular problems that it faces. These methods of problem-solving have become so basic that, like breathing, people no longer think about how they do it. For an outsider, these basic assumptions can be very difficult to recognize.

UNDERSTANDING
THE DIFFERENT MEANINGS

On arrival in your foreign destination to begin your professional assignment, you will immediately be aware of differences arising from the outer and the middle layers of culture. The importance of the inner layer of culture is that different cultures may give a different meaning to the same thing.

You are likely to find differences in the following areas, among others:
● the status accorded to older people
● the relationship between men and women
● the respect given to the law (and even simple rules)
● the degree to which your working relationship is, or becomes, more personal.

It is very important that you do not make the mistake of assuming that cultural differences are just about such visible elements as clothes, food, and houses. You may embarrass yourself, or your host, because you give different meanings to the same things. If you have some understanding of these differences, and learn how to cope with them, your experience of working in a different culture can be enhanced and made much more effective – and enjoyable.

UNDERSTANDING
THE BASIC ASSUMPTIONS

Every culture has developed its own set of basic assumptions, which can be categorized into different dimensions. In dealing with universal human problems, each cultural dimension can be seen as a continuum: at one end there is a basic value, which contrasts with the value at the other end. The continuum will cover every possible combination between the two contrasting basic values.

All cultures need to deal with the challenge of these extreme choices. They face a continuous series of dilemmas, because by itself each alternative is either unsatisfactory or insufficient. In business, for example, do we go only for the short term or the long term? For stability or change? For market-led or technology-led products? For rewarding individuals or teams? Transnational organizations respond to these dilemmas in different ways, according to how they stand on each separate dimension derived from their cultural heritage.

Seven cultural dimensions can be distinguished, as follows.

UNIVERSALISTIC VERSUS
PARTICULARISTIC

People in universalistic cultures share the belief that general rules, codes, values, and standards take precedence over particular needs and claims of friends and relations. In such a society, the rules apply equally to the whole "universe" of members. Any exception weakens the rule.

For example, the rule that you should bear truthful witness in a court of law, or give an honest account of an accident to an insurance company before it compensates, is more important here than particular ties of friendship or family obligations. This does not mean that, in universalistic cultures, particular ties are completely unimportant. But the universal truth – that is, the law – is considered logically more significant than these relationships.

The United States is a notable example of a universalistic culture, which explains the high number of lawyers per head of population.

Conversely, particularistic cultures see the ideal culture in terms of human friendship, extraordinary achievements and situations, and in a network of intimate relationships. The "spirit of the law" is deemed more important than the "letter of the law." Obviously there are

IDENTIFYING DIFFERENT CULTURAL VALUES

A single incident can have different meanings in different cultures, depending on the prevailing values of the society concerned. You need to learn to distinguish these.

As an example, imagine that you are a passenger in a car driven by your friend in an area of the city where there is a speed limit. Your friend drives too fast and hits a pedestrian, causing serious injuries. Your friend has to go to court, and you are the only witness. Do you tell the truth, or adapt what you will say to help your friend?

The choice is between the law (impelled by universalism – everyone should be treated equally) and friendship (your relationship with your friend is more important).

rules and laws in particularistic cultures, but these merely codify how people relate to each other. Rules are needed, if only so that people can make exceptions to them for particular cases, but generally individuals need to be able to count on the support of their friends.

South America and parts of Africa are examples of cultures where, typically, relationships between friends and family members are deemed more important than the letter of the law.

INDIVIDUALISTIC VERSUS COMMUNITARIAN

In predominantly individualistic cultures, people place the individual before the community. The pace is set by individual happiness, welfare, and fulfillment. People are expected to decide matters largely on their own, and to take care primarily of themselves and their immediate family. The quality of life for all members of society is seen as directly dependent on opportunities for individual freedom and development. The community is judged by the extent to which it serves the interests of individual members.

The United States and, to a similar extent, the United Kingdom, are examples of cultures that encourage the individual. Pay and performance systems in organizations are often based on this.

At the other end of the continuum, a predominantly communitarian culture places the community before the individual. It is the responsibility of the individual to act in ways that serve society. By doing so, individual needs will be taken care of naturally. The quality of life for the individual is seen as directly dependent on the degree to which he or she takes care of fellow members, even at the cost of individual freedom. People are judged by the extent to which they serve the interests of the community.

For example, in both China and Japan, working in a team and contributing to the group or society have a higher priority than individual performance.

SPECIFIC VERSUS DIFFUSE

People from specific cultures start with the elements, the specifics. First they analyze them separately, and then they put them back together again. In specific cultures, the whole is the sum of its parts. Each person's life is divided into many components: as a newcomer, you can enter only one component at a time. Interactions between people are highly purposeful and well defined.

The public part of specific individuals' makeup is much larger than their private space. People are easily accepted into the public area, but it is very difficult to get into the private space, since each area in which two people encounter each other is considered separate from the other, a specific case.

Individuals within a culture that is specifically oriented tend to concentrate on hard facts, standards, measures, contracts. In specific cultures (such as the United States and Australia) business can be done without individuals having to form a relationship first.

People from cultures that are diffusely oriented start with the whole and see each element in perspective to the total. All elements are related to each other. These relationships are more important than each separate element, so the whole is more than just the sum of its elements.

Diffuse individuals have a large private space and a small public one.

Newcomers are not easily accepted into either. But once they have been accepted, they are admitted into all layers of the individual's life: work, sports, domestic life, and so on. The various roles that someone might play in your life are not separated. Diffuse cultures cherish such qualities as style, demeanor, empathy, trust, and understanding.

In diffuse cultures such as in the Gulf countries, you have to develop a relationship first before you can do business. A high level of involvement is required as a precursor.

AFFECTIVE VERSUS NEUTRAL

In an affective culture, people do not object to a display of emotions. It is not considered necessary to hide moods and feelings and to keep them bottled up. Affective cultures may interpret the less explicit signals of a neutral culture as less important. They may be ignored – or even go unnoticed. For example, Italian and French cultures display their emotions – expressed, some would say, particularly in flamboyant driving! But this cultural bias is also revealed in their beautiful car designs and haute couture.

In a neutral culture, people are taught that it is incorrect to show one's feelings overtly. This does not mean they do not have feelings; it just means that the degree to which feelings may show is limited. They accept and are aware of feelings, but are in control of them. Neutral cultures may think the louder signals of an affective culture too excited, and overemotional. In neutral cultures, showing too much emotion may erode your power to interest people. For example, it may be difficult to tell what business partners in Japan are thinking, as they exhibit little body language.

ACHIEVED VERSUS ASCRIBED

Achieved status is a reflection of what an individual does and has accomplished. In cultures that are achievement-oriented, individuals derive their status from what

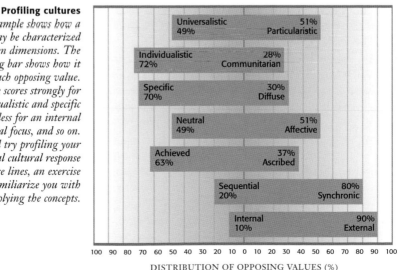

Profiling cultures
This example shows how a culture may be characterized along the seven dimensions. The measuring bar shows how it scores on each opposing value. The culture scores strongly for an individualistic and specific focus, rather less for an internal and sequential focus, and so on.
You could try profiling your own personal cultural response along these lines, an exercise that would familiarize you with applying the concepts.

Universalistic 49% — Particularistic 51%
Individualistic 72% — Communitarian 28%
Specific 70% — Diffuse 30%
Neutral 49% — Affective 51%
Achieved 63% — Ascribed 37%
Sequential 20% — Synchronic 80%
Internal 10% — External 90%

100 90 80 70 60 50 40 30 20 10 0 10 20 30 40 50 60 70 80 90 100
DISTRIBUTION OF OPPOSING VALUES (%)

MATCHING CULTURAL NORMS TO BUSINESS ACTION

The way that people in different societies interact with each other has important repercussions for business practice. To take an everyday example, consider buying food at a delicatessen. If you are in, for example, the US, the UK, or the Netherlands, you might collect a numbered ticket that shows your place in line. You patiently wait your turn in an orderly sequence. The sales assistant serves you with everything you need before the next customer, and this is an efficient system.

But if you are in, say, Italy, and you ask the assistant for salami, he or she will serve you and then shout, "Who else wants salami?" Other customers will then be served accordingly, before the assistant again asks you what else you want. This is also an efficient system. The salami is unwrapped just once, and the knife does not have to be washed again. This process also promotes social interaction between the cluster of customers who have a common bond (in this case, a need for salami).

Now imagine that you are running the computer services for a global hotel chain. You commission a computerized database system for the checkout system, which has been written by a US-based software house employing programmers with a sequential ethnic/cultural background. The desk clerk asks guests for their room number and retrieves their accounts from the database. This is a sequential system that works well in the US, the UK, Germany, and other countries.

But this system is not customer-friendly in the synchronic cultures of South America, Spain, or Italy. Here, the desk clerk and one guest expect to examine the account for extras (telephone, minibar, and so on) while the guest in front is paying and the guest behind is shouting their room number. Sequential culture is actually built into the internal architecture of database software that originates in sequential cultures. It is difficult to make such a database work in synchronic contexts.

they have accomplished. An individual with achieved status has to prove what he or she is worth over and over again: status is accorded and maintained on the basis of his or her actions.

The Dutch culture is a good example of one that encourages people to achieve results, while family background is less important. It is what the individual does that is significant.

Ascribed status is a reflection of what an individual is and how others relate to his or her position in the community, in society as a whole, or in an organization. In an ascriptive culture, people derive their status from birth, age, gender, or wealth. People with ascribed status do not have to achieve results to retain status: it is accorded to them on the basis of their being.

In the Middle East and Far East, for example, who you are has to be taken very much into consideration.

SEQUENTIAL VERSUS SYNCHRONIC

Every culture has developed its own response to time. The time-orientation dimension has two aspects: a culture's approach to structuring time, and the relative importance it gives to the past, present, and future.

Time can be structured in two ways. In the sequentialist approach, time moves forward, second by second, minute by minute, hour by hour, in a straight line. In the synchronistic approach, time moves around in cycles: of minutes, hours, days, weeks, months, and years.

People structuring time sequentially tend to do one thing at a time. They view time as a narrow line of distinct, consecutive segments. Sequential people view time as tangible and divisible. They strongly prefer planning and keeping to plans once they have been made, rather than extemporizing and adapting. Time commitments are taken seriously, and staying on schedule is a must.

Sequential cultures include Canada, Australia, and Switzerland.

Conversely, people structuring time synchronically usually do several things at a time. To them, time is a wide ribbon, allowing many things to take place simultaneously. Time is intangible and flexible. Time commitments are desirable rather than absolute. Plans are easily changed. Synchronic people especially value the satisfactory completion of interactions with others. Promptness depends on the type of relationship.

The whole philosophy of "Just-in-Time" management derived from the highly synchronic Japanese.

Past-oriented cultures

If a culture is predominantly oriented toward the past, the future is seen as a repetition of past experiences. Respect for ancestors and collective historical experiences are characteristic of a past-oriented culture.

Present-oriented cultures

A culture that is predominantly oriented toward the present will not attach much value to common past experiences, nor to future prospects. Rather, day-by-day experiences tend to direct people's thinking and action.

Future-oriented cultures

In a future-oriented culture, most human activities are directed toward future prospects. Generally, the past is not considered to be vitally significant to a future state of affairs. Detailed planning constitutes a major activity in future-oriented cultures.

INTERNALLY OR EXTERNALLY CONTROLLED

This dimension is concerned with relationships to nature. Every culture has developed an attitude toward the natural environment. Survival has meant acting with or against it. The way people relate to their environment – internalistically or externalistically – is linked to the way they seek to have control over their own lives and over their destiny.

Internalistic people tend to have a mechanistic view of nature. They see nature as a complex machine, and machines can be controlled if you have the right expertise. Internalistic people do not believe in luck or predestination. They are "inner-directed": one's personal resolution is the starting point for every action. You can live the life you want to live if you take advantage of the opportunities. People can dominate nature, if they make the effort. Many Israeli people, for example, are highly internally controlled.

Externalistic people have a more organic view of nature. Mankind is one of nature's forces, so should operate in harmony with the environment. Man should subjugate himself to nature and go along with its forces. Externalistic people do not believe that they can shape their own destiny. "Nature moves in mysterious ways," and therefore you never know what will happen to you. The actions of externalistic people are "outer-directed": adapted to external circumstances. Russians and Singaporeans are notably externally controlled.

MANAGING THE CULTURAL DIFFERENCES

DEALING WITH DIFFERENT CULTURES IS NOT ABOUT TRYING TO EMULATE OR DENIGRATE WHAT YOU FIND DIFFERENT. DOING BUSINESS AND MANAGING ACROSS CULTURES IS VERY MUCH ABOUT INTEGRATING THE STRENGTH OF ONE CULTURE WITH THAT OF ANOTHER.

DEALING WITH DILEMMAS

Major business and management problems can be expressed as a dilemma: on the one hand, this, but on the other hand, that. For example, we need to work more in teams, but our reward system recognizes individuals. In working across cultures, dilemmas arise from each of the seven dimensions of culture.

DEVELOPING TRANS-CULTURAL COMPETENCE

To work effectively in a multicultural environment, the key is reconciliation. You will need to be able to reconcile values that are seemingly opposed. These dilemmas arise on a continuing basis.

As a manager, you have to inspire your workforce, and you also have to listen. You need to follow the orders of HQ to fulfill the global strategy, and you need to have local success by adapting to regional circumstances. You have to decide when to act yourself, but also when and where to delegate. You need to input your own day-to-day contribution, and at the same time be passionate about the mission as a whole. And you need to simultaneously use your powers of analysis while enabling the contribution of others.

RECONCILING STANDARD AND ADAPTATION

This dilemma can be found in many forms. Should you globalize or localize your approach? Is it better for your organization to mass-produce or to focus on specialized products?

Good leaders in transnational organizations are effective at finding resolutions whereby locally learned best

THE IMPLICATIONS OF CULTURAL DIFFERENCES

When you are in a foreign country, and you encounter something familiar, it is all too easy to assume that your host culture gives it the same meaning as you do. As an example, consider a "global" product: the MP3 player.

The technical specification of the "portable RX MP3 player" is the same everywhere it is sold throughout the world: it is the same size, it has the same performance, memory, and so on. You transfer MP3 files from your personal computer to the player, and the music comes out of the headphones.

A test group of consumers in the United States was asked if they liked it. "It's great," was the typical response, the reason being: "I can listen to my favorite music without being disturbed when I'm traveling." In China, the test group typically said: "It's great. I can listen to my favorite music without disturbing others when I'm traveling."

It may be the same product technically, but it may be perceived differently from one culture to the next. Therefore, it has to be marketed to satisfy different needs in different cultures.

practices are globalized. Thus activities might be decentralized, but information about them will be centralized. The universalistic approach promotes common systems, global brands, and human resources principles around the world. It fuels the search for the one best way of doing things and releases the synergy of a global corporation. Without this, you can lose the benefits of operating globally.

At the same time, taken too far and not balanced with a healthy dose of particularism, it can lead to extremes with "one best way" being pursued at the cost of flexibility to the particular needs and circumstances of the local situation.

RECONCILING INDIVIDUAL CREATIVITY AND TEAM SPIRIT

The effective manager knows how to mold an effective team out of creative individuals. In turn, the team is made accountable to support the creative genius of individuals as they strive to contribute the best for the team. This has been described as "coopetition."

In many companies, there is no problem finding enough individuals to generate enough ideas. The challenge lies with the "business system" or community, which has to translate those ideas into the reality of viable products and services. While ideas originate with individuals, it is not enough to simply pass these down for implementation to subordinates, who may be inhibited in their criticism. It is far more effective for the originator to work with critics, implementers, and builders of working prototypes to help to debug the idea, where necessary. It is a question of reconciling idealization with realization, which is at least as important.

In this dilemma concerning individual versus community, the membership of teams must be diverse, consisting of people whose values and endowments are different, yet these teams must achieve a unity of purpose and shared solutions. The problem with highly diverse competing individuals is that they may behave like so many prima donnas.

The problem with unity and team spirit above all is that diverse and novel inputs get squeezed out. A way of reconciling these polarized opposites is to make the ultimate goal so exciting, and the process of creating new shared realities so enjoyable, that diverse members overcome their differences to realize a unity of diversities, which makes the solution far more valuable.

RECONCILING PASSION AND CONTROL

Is a good manager an overtly passionate person, or rather a person who controls his or her display of emotions?

Two extreme types can be recognized. Passionate managers without reason are seen as neurotics. Overly controlled managers without emotions are seen as robots or control freaks. Both these types are unsuccessful in a multicultural environment. Effective managers check passion with reason; conversely, they give meaning to control by showing their passion at specific, well-chosen moments.

RECONCILING ANALYSIS AND SYNTHESIS

If a manager uses pure analysis to address a problem – chopping the larger whole into piecemeal chunks – this can lead to a kind of paralysis. Conversely, a synthesis, putting everything into a larger context, can be overdone and lead to aimless holism and a resistance to action. An important ability of the modern manager is to transcend any problem by elevating thought to higher levels of abstraction, while retaining the ability and drive to zoom in on certain aspects of the problem.

RECONCILING BEING AND DOING

Research shows that what leaders *are* is not different from what they *do*. They seem to be one with what they do. It is recognized that an important source of stress is when being and doing are not integrated. Successful leaders do things in harmony with who they feel they are, and vice versa. They have reconciled their private and professional lives.

RECONCILING SEQUENTIAL AND SYNCHRONIC

Effective leaders can plan sequentially, but they also have a strongly developed skill in stimulating parallel processes. "Just-in-Time" management is widely recognized as the approach in which processes are synchronized to speed up the sequence. Furthermore, an effective international leader is able to integrate short and long term, and past, present, and future: tradition and potential.

RECONCILING INNER AND OUTER FORCES

The final core quality of an effective manager is the ability to integrate the feedback from the market with the technology developed in the company.

Again, it is not a competition between technology push and market pull. A push of technology will eventually lead to the ultimate niche market: one without customers. A monolithic focus on the market will leave the business at the mercy of its clients. Values are not "added" by leaders or managers, since only simple values "add up." Leaders combine values: a fast and a safe car; good food yet easy to prepare; a computer that makes complex calculations but is also customer friendly.

Combining values is not easy, but it is possible. The more extended system of values is the context where international leadership will prove its excellence.

Responding to different cultures
The most productive response to other cultures is to reconcile yours with theirs. The global approach, where a company operates in the same way around the world, is the polar opposite of the multi-local approach, which tries to be different everywhere. The multinational approach is only a compromise, and does not achieve the win–win position of the transnational approach.

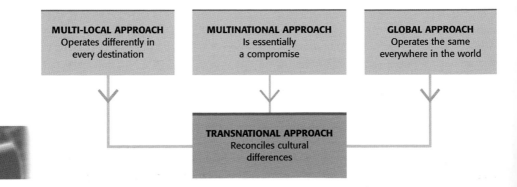

MULTI-LOCAL APPROACH	MULTINATIONAL APPROACH	GLOBAL APPROACH
Operates differently in every destination	Is essentially a compromise	Operates the same everywhere in the world

TRANSNATIONAL APPROACH
Reconciles cultural differences

WORKING WITH CULTURAL DIFFERENCES

BEING AWARE OF CULTURAL DIMENSIONS, AND THEIR IMPACT ON AN ORGANIZATION'S STRATEGY, YOU NEED TO CONSIDER HOW TO WORK AS A MANAGER ACROSS CULTURES. HOW CAN YOU BECOME MORE EFFECTIVE IN IDENTIFYING AND DEALING WITH DILEMMAS THAT ARISE FROM CULTURAL DIFFERENCES?

RECOGNIZE THE DIFFERENCES
Your first task is to recognize the differences integral to particular cultures. Use the seven dimensions of culture to help you understand and interpret what you see (*see* pp.235–9).

RESPECT THE DIFFERENCES
One culture is not better than another. There is no correct way or ideal position on each dimension. Cultures are just different. Learn to respect other cultures and accept they have the right to give the meaning they choose to their world.

RESPOND TO THE DIFFERENCES
There are several options for you to respond. First, you can ignore cultural differences and "do your own thing," like a tourist on a short vacation. You face the danger of being misunderstood and your hosts may not welcome you. Or you can abandon your own culture and try to behave as the destination culture: "When in Rome, do as the Romans do." However, this is simply putting on an act and it will be difficult to maintain. Your hosts may mistrust you and be suspicious. You can decide to compromise and try to adapt to some aspects of the differences.

However, what do you choose to compromise on? This is still a lose–lose option, satisfying neither party.

The most productive approach is to try to integrate your culture with the culture of your hosts. Try to get a win–win position: that is, reconciliation. It is about using the strengths of your culture and the strengths of theirs. For example, if you are basically an individualist and you are working in a team or group culture, why not join in with the group spirit to develop your own individual strengths? Then help members to see that high-performing individuals can contribute to their team.

SUPPORT INTERCULTURAL COMPETENCE
The ability to reconcile dilemmas is not just learned or innate. It needs a systemic approach. The whole organization should build a framework to support, stimulate, and facilitate people to reconcile.

Some individuals with high potential may not be able to progress further than a (lose–lose) compromise, as their work environment does not appreciate creative solutions. Conversely, less effective people may have achieved significant reconciliation by a stimulating and supportive environment.

How can such an environment be created? It begins with leaders and managers who practice what they preach. And it is of the utmost importance that rewards are created that will motivate individuals and teams to do the same.

GLOSSARY

Balanced scorecard Method of rating corporate and sub-unit performance on financial/nonfinancial criteria.

Benchmarking Using operating standards of other companies and departments as guides to judging and then improving performance.

Brainstorming (1) Organized exploration of unorganized ideas to stimulate creativity. (2) Used loosely to cover any meeting called to discuss an unresolved issue.

Business Process Reengineering (BPR) Fundamental rethinking and radical redesign of business processes to achieve dramatic improvements in performance.

Change management Approach required to design radical change programs and bring them to fruition.

Core competencies The unique abilities that give a business its competitive advantage – vital to core (indispensable) activities.

Corporate strategy The company's objectives over the short, medium, and long terms in relation to its products and plans for expansion.

Critical path analysis Mapping the route through any network of events that governs the total time taken from the start to the finish of a process.

Culture change Programs intended to alter behaviors by instilling new attitudes into the workforce.

Customer focus Making customer needs central to all products and processes.

Customer loyalty The prime aim of marketers, since retained customers are the best source of profitable sales.

Customer Relations Management (CRM) Using specialized techniques (mostly IT) to increase customer loyalty (*qv*).

E-business Business transactions of any kind using the web.

E-commerce Trade conducted over the web, both business-to-business (B2B) and business-to-consumer (B2C).

Economic Value Added (EVA) Deducting the total cost of equity and other capital from recalculated profits to determine the true economic return of the enterprise.

Empowerment Giving employees greater control and responsibility to increase their satisfaction and motivation.

Extranet Private network linking a company with outside suppliers, customers, etc.

Feedback The organized relay of information (from workers, customers, etc.).

Horizontal (1) A company organized around specific competencies. (2) A flat structure with few levels – the opposite of vertical organization (*qv*).

Intellectual capital General and specific knowledge that a company possesses and builds in its staff and databases.

Intranet Private network that links management and staff and provides information, training, and interchange.

Knowledge management Management of the firm's intellectual capital (*qv*) to optimize the return on these assets.

Knowledge workers People employed for their own individual knowledge rather than for collective work.

Learning organization One that develops to reflect and pass on new knowledge.

Life-cycle cost Total costs, direct and indirect, of buying and using a product over its entire economic life.

Management by Objectives (MBO) Improving performance by developing corporate objectives and ensuring managers' goals are consistent with those aims.

Marginal costs Costs associated with raising production or sales by one unit more.

Mission statement The setting out of the company's priorities, tasks, and objectives to realize the corporate vision (*qv*).

Outsourcing Using outside suppliers for products and services previously obtained from internal sources.

Portfolio career Instead of a single employer, having several employers, for either the same work or a collection of different activities.

Price/earnings (P/E) ratio Dividing the market price per share by net earnings per share to calculate the most widely accepted measure of a firm's valuation.

Profit centers Units within large companies that are held responsible for minimizing costs and maximizing revenue.

Scenario planning Planning based on a range of possible future outcomes.

Shareholder value The worth of a company to its owners, generally equated with its equity's market value.

Six Sigma Standard of quality performance: no more than 3.4 defects per million parts or operations are acceptable. Also name adopted for a variant of Total Quality Management (*qv*).

Stakeholder Anybody or any group with an interest in a business or organization.

SWOT analysis Evaluating a company's Strengths, Weaknesses, Opportunities, and Threats as a foundation for forming strategies.

Team briefing (360-degree review) A method of review where feedback is sought from everyone who has worked with the person being reviewed.

Total Productive Maintenance (TPM) Achieving improved manufacturing performance by using similar techniques to those of Business Process Reengineering (*qv*).

Total Quality Management (TQM) Company-wide system that trains people in relevant techniques and sets them working toward achieving perfect quality.

Value added Difference between the cost of all purchased goods and services, and processing them, and the revenue obtained from selling them to outside customers.

Value chain Linked processes that represent the stages from design, through engineering and manufacture, to delivery to the final customer by the marketing and sales operations.

Values The fundamental beliefs that animate and govern the organization.

Venture capital Funds provided as risk capital for ventures in which the provider takes an equity stake.

Vertical (1) Organizing a company in hierarchical mode. (2) Undertaking all activities in the value chain (*qv*) in-house; opposite of horizontal (*qv*).

Virtual organization A company that undertakes only its core activities, outsourcing all the others, and treating its main suppliers as extensions of the "parent" organization.

Vision statement The setting out of a company's basic purpose and its overriding philosophy.

Win–win Seeking or agreeing on a solution or plan that should satisfy all parties.

BUSINESS DIRECTORY

The leading organizations for general and specialized management services are an invaluable source that managers can tap whenever they need wider or deeper knowledge and research. Readers seeking the right and rewarding information will find these bodies responsive and helpful.

The Business Directory is divided into nine sections representing key areas of management in the US and Canada.

GENERAL

Harvard Business School Resources
www.hbsp.harvard.edu/tools_resources/index.html
Harvard Business School hosts an online information database for managers, entrepreneurs, and educators.

National Alliance of Business
Suite 700
1201 New York Ave. NW
Washington, DC 20005
Tel: (202) 289-2888
Fax: (202) 289-1303
The National Alliance of Business is a nonprofit organization aiming to encourage lifelong learning among business professionals, and to offer students at all levels an opportunity to gain experience of business.

United States Chamber of Commerce
1615 H Street NW
Washington, DC 20062
Tel: (202) 463-5869
www.uschamber.org
The US Chambers of Commerce is a lobbying body that offers benefits and information resources to its members. It also has a useful Business Resources section on its website.

CAREERS INSTITUTIONS

American Society for Training & Development (ASTD)
Box 1443, 1640 King Street
Alexandria, VA 22313-2043
Tel: (703) 683-8100 or (800) 628-2783
Fax: (703) 683-1523
www.astd.org
The American Society for Training & Development is dedicated to helping improve workplace conditions through training and education.

Edward Lowe Foundation
PO Box 8
Cassapolis, MI 49031
Tel: (800) 232-5693
www.lowe.org
The Edward Lowe Foundation is a nonprofit organization providing services and peer-learning opportunities to would-be entrepreneurs, as well as a publishing and information program and a calendar of conferences and events.

FINANCIAL INSTITUTIONS

Association of Chartered Certified Accountants (ACCA)
www.accaglobal.com
The Association of Chartered Certified Accountants holds an annual general meeting, creates and presents programs of interest on international business issues, and distributes ACCA press releases and a quarterly newsletter to members. It also has offices in Canada.

American Institute of Certified Public Accountants
1211 Avenue of the Americas
New York, NY 10036
Tel: (212) 596-6200
www.aicpa.org
The American Institute of Certified Public Accountants is a membership association offering training and accreditation, publications, and legal representation to certified public accountants.

Financial Executives International
www.fei.org
Financial Executives International is a membership organization offering networking opportunities, personal and professional development and advocacy services to senior finance professionals and academics. See website for contact details of individual chapters.

Financial Management Association International (FMA)

University of South Florida
College of Business
Administration
Tampa, FL 33620-5500
Tel: (813) 974-2084
Fax: (813) 974-3318
www.fma.org
The Financial Management Association International is a research and educational institute serving senior level financial professionals. It runs a publishing program and provides opportunities for students and academics to network with professionals.

Financial Management Service

401 14th Street NW
Washington, DC 20227
Tel: (202) 874-7050
www.fms.treas.gov
The Financial Management Service is a government body that provides a useful indicator to the public and private sectors of government fiscal and monetary policy, in the form of reports on government spending.

Institute of Management Accountants

10 Paragon Drive
Montvale, NJ 07645-1718
Tel: (800) 638-4427
Fax: (201) 573-0559
www.imanet.org
The Institute of Management Accountants is a professional organization that hosts seminars and conferences, runs educational courses, and offers certifications.

MANAGEMENT INSTITUTIONS

American Management Association (AMA)

1601 Broadway
New York, NY 10019
Tel: (212) 586-8100
Fax: (212) 903-8168
www.amanet.org
The American Management Association is an educational organization offering training in the Americas, the Pacific Rim, and East Asia.

Institute of Certified Professional Managers

James Madison University
MSC 5504
Harrisonburg, VA 22807
Tel: (800) 568-4120
http://cob.jmu.edu/icpm/default.htm
The Institute of Certified Professional Managers aims to raise competency and professionalism through the certification of managers. It also conducts research in the areas of management, business education, academic assessment and certification.

Institute of Management Consultants USA

Suite 800
2025 M Street NW
Washington, DC 20036-3309
Tel: (202) 367-1134 or (800) 221-2557
Fax: (202) 367-2134
www.imcusa.org
The Institute of Management Consultants USA is a representative and educational organization serving the management consulting sector. It offers representation and professional accreditation to members, and seeks to uphold ethical standards within the industry.

Institute of Management and Administration (IOMA)

29 West 35th St.
New York, NY 10001
Tel: (212) 244-0360
Fax: (212) 564-0465
www.ioma.com
The Institute of Management and Administration publishes a broad range of information products for business professionals in print and electronic formats. The website contains news, articles, discussion groups and a list of over 600 links to related sites.

National Management Association

2210 Arbor Boulevard
Dayton, OH 45439-1580
Tel: (937) 294-0421
www.nma1.org
The National Management Association is a membership association for managers across the United States. It encourages development through coaching, mentoring, and certification.

Project Management Institute

Four Campus Boulevard
Newtown Square, PA 19073-3299
Tel: (610) 356-4600
Fax: (610) 356-4647
www.pmi.org
The Project Management Institute is a representative and

educational organization with an international membership. It offers a variety of services from professional standards and certification to research, publications, education, and training.

SALES AND MARKETING INSTITUTIONS

American Marketing Association
Suite 5800
311 South Wacker Drive
Chicago, IL 60606
www.marketingpower.com
The American Marketing Association is a professional organization for those involved in the practice, study, and teaching of marketing. It represents the interests of members, offers training and accreditation, and provides conferencing and networking opportunities.

Public Relations Society of America
33 Irving Place
New York, NY 10003-2376
Tel: (212) 995-2230
www.prsa.org
The Public Relations Society of America aims to advance the standards of the public relations profession and to provide members with professional development opportunities.

Sales & Marketing Executives-International, Inc.
PO Box 1390
Sumas, WA 98295-1390
Tel: (312) 893-0751
Fax: (604) 855-0165

Sales & Marketing Executives-International is a worldwide association of sales and marketing managers. It provides training and development opportunities, networking events, and publications for members.

HUMAN RESOURCES INSTITUTIONS

National Human Resources Association (NHRA)
www.humanresources.org
The National Human Resources Association aims to provide high quality programs and services for HR professionals, to advance their interests, to encourage and assist the professional development of members, and to provide a forum for the exchange of information and ideas.

Society for Human Resource Management (SHRM)
1800 Duke Street
Alexandria, VA 22314
Tel: (703) 548-3440
Fax: (703) 535-6490
www.shrm.org
SHRM is a representative body serving the human resources profession primarily in the United States. It also takes members from international HR companies across the world, and aims to provide a framework for discussion and the circulation of ideas.

World Federation of Personnel Management Associations (WFPMA)
c/o of Chartered Institute of Personnel Development
CIPD House
Camp Road
Wimbledon
London SW19 4UX
United Kingdom
Tel: +44 (20) 8971-9000
Fax: +44 (20) 8263-3333
www.wfpma.com
The WFPMA is a global network of HR professionals. It links the personnel of more than 50 national HR associations, and commissions research projects, publishes a quarterly newsletter, and holds an international congress every two years.

INFORMATION TECHNOLOGY INSTITUTIONS

Association of Information Technology Professionals (AITP)
Suite 200
315 South Northwest Highway
Park Ridge, IL 60068-4278
Tel: (847) 825-8214 or
(800) 224-9371
Fax: (847) 825-1693
www.aitp.org
The Association of Information Technology Professionals acts as a link between industry, government and academia. It allows professionals, academics and students to share ideas and experience, and also provides IT related education, and information on relevant IT issues.

Information Technology Association of America (ITAA)

Suite 1100
1401 Wilson Boulevard
Arlington, VA 22209
Tel: (703) 522-5055
Fax: (703) 525-2279
www.itaa.org
The Information Technology Association of America is a trade association representing the US IT industry. It runs education programs, publishes a wide range of material and hosts meetings and seminars for members.

International Association for the Management of Technology (IAMOT)

The Department of Industrial Engineering
University of Miami
P.O Box 248294
Coral Gables, FL 33124-0623
Tel: (305) 284-4100
Fax: (305) 284-4040
www.iamot.org
The International Association for the Management of Technology is a membership organization that meets biennially at different locations across the globe. It hosts conferences, publishes a monthly newsletter and research reports, and provides information and resources to members.

Society for Information Management (SIM)

401 N. Michigan Avenue
Chicago, IL 60611-4267
Tel: (312) 527-6734 or
(800) 387-9746
Fax: (312) 245-1081
www.simnet.org
The Society for Information

Management is a grouping of information technology experts. It offers development programs and provides an infrastructure for members to pool their ideas.

OPERATIONS MANAGEMENT INSTITUTIONS

The Educational Society for Resource Management (APICS)

5301 Shawnee Road
Alexandria, VA 22312-2317
Tel: (800) 444-2742 or
(703) 354-8851
Fax: (703) 354-8106
www.apics.org
The Educational Society for Resource Management is an institute offering educational courses and professional certification in areas including materials management, information services, purchasing, and quality control. It also runs a publication program and hosts networking events.

Institute for Operations Research and the Management Sciences (INFORMS)

Suite 400
901 Elkridge Landing Road
Linthicum, MD 21090-2909
Tel: (800) 464-6767
Fax: (410) 684-2963
www.informs.org
INFORMS runs training courses and publishes material, represents the interests of operations management professionals, and maintains INFORMS Online, a web-based information resource.

Institute for Organization Management

www.uschamber.com/Institute
The Institute for Organization Management runs a variety of educational courses in chamber/association management at different sites across the United States. For contact details see website or contact the US Chambers of Commerce.

Logistics Management Institute

2000 Corporate Ridge
McLean, VA 22102-7805
Tel: (703) 917-9800
Fax: (800) 213-4817
The Logistics Management Institute is a nonprofit consulting service aiming to improve the operations of companies and organizations across the United States.

Production and Operations Management Society (POMS)

POMS Executive Office
College of Engineering
Florida International University
EAS 2460
10555 West Flagle Street
Miami, FL 33174
Tel: (305) 348 1413
Fax: (305) 348 6890
www.poms.org
The Production and Operations Management Society offers a number of benefits to members, from networking and conferencing facilities to printed and web-based reference material.

CANADIAN INSTITUTIONS

Association of Chartered Certified Accountants (ACCA)
ACCA Canada Center
55 St. Clair Ave West
Suite 255
Toronto
ON, M4V 2Y7
Canada
Tel: (416)966-2225 or
(888) 801-0011
Tax: (416) 967-6320
www.accaglobal.com
A worldwide association for chartered certified accountants, the Association of Chartered Certified Accountants has offices in Canada and the US. It holds an annual general meeting, creates and presents programs of interest on international business issues, and distributes ACCA press releases and a quarterly newsletter to members.

Canadian Council of Human Resource Associations (CCHRA)
P.O. Box 1227, Station 'B'
Ottawa
ON, K1P 5R3
Canada
Tel: (416) 618-0052
www.cchra-ccarh.ca
The Canadian Council of Human Resources is an association of human resource organizations across Canada. It aims to establish national core standards for the human resource profession, foster communication among participating bodies, and represent the interests of members on a national and international

level. It is also a member of the North American Human Resource Management Association (NAHRMA).

Canadian Institute of Chartered Accountants (CICA)
277 Wellington Street West
Toronto
ON, M5V 3H2
Canada
Tel: (416) 977-3222
Fax: (416) 977-8585
www.cica.ca
The Canadian Institute of Chartered Accountants is a representative organization that conducts research into business issues and sets accounting and auditing standards for business, nonprofit organizations, and government. It issues guidance on control and governance, publishes professional literature, develops education programs, and represents chartered accountants nationally and internationally.

Canadian Institute of Management (CIM)
Toronto Branch:
2175 Sheppard Avenue East
Suite 310
Toronto
ON, M2J 1W8
Canada
Tel: 416-493-0155
Fax: 416-491-1670
www.cim.ca
The Canadian Institute of Management offers training and representation to management professionals in Canada.

The Society of Management Accountants of Canada (CMA Canada)
Mississauga Executive Centre
One Robert Speck Parkway,
Suite 1400
Mississauga
ON, L4Z 3M3
Canada
Tel: (905) 949-4200 or
(800) 263-7622
www.cma-canada.org
The Society of Management Accountants of Canada is a membership organization that represents the interests of certified management accountants in Canada. It maintains standards and codes of conduct, hosts conferences and provides a resource of print and electronic information.

Canadian Marketing Association (CMA)
1 Concorde Gate, Suite 607
Don Mills
ON, M3C 3N6
Canada
Tel: 416-391-2362
Fax: 416-441-4062
www.the-cma.org
The Canadian Marketing Association represents the interests of its members, encourages development through training, and hosts conferences and events.

INDEX

ACKNOWLEDGMENTS

Authors' Acknowledgments

George Boulden drew on the following publications: *Action Learning: A Practical Guide*, Krystyna Weinstein (1999); *Action Learning: New Techniques for Management*, R. W. Revans (1980); and his own *In-plant Action Learning* (1993).

Terence Brake thanks all his colleagues at Transnational Management Associates (TMA) for their important work in developing global minds, and everyone at Dorling Kindersley for their commitment to producing quality publications.

Sue Clemenson wishes to thank the Careers Research Forum, Sir Thomas Boyd-Carpenter, David Laughrin, John Toplis, David Whyte, and colleagues at Archangel; and acknowledges the work of Meredith Belbin and Charles Handy.

Paul Donkersley is grateful in particular to Working Futures and Sanders & Sidney for their help in his research, and to the human resources departments of progressive employers like H. P. Bulmer and Churchill Insurance. He also acknowledges the influence of leading lights such as Handy, Black, and Goldman on his thinking. Finally, the opportunity given to him by Corporate Research Foundation to twice edit and write the book *Britain's Best Employers* allowed the valuable field research into the role that leading companies are playing in the ever-changing career equation.

Chris Downing wishes to thank Steve Tonge, Robert Heller, Paul Spenley; and Nik Fuchs, Sven Awege, and Maria Luisa Rodriguez of e>>co consulting in Paris.

Bob Garratt drew on his books *The Learning Organization* (2000), *Twelve Organizational Capabilities* (2000), and *The Fish Rots from the Head* (1996). He also acknowledges the work of Jan Carlzon (*Moments of Truth*, 1989), Reg Revans (*The ABC of Action Learning*, 1998), and Hesketh, Sasser, and Schlesinger (*The Service Profit Chain*, 1997) in helping frame his sections.

Terry Gasking wishes to acknowledge those who are the sources of his understanding of finance and the ways in which it is actually practiced: that is, his clients from many parts of the world with whom he has shared so many successful and happy tasks and warm memories.

Angela Pinnington thanks her colleagues at Kepner-Tregoe, and the many individuals among her clients who have made the ideas discussed in her chapter come alive. In particular, she would like to mention Ben Tregoe, whose work in this area has been an inspiration.

Paul Spenley wishes to acknowledge Ivor Tiefenbrun MBE, MD of Linn Products; Tony Belisario, CEO of Ascent Investments; and Steve Collyer, MD of W. K. Test.

Publisher's Acknowledgments

Dorling Kindersley would like to thank the following for their contributions:
Editorial: Amy Corzine, Clare Hill, Mary Lambert, Daphne Richardson, Hazel Richardson; **Design**: Nigel Duffield; **Jacket Editorial**: Beth Apple; **Jacket Design**: Chris Drew; **Index**: Hilary Cooper; **Proofreading**: Stewart J. Wild; **Picture Research**: Sarah Duncan; **Picture Library**: Melanie Simmonds, Neale Chamberlain, Lee Thompson.
TEXT CREDITS **The Service Profit Chain** (page 40), reproduced from Heskett, J. L., Jones, T. O., Loveman, G. W., Sasser, W. E., and Schlesinger, L. A., "Putting the Service Profit Chain to Work", Harvard Business Review (March-April 1994) page 166, with kind permission from the Harvard Business Review.
PICTURE CREDITS
Key: *a* above, *c* center, *b* below, *l* left, *r* right, *t* top
Ardea London Ltd.: 4 *cr*, 32–3 *c*; **Comstock**: 81 *c*; **The Image Bank / Getty Images**: 116 *c*, 188 *c*; **Pictor International**: 1 *c*, Robert Llewellyn 100 *c*, 232 *c*; **Corbis Stock Market**: Lester Lefkowitz 5 *cr*, 216–17 *c*; Jose Luis Pelaez Inc. 134 *c*; 201 *c*; **Stone / Getty Images**: 2–3 *c*, 5 *bl*, 14 *c*, 34 *c*, 146–7 *c*, 148 *c*, 166 *c*, 218 *c*; **Superstock Ltd.**: Miles Schuster 56 *c*; **Telegraph Colour Library / Getty Images**: 4 *tr*, 12–13 *c*. Jacket photography: **Superstock Ltd.**, Richard Heinzen.